We Can Live Like This

We Can Live Like This....a Memoir of a Culture

BillieBooks
PO Box 3828
Berkeley, CA 94703

Cover Design by Cynthia Clabough
Cover Photographs by Desdemona Burgin
Book Design by Cynthia Clabough

Paperback ISBN 979-8-9906737-4-8
Hardback ISBN 979-8-9906737-1-7
Ebook ISBN 979-8-9906737-2-4
Audiobook ISBN 979-8-9906737-3-1

Library of Congress Control Number: 2024909029

We Can Live Like This

...a Memoir of a Culture

To all the sisters who forged a new
life in the woods of Michigan.

Lisa Vogel

BillieBooks
LisaAVogel.com

CONTENTS

PART FOUR

PART FIVE

ACKNOWLEDGMENTS

I am fortunate to live in a community of smart, perceptive, and kind womyn. I worked on this book for seven years, and so many sisters added their wisdom and insight to various stories as they unfolded. I will be forever grateful to Judy Grahn for welcoming me into her memoir group, where the very fact that we needed to bring something to class was my impetus to keep writing. When I thought I was drafting therapeutic stories that I might blog one day, my core classmates for many years — Sara St. Martin Lynne, Dianne Jenett, and Joellen Hiltbrand — kept telling me I was writing a book. There in Judy's house, with her forever wisdom and her bone broth soup, I started to imagine this book.

I phoned dozens of womyn over these years to check memories and confirm events, and I appreciate everyone who got into the time machine with me. Sara St Martin Lynne read and reread so many early versions of stories, always patient, supportive, and kind. Early in the pandemic lockdown of 2020, Elvira Kurt joined me for two months of live-streamed readings I called Fireside Chats. My intention was to help break isolation, and at the same time I found these readings invaluable to me because they let me experience how the stories were received by our community. Many thanks to all who came. I told Judy when I entered her memoir class that I wanted to write like I was telling a story around a campfire and asked for her help keeping me in that zone. We all created that zone together.

Each public reading I was fortunate enough to do with Elvira was a ripe, fast-paced co-editing opportunity, as she often put her eyes, mind, and heart into the stories that were to be shared. Pat Simon tenaciously read every story and spent hours on the phone giving me her corrections and feedback while she kept her pencil sharp and her heart open.

Cyn Clabough was the Festival's graphic artist for its last 15 years. I was scanning art in the spring of 2023 and dropped her a note of appreciation for the incredible body of work she created over time. When I told her I was looking at things for potential inclusion in my book, she said, "Um, I have designed a few books lately." Me: "She said 'books.'" Cyn: "You had me at hello." I feel completely blessed to have her creative talents in the creation of the art and design for this book.

Many talented photographers' photos appear throughout the book, all credited on their pages unless, as in the early years, the photographer is unknown. Both the front and back cover photographs were shot by the talented Desdemona "Bunty" Burgin, a primary Festival photographer for the last 10 years.

I could not have done this book without the support of my community. Your support allowed me to self-publish — complete with color photographs and collaborating with editors and designers of my choice from within the Festival community, who had respect for the content and intent of the stories. Thank you, Amazons!

I have such deep appreciation for Holly Pruett and Kiki Reinecke for their editing skills and their amazing insights. This book is better because of each of their contributions. I am not a traditional writer. They each edited these stories with their hearts set on making things clearer and more concise, but always keeping my singular voice. They each brought their deep understanding and love of the Michigan community to the work, and it showed in every edit brought to the table. Thank you and bless you both. No matter how many eyes combed this text, Carol Vitelli, you rocked the missing pieces in the last read-through — bless you!

Billie — the most beautiful dog of all time, with the gentlest spirit and deepest eyes — thank you for staying with me through all the phases of the book.

Finally, my deepest love and appreciation to my partner, Lia Willebrand, for her love and support, her fearless feedback, and every single suggestion that I could not hear for days. Thank you for standing by me through all of it. You are the gentle wind at my back.

PROLOGUE

I started to write these stories in the fall of 2016 as a chronicle of the womyn who built and loved the community of the Michigan Womyn's Music Festival. I wanted something that Michigan sisters could see themselves in, to be celebrated as the ingenious, radical, joyous, hardworking womyn who forged a revolutionary reality in the woods of Michigan for 40 years. I also was inspired to bring the stories of this community to the womyn who were never part of Michigan but who are pulled to know what we manifested for four decades. And most of all, I wanted to leave breadcrumbs for the womyn who come after us, so that who we were and what we created may be an inspiration for the vision they might want to create next.

These are my experiences, both internal and external, of producing the Festival from its inception in 1976 to its final year in 2015. This is just one woman's experience. It is 100% reasonable that you could have been right there, exactly in the story I am telling, and have a different experience. I'm not telling the global herstory of the Festival. I am sharing my experiences. I produced the Festival from the ages of 19 to 59, and how I influenced the Festival was so much less than how it shaped everything about my life. Everything of value that I have learned in my life I learned on that Land. I say that with deep gratitude for having had this as my life's work, and to have received the gift of being part of this beautiful and profound community.

It is important to me that the legacy of the culture and womyn of the Michigan Womyn's Music Festival be remembered for the phenomenally radical, innovative, soulful community that it was. A community that was deeply intergenerational, multicultural, gender-radical, and that lived in harmony with the Land. Together, we created a space where womyn and girls felt some of the first freedom in their lives, to live in the forest without fear of assault or harassment, to be free in their bodies, and supported in expanding their hearts.

You will find that I don't write very much about the music and performances of the Festival, though I have deep love and respect for the thousands of artists who expanded our hearts and minds over these 40 years. I was driven to write stories that reflect how living together in a womyn's community in the woods, at one with nature, shaped our values and expanded our shared understanding of the world we wanted to create. The values that we developed and held on the Land are what changed our lives. Together, we created a matriarchal, woman-centered world, one this planet had scarcely seen for centuries.

Of course, it is impossible to tell every story. The complexity of our living community, the years we were blessed to be together, and the sheer intensity of what we created together is endless.

To everyone I have named, you stand in for all the sisters not named, because truly, on that Land, we miraculously became one life force.

The contributions to this book have been many and the errors are all on me.

Now walk the paths with me into these tales of a 40-year community created by womyn from throughout the world. Whether or not you've physically walked the Land, see yourself here. These stories offer a glimpse into the potential of a world shaped by womyn.

We can live like this.

CHAPTER 1

MY FIRST FESTIVAL

It was 1976, a couple of weeks before our first Festival. I was in my 20-year-old Rambler on a weekend trip to Detroit, Ann Arbor, and Lansing to pass out our newly minted brochures and meet with our sound company. I pulled up to their warehouse, a 12-pack of cheap beer in tow, and proceeded to act like I knew what I was doing, even though this was the first concert I had ever produced.

I hit it off with Mr. Sound Dude as we talked about shows we had both been to in recent years. Jefferson Airplane. The Eagles. Buddy Miles. Bonnie Raitt. The Rolling Stones with Stevie Wonder. Everything was going great with our shared rock-and-roll hippiedom until he asked me how many people we thought we would have at the show.

"I think we might have as many as 1,000 womyn," I said, still not believing my own number.

"How many men?"

"Ahh. None. It's an all-womyn's festival. No men."

Our San Francisco sound engineer, who had booked the Michigan sound company, had not discussed this fact, and right there, three-quarters of the way through my 12-pack of beer, the sound for our Festival was canceled. No men, no sound. We had absolutely no idea what we were doing when we produced the first Festival. None. I personally had produced nothing more than a few major keggers. From our hometowns in the middle of Michigan, we had been swimming in the electrifying energy of lesbian feminism that we devoured in books and found on trips to cities like Chicago, Boston, Lansing, and Cleveland. We wanted to experience that magic on our home turf. But creating a womyn's gathering space bigger than our living room — and doing it with zero money — meant that creativity and sketchy, old-school, working-class skills had to come into play.

To buy postage, we had yard sales. We first promoted the Festival with flyers we made on the ditto machine at the local university after sneaking in at night. To print a real brochure, we had a car wash, ran a kegger, and borrowed money $20 at a time.

To get a baby grand piano from 100 miles away delivered for $150, I offered, "We will happily hand out flyers promoting your piano company and announce your company between each performance. This Festival is pretty much a festival of pianists. The performers and the audience. All pianists."

We decided we would build the stage like the ones we'd seen at many rock shows: scaffolding with lumber laid flat then covered with plywood. My sister, Kristie, and I did reconnaissance one afternoon as workers set up for an Alice Cooper show at the Saginaw Arena, 45 miles from our home in Mt. Pleasant. It looked doable.

We didn't see how they did the stairs, though, and we started to wonder how we were going to get up on that stage. Anyone we know ever built stairs? The scaffolding was more than 6 feet high. Hmmm. Have to figure that out soon.

The problem was solved when Digger rolled in with two zigzag stair stringers hanging out of her car window after "borrowing" them from a building site the night before.

We didn't have the money to buy the wood to build the stage, so we convinced the lumberyard to rent us the two-by-10s at a dollar per board. "We'll only put two little nail holes on each end. No one will even notice them," we told them.

Most of our asks were so weird — and frankly, desperate — that we got confused "yeses" before anyone knew what hit them.

Manifesting Water

The land we rented had no water and no electricity. We thought we could "drill" our own well. Off we went, with a couple of friendly guys from the water department where Kristie worked and a 2-inch pipe to bang into the ground by hand until we reached water. It was one of our massive early failures, accented by massive blisters all around. I called milk companies, farmers, and anyone else I could think of who might use huge potable water containers. In that time before bottled water was anyone's idea, we were sure we'd have to haul in drinking water, and lots of it.

The Army! They must haul everything — water for sure — and tents!

I discovered that if I was (in theory) a reservist, I could buddy up to the local commander and borrow all kinds of things. I collected the names of the lieutenants and commanders within a 150-mile area. I would call one post and say, "Captain Big Dude from Grayling said to call you, that he thought you had a water tank I could borrow for this community event." Or some big tents, or some cots. The Army guys really helped each other out, and I found they were very nice to one of the few (faux) female reservists who was in the know about all the officers. We pulled off the Army borrowing trick for three years before they caught up with us.

That first Festival ran Friday through Sunday. On opening day, while Digger and Kristie were both off on an airport run, I watched as womyn flooded onto the Land. From everywhere! And these womyn! Wow! They were so much more sophisticated, political, and just generally more awesome than we were. They were from Chico and D.C., Toronto and St. Louis, places I couldn't begin to find on a map. I was intimidated just to talk to some of them.

As that reality was registering for me, up the dirt road this huge Army truck decked out in full fatigue was turning onto the property, with a totally iconic jarhead behind the wheel. Panic rippled through the radical '70s hearts and minds of the newly arrived womyn. Our worst fear: We were being invaded by the fucking Army! I could feel the vibe of retaliation rising through the sisters in the field.

I was the only one who understood this guy was delivering a tank of water for us. I jumped up on his running board, one foot on the step-up, one arm slung around the driver's mirror. I told him, "Just keep driving, 5 miles an hour, and let me talk to the womyn. Keep your eyes straight ahead, don't talk to anyone but me, and you'll be safe."

The irony was that we no longer needed the damned water truck. Literally days before the Festival was to start, a local well-driller, the father of a straight-but-not-narrow womon we drank and flirted with at local bars, heard his daughter's story of us believing we could manifest water by banging away on that pipe. He took pity on us and put a well down, with a pump and a few spigots. We used it for a few days, then he pulled it back up. It took the perspective of four decades later — once we'd had eight wells drilled and paid for them — to realize what a miracle that really was.

Who Brings a Machete?

Everything was a miracle, and every single thing was happening in such a slipshod way and at such a frenetic pace. We just kept moving until the next thing blew up in our faces, a mixture of terror, bravado, and cheap beer pumping steadily through our veins.

Take the location of the showers, for example. Deciding where to put the well had seemed logical. It needed to be near the generator we were renting to run the electricity for sound and lights, so, how about near that hill? We can put the showers on top of the rise and the water can drain down.

It was an excellent idea when it was just a handful of us out on the Land, putting the stage together just days before the womyn were to arrive. But that sleepy 120 acres in what we thought was very remote country — where we never saw or heard a car go by in the days leading up to Fest — was suddenly bumper-to-bumper with locals gawking at nearly 2,000 womyn as they arrived, spread out their pup tents, and started to rinse off in the freezing cold water of that funky little shower on wooden pallets up the hill.

Some enterprising guy sold time on his telescope on a hill across the road, a straight shot to our showers, and whole families pressed their faces to their car windows to get a good look at the "international gathering of weirdos," as we were called in the local county paper. The gawking turned to name-calling, which morphed into sisters who were not having it.

"Always wanted to give a dyke 10 inches," said one of the guys, safely behind his truck door. "If you want to leave with those 5 inches of yours, you better get out of here now," said one sister, brandishing a machete like she knew how to use it.

Who the fuck travels to a festival with a machete?!

We were in over our heads.

We were in the crazy position of running interference between the local dudes who were trying to prove their manhood on the road and the dykes who were ready to send their manhood home with them in a bag.

A womon from Lansing named Keyosha had a Doberman, a van, and a calm that was lacking in most of us. We hadn't thought of anything remotely like security, but Keyosha threw together an idea that seemed to match the seriousness of the situation. If you heard a car horn, everyone who'd come from east of the Mississippi would go to the front gate road, everyone from west of the Mississippi go to the south road, and so on. Every time a horn blasted, womyn scrambled to their positions.

It was overkill — intense and kind of insane — but we were protecting our newly formed Lesbian Nation, and all methods were reasonable.

I didn't own a tent or even use one that first year, but that was OK. I was so afraid someone would party on the Kawai grand piano late at night that my plan was to sleep right there, on the stage, directly under the piano. I was so screwed if anything happened to that piano.

On Saturday night, Be Be K'Roche, a rock band from San Francisco, played the closing set. Following their set, the band headed out through the woods to do a security shift at a perimeter location where we had discovered guys coming through earlier. I joined them, and we proceeded to party and get to know each other in the dark of the night. None of us were particularly nervous about the situation, so when we heard some noise in the woods, Peggy, the bass player, went off by herself to check it out. She came back with a man — barefoot, drunk, and scared out of his mind — hanging from his shirt collar at the end of her hand.

He had come into the Land on a dare, gotten lost, and was roaming around in the pitch-black woods getting his feet cut up. We put a hooded sweatshirt over him and told him, "Keep your eyes down, and don't say a word. We'll take you to the road and then you should run like hell." As we were exiting the woods the horns went off. Womyn everywhere started scrambling to respond, making the guy absolutely shake.

I told the band I was heading over to the stage to secure the piano, and off I went through the half-asleep, half-drunk trails of womyn heading to their positions. A sister ran up to me demanding, "Where are you from?! Where are you from?!" "Uh, Michigan?" "You're going the wrong way! Michigan's station is at the front gate, it's thataway!"

A 40-Pound Block of Cheese

We were freshly politicized lesbian feminists in 1975 and 1976 as we began to scheme about a Festival, but we were also dyed-in-the-wool leftist hippies. Both truths influenced a lot of how we wanted to do things. From the beginning, one of the clearest directions we went in was deciding to have communal food. It didn't matter that we had no idea how to do this. We hit learning curve after learning curve, mess over madness.

Lucky for us that in the glow of '70s feminism, expectations from our sisters were extremely low. Corn and potatoes cooked over an open fire in a 55-gallon drum, salad, fruit, bread, cheese, lemon juice and water. I had originally asked one of the womyn from the local food co-op to be part of the first Collective because she loved music and knew food. She passed. I came back around and asked a group of womyn from the co-op if they would organize the food. I would do the ordering; they would prep on site. They agreed! They were music lovers, straight, but they mixed well with the local co-op dykes, and they could all do it together.

We got the celery from the celery farmer. We got a 40-pound block of cheese from the co-op. We rented a little milk truck, no bigger than a pickup, to keep the dairy cold. We got bread from the bread delivery truck. We bought knives at Kmart. We had one borrowed table. Late in the morning on Saturday, before the first "meal" was to be put out, it was already getting hot in the sun, and the kitchen womyn headed out to the nearby swimming hole to cool off.

They never came back.

I started the fire under the metal drum to boil the corn and potatoes and went to the stage to continue to try to smooth the revolving arguments flaring up between Margo, the sound engineer, and a womon I had found at the last minute, who came in from Chicago with her brother's sound gear. I looked back toward the little kitchen area to see a steady line of fire making its way from the potato drum to the stage, licking at all the dried grass in between. We didn't have a single fire extinguisher, but stomping feet and a single shovel handled the fire.

The potatoes were never really cooked that year. We had that 40-pound block of cheese on the table with a knife stuck into it. Cut what you need, sisters! We had watermelon, carrots, and beautiful celery from down the road. We had the start of home.

Sunday morning came and I realized we had to organize the money so we could pay the artists. We didn't have a box office trailer or even a tent, just a little table with a tarp over it to block the blazing sun. I stored the money in my boots in the trunk of my Rambler.

I got my boots, headed out to the back of the listening area, grabbing a few womyn out of the audience as I went. "Got a few minutes to help me count money?" We sat in the back of the grassy bowl during the Meg Christian, Holly Near, Linda Tillery, and Teresa Trull concert, sorting fives, tens, and twenties, catching them as they floated in the wind.

Teresa, Holly, Meg, and Linda, 1976 photo by Diana Jo Davies

After we paid for the artists, sound, lights, and food, we had roughly $400 left. We could divide that up as our pay for our months of work, but there was a problem we hadn't considered: We had a huge mound of garbage bags that had collected over the past three days — the trash of 2,000 womyn — and this was before recycling was part of anyone's program. The garbage had sat in the 90-plus degree heat for days now, and the bags were exploding. It was a shitty, gross mess.

We decided that as badly as we needed the money, we would hire a garbage company to haul the bags. We called all the local haulers. We were told they would not come and get lesbian garbage. While we were on the Land and having our little private Festival in the woods, we had become infamous in the county.

There were five womyn who were the Festival's first "cling-ons," who just stayed on after everyone left on Sunday, bless their hearts. With a truck borrowed from a neighbor — we didn't have a pickup between us — we tore down the stage, returned the rented lumber, made plywood sides so we could pile the garbage high, and started the long, gross process of hauling exploding garbage bags crawling with maggots to the dump.

We were Amazons. We could do this. Rags wrapped around our mouths and noses, exhaustion as our bond, we could do this. Gagging as we worked, we would do this.

But there was no doubt in any of our minds. We would never attempt to do this Festival thing again.

CHAPTER 2

2,000 LESBIANS TO CONVERGE ON OCEANA COUNTY

Stage, 1977-78 photo by C. Elliot

The first Festival came and went and blew a hole in the quiet town of Mt. Pleasant. I can confirm that it is indeed very hard to go back to the farm once you've seen Gay Paree. It was an absolute bummer to do a deep dive back into semirural Patriarchy after the Matriarchy had pulled up tent stakes and left town.

As magical and beautiful and liberating as the first Festival was, there wasn't a single thought that we would do another. The confluence of decisions, the abundance of willingness, and the deep well of ignorance that made it possible for us to do that first Festival was a magical trifecta. We were in the right place at the right time. How else could we have done it? But the technicolor band-aid of naïveté had been ripped off and there were no takers for another round.

Personally, I was beyond broke from having spent the summer working for no pay, and I had to hustle immediately to find work to pay my $46.25 rent in our group lesbian house, and to put food on the table and a little beer in the cooler. I looked for weeks and eventually took the only job I could get, selling magazines door-to-door in the deep country.

Riding around in my old Rambler on dusty back roads, chased away from porches by German shepherds, goats, and honking geese, I earnestly tried to get my binder through the door to show another disinterested person the deal I could offer on *Ladies' Home Journal, Michigan Sportsman*, or *Car and Driver*. My Amazon-proud high from doing the Festival was soon ground down to wretched humiliation from the demeaning way people spoke to me as I started my sales pitch, mixed with abject shame when I eventually took checks from the only people buying, people too poor to be buying fucking magazines.

My Second Favorite Job

Early that winter I applied for a job with the city, sponsored by the CETA program to give training to low-income and unemployed people. I snagged a three-month job as the first female laborer in the city: Pumper Class 1 for the wastewater treatment plant. It turned out to be the second favorite job of my life. I was being paid union wage and it was the first time since I had quit selling drugs full-time that I had money in my pocket.

My mind would drift off to the idea of a second Festival, but it just felt too huge. There was no way we could do it around Mt. Pleasant since we had freaked out the county so completely. But as I repaired the pumps that moved the shit of the city up and down the sewers and into the huge putrid vats that were my new domain, the dialogue in my head continued and the idea would just not let go.

When my three-month job at the plant was ending, my boss told me about a full-time job opening up as a pump operator for the Water Department. "Same job really, Lisa, except our business is honestly a little cleaner." I applied for the job, took the math test necessary to do the calculations for the chlorine gas and fluoride treatments at each pumping station, and headed into my interview.

"Do you know that this job runs 3-11 p.m., and you'll be out there on your own? Even the men get scared out at the Rainey Station, it's so isolated and dark."

"Yes, the job description was clear it was second shift, and that I'd be the only one working in the entire water department after 5 p.m. I'm OK with that. As for the work at the Rainey Station, I imagine if everyone gets scared out there, I will too. But I'll do it."

He told me that I had scored highest of all applicants on the math, that he knew I had learned to take apart the large pumps and replace parts, that I had already worked with chlorine gas, but he still wasn't going to offer the job to me. "It should go to a man."

That night, shooting pool at The Bird, I approached a womon who had been a philosophy instructor of mine in the year and a half I had attended college. She was on the City Council and was a feminist. "Hey, I was just told that I wasn't going to get this job with the Water Department, even though I was trained through the CETA program to do pretty much the same work and scored the highest in the math. He flat out told me he didn't want a womon in the job. I am going to sue the city. I thought you might like to know."

"Excellent", she said, "I have been waiting for just this much of an obvious case to slam these guys against the wall. I'm on it."

She made a few calls, and I got the job. I thought I looked great in the yellow pickup driving around at night, testing wells, repairing little bits here and there, hiding the truck in alleys so I could stop into the lesbian parties that carried on without me. But I was completely loathed by all the men I worked with.

First, presented on the lunch table was a copy of the infamous *Hustler* magazine, the one with the womon going through the meat grinder. And then the naked pinup calendars appeared. As soon as I threw them away, they would reappear — fresh copies, not the ones I had ripped up on the way into the trash can. My car was pissed on. My tires were slashed. A shotgun went off when I was on my way into the Rainey well one night. I returned to the shop another night and my timecard had been stamped every minute for almost an hour. I was the only one working, but someone was letting me know I wasn't alone. As much as I appreciated the payday, I had not signed up for this.

'2,000 Lesbians'

Meanwhile, sisters from all over North America were writing to 1501 Lyons St. to ask if we were doing another Festival and to tell us how life-changing the first one had been for them. Our resolve to never try that Festival again was softening, and as for me — completely covered in patriarchal hostility at the job I had fought so hard to get — I needed sisterhood now more than ever.

We found the land for the second Festival by poring over phone books in the library and writing to every single real estate agent in rural areas throughout the state to ask if they knew of land that could be rented for a "womyn's musical retreat."

We received one response, from an aged-out hippie from Oceana County wanting to make a little money from some empty land he had dreamed of subdividing. We rented it immediately. It was located about two hours from where we lived, so Kris and I drove over in late June to find a house to rent in order to install a phone and have a crash pad, and start to get a feel for Oceana County and the town of Hesperia. We thought it would be a good idea to stop into the sheriff's office and find out if there were any regulations we needed to know about to start off on the right foot.

As we entered the sheriff's office, a little surprised that we were let in to see him right away, we started our sister act.

"Hello, I'm Lisa Vogel and this is my sister Kris, and we are here ..."

"I know who you are."

"O-K. Well, great. We are here because we are organizing a womyn's musical retreat (religious undertones implied) and we would like to find out ..."

"I know who you are and I know where you came from."

"Oh. OK. We came here today to find out if there is anything we need to know to work within the guidelines of the county ..."

"I KNOW who you are. I know everything about you," he repeated, this time slamming a newspaper down on his desk.

"2,000 LESBIANS TO CONVERGE ON OCEANA COUNTY" ran across the top of the front page.

"Go ahead, read it."

The paper had been printed the day before, and in it, the sheriff whose office we were standing in was quoted as saying he heard that what we did the year before was run around naked, lure men into our campground, and then beat them up. "I heard they even used knives on some of them."

I lost it.

"Do you realize what you just did? You threw down a challenge to every redneck man in the county to come out and challenge us. Someone is going to get hurt, and if I were you, I would be concerned for those rednecks."

Kristie remained calm as I continued to blow smoke all around the room. We had every desire to fly so far under the radar that we would come and go before people even knew we were there. But this. This was a gauntlet thrown down on the dirt road leading to our sleepy 160 acres in Newfield Township. It was 1977, and even using the word lesbian was a gauntlet of sorts: "I am a womon who does not need or want a man."

"Oh yeah?! I'll show you that you want a man!"

We had all been there.

It turned out that Oceana County had increasingly become a place for biker groups to gather, and that the county officials were trying to get an outdoor gathering ordinance passed to regulate them the hell out of the county. But they couldn't get enough support because so many people had a biker somewhere in their social or family group. But lesbians — lesbians who lured men into their lair and beat them up, even used knives on a few — this was both titillating and galvanizing.

"You do whatever you want, I'm not going in there with 1,500 of them," the sheriff was quoted as saying in the paper.

We had survived the encounters on the road at the first Festival, and we knew well that the sisters would not be passive if men came to challenge our world.

We were in a shitstorm of trouble.

I got nowhere with the sheriff when I suggested that the only solution was for him to write a retraction. Fuck it, I would write to the paper myself.

It was the first round in decades of attempting to correct misinformation about the Festival. As I read it now, I can still feel the tremble in the typewriter as I wrote that letter, a 20-year-old with one Festival under my belt.

"It is entirely false that we have a desire to do any harm to anyone in the community: more realistically, we come to the community as friends, to do business and to create an environment where womyn can share their music and knowledge with each other. We have respect for your community and the land where we are holding the event and for the people who we have done business within this area. It is true that this is a unique event held for womyn and children only; we fully intend for it to remain this way.

"Our hope is that the people of this community will take us at face value and not judge us on the unfounded rumors circulating through the area. We will respect the people and the land of this community, and we ask for mutual respect of our land and the womyn and children attending this event."

The newspaper printed my letter, and it was discussed at breakfast counters, hardware stores, and backyard barbecues. The story of 2,000 lesbians converging on Oceana County went statewide, and I even heard it on the radio as I drove about in my van.

One day right before the Festival, the sheriff stopped by and said he had been contacted by the FBI. Someone embedded with the Devil's Disciples motorcycle gang had informed them that the Disciples and Hell's Angels were planning to descend on the Festival and "kick some lesbian ass."

I stared into the sheriff's eyes and had no intent of giving this jackass a pass on what he had manifested with his article. "You did this, you know that, right?"

"I know we have an issue now," the sheriff said as he glanced around the land, peppered with womyn building a stage to his far right, others setting up a large Army tent just behind us.

I cracked open an Old Milwaukee and said, "I really don't know what else there is to do except for you to close off the county roads leading to the Festival, and only allow womyn through. Otherwise, there's going to be mayhem. And I just want to say, though we come in total peace, we will not take shit from men who come to threaten us."

"We can't really entirely close the county road down, but we, I guess we have to set up checkpoints, or I can see something might really happen."

"You think? The FBI told you that biker gangs from here to Chicago were coming to cause trouble, based on your false information, and you are still wondering if it's a real issue? We think we also need to have a squad car right on the road, 50 yards from the gate at all times. You caused this problem and you must be part of solving it."

"We don't have the men or the budget to do all of that. I can't have a squad car just sitting there."

Kris and I offered to pay for it. We just couldn't afford to have womyn be threatened by bikers who'd gotten all ginned up by this explosive article. "We will pay for the coverage right outside our gate, you cover the checkpoints to make sure that none of these biker groups get anywhere near our event."

From that point forward, for the next 38 years we paid to have a squad car outside our gate at night, connected to our security coordinator by CB radio. The man who had started the showdown was Sheriff John Smith, who later retracted what he had said in the paper. Over time he became one of our biggest supporters, starting with his reluctant respect for how we handled this incident in our second year.

Bob Farwell, a young recruit who did much of the road duty that year, became a favorite of our Communications/Security Crew, so much so that every deputy who was on shift was simply called Road Bob by our crew. Eventually they would all do their CB check by saying "Road Bob checking in." Road Bob eventually became the sheriff and like so many in Oceana County, came into his full adulthood and then into his own community leadership with the Festival being a fact of life in Oceana County.

Odd '70s game
with accordion
photo by Jill Ferson

CHAPTER 3

MY MOTHER ON THE LAND

Lisa Vogel and Edith Vogel, 1977

This is me, as a young dyke on the old Land, in this tattered photo in my hand. The labrys around my neck tells me it's the second Festival. The womon next to me doing magic with that super-long cigarette ash is my mother, Edith. The chair she's sitting in was also magic because this was long before there were chairs on the Land. Some sister was kind and loaned it to her, and another sister brought her that flower. We had never known someone's mother to be on the Land at that time. I was pretty surprised the first was mine.

Edith had surprised me, arriving after a solid day of rain on Saturday, when all shows had been canceled due to the storm. My mind was on everything and anything but my mother at that point.

We had one stage running five sets of performances per day. The huge storm had literally collapsed the stage as we clambered to move all the equipment to the center. I have no idea how many of us were right there on the stage, but a lot. Back then, we all got involved in everything, and this was an all-out emergency. The high winds had taken ahold of the tent fabric, pushing the canvas against the speaker tower, which swayed backwards with every large gust. I scrambled up the speaker cabinets (we could not find our single ladder) to reach the speaker horns at the very top. When the winds gusted and the canvas pushed the stack, the stack pushed me, and the sisters behind me pushed back, trying to keep us all erect. In the breaks between gusts, we got that first horn cabinet down, then the next, and in the middle of our dyke Keystone Cops disassembling of the speaker stacks, the stage just gave way.

We were determined to teach ourselves all the skills that were denied females, but at the beginning, we still hadn't found womyn who had those skills to be our guides. Instead, we got our ideas from all kinds of unlikely places. For example, the inspiration for the stage construction that eventually was perfected over the years came late one night in Mt. Pleasant. I was parked on a side street with a friend, drinking peppermint schnapps and snorting lines from a quarter gram of coke. We just happened to be across from a house that was jacked up off the ground to prepare it for being moved. The entire house was sitting on cribs of 4-foot-long four-by-fours.

"Wow!" said my hyper-alert, bedazzled brain. "If they can do that with a whole house, we can do that with a stage!" It had been such a hassle the year before, leveling the scaffolding for the stage and cutting the little square feet to stop the scaffold legs from grinding into the dirt. We didn't even know they rented feet and leveling legs — we just did it all by digging and swearing. With this jacked-up revelation, we designed the stage to sit on cribs of four-by-fours, with two sets of framing grids made from two-by-twelves sitting on the cribs instead of scaffolding.

What we hadn't realized was something the storm showed us — the importance of those cribs being under the critical areas where the framing structures met.

The year before we had rented lumber from the nearby local lumberyard, impressing them with our assurance that we would return the wood with very few nail holes. For the second Festival, we planned a larger 32-by-20-foot stage using 16-foot-long two-by-twelves. When the wood arrived, it was just dumped on the ground: black oak, wet, heavy as hell, and rough-cut (which means it was not cut to size or cut square). We quickly burned out our two circular saws attempting to square off the pieces to build the grid, and our one chainsaw didn't work either. The lumber was so heavy it took four womyn to carry each board. What had started as a fun ballet continued through the hours as a grinding, sweaty catastrophe.

At 7 p.m., after a long, exasperating, and completely unproductive day, I walked into the sawmill where the guys were now playing poker and drinking beer. A fried circular saw in each hand, I asked, "Are you deliberately fucking with us?" Tears of frustration and exhaustion rolled off my filthy, 21-year-old face. They stopped their game. They listened. They agreed to come out and get the wood in the morning and bring it back square cut by the afternoon. They offered me a cold beer and had a few laughs at my expense, but they kept their word the next day. They ended up being the only people we bought framing lumber from for the next 38 years.

Even with the correctly cut wood, the wet black oak was almost impossible to get a 16-penny nail through unless you really knew how to drive a nail. We had dozens of bent nails everywhere. We were still learning how to nail, level, and shim, and it sorely showed. It didn't help matters when someone brought out their bag of peyote and we tripped as we banged away. One board had about 15 bent-over nails in it, with the scribbled slogan: "Even cowgirls get the shakes."

After riding this crazy roller coaster, we nailed it. We had built a stage. The process had been a hot mess. And now when the storm landed on us, it was our hot mess to deal with, caved-in in the dark of the night, sound and lighting equipment piled in the middle.

We stayed up all night, drying connections, rebuilding. When we realized that this would be an all-nighter, I asked a womon nicknamed Peanut Butter if she could find us some booze. Off she went, tent to tent, rousing sisters and asking for alcohol for the Collective. She came back, arms loaded with half-full bottles. Even with that long night of frenzied work, we would have to cancel the next day's shows, working round the clock to rebuild the stage, dry out the equipment, and prepare for our final day of Festival. Once we had rebuilt the stage, we would have to run 10 sets on the last day.

Early that morning, after a night of no sleep, I was at the house we had rented for a phone line a couple of miles away. In the midst of making equipment calls to repair or replace gear damaged in the storm, the phone rang. I assumed it was a return call. Instead, it was my father, calling to say my mother, Edie, was on her way. She and Linda, my brother's wife, were already on the road. They'd left early and would arrive by 11.

I wasn't out to my mother. Hanging up from my father's call, I didn't know what was worse, that she was coming to the #%!# Festival and I couldn't stop her, or that I would have to face all these new womyn in my life, my sudden family and co-conspirators in building our radical, self-loving lesbian town, to say, "Argh … say hello to my mother, and oh, by the way, she doesn't know I'm a lesbian."

Some things take time.

I remember the look on her face, a mix of pride and horror. I remember her watching the butt-naked game of London Bridges happening in the mud-filled concert bowl — so beautiful when they all went tumbling down. I ran out to join in for a brief moment, and when I returned to check on Edith, she was trying to keep it together. "Lisa — don't you think you could at least put some shorts on?"

I remember the two sisters sitting right in front of her who fell backward, making out, both heads resting on Edith's feet, who then proceeded to pass out right on her slippers. She just kept drinking her beer, smoking her unfiltered Chesterfields, and smiling. She looked at me and said, "You know Lisa, someone could get the wrong idea about this Festival. They would think it was only for a certain kind of womon." She couldn't say the word lesbian. She hadn't wrapped her mind around what was really happening and was valiantly working to keep her denial in place, even in the midst of Lesbian Nation.

Most of all, I remember the line of sisters, a steady dozen long, stopping by to say hello, wondering if their mothers would ever come to the Land. It was only the second year and it was already our home.

CHAPTER 4

IT'S ALL ABOUT THE HUSTLE

I've been asked hundreds of times over the years what made us start the Michigan Womyn's Music Festival, and what previous experience we brought to the task. I often felt like the answer should have included a background in business, or a job working special events, a deeply drawn epiphany about womyn's space and safety, maybe a radical plan to overthrow Patriarchy. It was never that satisfying to reply with some version of, "We were tired of driving to get to a womyn's event," or that our skills were "complete ignorance" and "total naïveté." There's nothing very sheroic in claiming, "It was somewhat of a lark that just kept happening."

But that's all true.

I can't claim that the Festival was my idea, even though the idea did come out of my mouth during a stoned trip in the back of a cargo van full of lesbians as we drove from Boston back home to Mt. Pleasant, Michigan. In later years I knew in my heart that when the goddess went looking for a few someones who would have the tenacity to do something like this, it made sense that I was on the short list. While I had a few good ideas along the way, it helped me keep my sanity and wear the proper size hat to know that the larger idea wasn't really mine. To say I was a channel of the goddess was not something I would say out loud. It sounded so pretentious. Instead, I would say, "I was willing to be of use."

We had gone to Boston to attend a womyn's music festival, and my naïveté was so thick that I thought at least if we organized something in Michigan, we wouldn't have to smash ourselves into the back of a borrowed cargo van for 1,500 miles.

None of us who initially said yes to this idea knew a single thing about what we were innocently starting. The one thing I brought to any table was hustle. Hustle, as in, I had determination, passion, and the ability to exert energy toward a goal, sure. But on a deeper level, I had lived my short life up until that time with the self-reliance of a street urchin, the get-over of a corner hustler, and the sleight of hand of a carnie. I liked people, and from all my years of hustling work, waiting tables, dealing drugs, and throwing parties, I knew how to talk with all kinds of people.

"You can't con a con" was how I owned my flimflam ways. With little phrases like this I let my friends know that I understood the slightly crooked route my blood took through my veins, that I had a loose hold on it, and would reserve the bite of it for dealing with The Man. I was confident that I could spot most people or businesses trying to pull one over on us, especially the type of male exploitation thrown at womyn trying to get something done. I knew to never take the offered price as what we would pay. I always negotiated to the point of exhaustion, and if I was on point, I could turn the quote around and get what we needed at the price we could afford while making them think it was their idea.

I grew up working-class poor white in mid-eastern Michigan, the very beginning of the Fan Belt, the corridor of our state that churned out automobiles. From as young as I can remember, I was shoveling snow and raking leaves for coins. I was probably around 9 years old when I began my progressive side-hustles.

It started with being a badass dirt marble player and amassing an apple basket full of puries, cat eyes, boulders, steelies, clearies, and aggies. I traded marbles for comic books that the kids on the corner pilfered from their dad's stash, and then I sold those 12-cent comic books for a nickel each, turning marbles to get cash. Then I would sneak across the river on my bike to the Mill End and buy fire-sale nickel candy bars for 3 cents and sell them at my stand on the playground for a nickel.

I didn't net that much, but anything was something, and I loved the hustle.

Hustle. Not fraud. Not completely innocent, but solid hustle.

I had one little business after another in my neighborhood. I'd clean your bike and get all the rust off your rims. I made skateboards out of abandoned roller skates and found boards, and made rubber guns and rifles with cut-up bike inner tubes stretched over a piece of wood, released by a "trigger" fashioned out of rubber bands and long tacks. I loaded up the Horses pinball machine at the tiny neighborhood arcade and sold the games I won at half price. I sold fireworks from my bike, and later, pot, speed, and mescaline from under my bed at my parents' house. I guess I was a little hood, but mostly, I was a little hustler, utilizing whatever contraband I could to make an exchange. It wasn't always for a buck.

After we decided to do a music festival there was an entire world to figure out, a whole universe of things to bring together, and without resources or money, we relied on our willingness and street smarts to move forward. This came into play in a million ways over the decades, but early on what we needed more than anything was some land.

I found an ad in the Mt. Pleasant *Daily Sun* for someone who was dividing up a 120-acre piece of property into 10-acre lots outside of Weidman, a little four-corners town 15 miles northwest of where we lived. I called the number. Planning a womyn-only gathering had become such a hot issue, even in our peer group, I knew I couldn't introduce the Festival like that.

"We are organizing a women's musical retreat" was the phrase I adopted and used for years. It got the word "women's" in there, but when combined with "retreat" it implied something religious, or at least spiritual, both of which were true within our reality. I already understood that a womyn's music festival struck fear and loathing in many people's hearts as much as it ignited excitement and yearning in others. It was subversive. It said we didn't need men. It said out loud that womyn were left out of popular music, that you all can go and have your music festivals, we will make ours. It was threatening. Some even said it was hateful.

"Women's music retreat" took the edge off of all of that. With that slightly passive turn of words, we were seen as nice young women rather than hateful ball-busters, and in the process, everything became possible when otherwise, doors had been closed. As long as we didn't let people know who we were, what we were doing and that we were dykes, so many folks wanted to "help the girls out."

Some of our schemes worked. Some, not so much. Sprouts for our salads at the Festival, for example. In the '70s, we all made sprouts in our own homes. It was before they were mass produced, and if you could buy them, they were very expensive. Since I was a weekly sprouter, I figured I could grow what we'd need for the Festival. I built two 8-foot-long by 3-foot-wide sprouting contraptions, covered them in window screen, and set them up under the willow tree to get the darkness they needed to sprout. It was all going great until the rain started. I ended up with two huge vats of moldy almost-sprouts.

Wherever I traveled, my eyes reliably landed on things that I could scavenge for use on the Land. A couple of discarded cinder blocks went into my truck. Odds and ends of pieces of wood on a building site could be used for shims. Hmm, it doesn't look like anyone is using that stack of pallets. I've seen that pile of milk crates in the same place for a week, let's go back tonight and tidy up.

And though we didn't straight-up steal many things of value, we were busted once for relieving the Farm Store of a part of their abundant pile of steel fence posts (we needed these posts for just about everything), along with some rolls of wooden snow fencing we used for wheelchair traction. We had strong ethics, but in the early years of little money and big vision, our code allowed for reallocating some of the goods of the Patriarchy to use in building our matriarchal town.

Sometimes it was what we spotted, apparently unused or underutilized, that we could repurpose. Other times it was all about the sweet talk. Before we had anything like Artist Shuttle, we would borrow vehicles from campers for artists to drive back and forth from where they stayed off-site. The artists' transportation coordinator position pretty much involved schmoozing sisters upon arrival to borrow their cars. One year, a particularly creative Amazon decided to borrow a car for Holly Near. Nine times.

"Hi! I'm wondering if you would be willing to loan your car to Holly Near for the weekend?" she would ask womon after womon. No one was the wiser until Monday morning, when nine different womyn showed up at the front gate to be reunited with the car they had lent to Holly Near for the weekend.

Our entire ecosphere ran on hustle.

I tell these stories fondly, and though the illegal get-overs fell by the wayside as we grew older and had a few more resources, I have no regrets. People — individually and collectively — do what they need to do to create a better life. Some doors were closed tight to us by sexism, and other doors, opened by class privilege, were shut to me and so many of the sisters who came to build the early Festivals. That hall pass was never mine.

But hustle — I owned that. While I lacked some foundational worldly information (universally mistaken as intelligence) that forms one of the building blocks of middle-class privilege, I excelled in street smarts, hustle, and get-over. And I was game to do just about anything to build a home for the growing Amazon Nation.

Old Land pallet path, circa 1978-79 photo by C. Elliot

CHAPTER 5

TRISH

On the Monday afternoon following the second Festival, I was in a game of chess with some womyn who wanted to take the Womb tent home with them, a tent with "U.S. Army" emblazoned along one side. Understandably they felt in their Amazonian arrogance that they were justified in lifting anything that belonged to the government. This is how we felt in the '70s, no reservations. But I was nurturing a relationship with Reserve posts all over the state to get free equipment for the Festival and I wasn't going to let these drifters ruin this sweet deal.

While they were busy making me into someone who supported the Army, I was checkmating them by explaining how the tent was used by witches and healers to teach non-allopathic healing to the sisters. We were in a bit of a standoff when someone ran up and said the State Police had a womon in the back of their car on the county road, and that the womon was naked.

Double checkmate.

My sister Kristie and I took off running to the front gate. The state bull cruiser was idling on the side of the road, with a dozen bedraggled post-Festival womyn wandering around. As we approached the squad car, we could see that there was a womon truly naked in the back.

"Hello officer, I understand there's a bit of a misunderstanding going on," I said.

He looked up at us like we were talking Pig Latin. Why was this a state bull instead of someone from the sheriff's office?! We now had good relations with the sheriff but had absolutely no direct contact with the state police.

He explained that he had gotten a call from an elderly womon down the road who was in a panic because a naked woman had run up to her house and started pounding on the kitchen window.

"I'm sure she was just lost and didn't mean any harm. We can sort this out if you release her to us."

More Pig Latin.

He explained he was waiting for the go-ahead to take her up to the psych unit in Traverse City, renowned in Michigan as the place you did not want to go if you were flipped out.

Ka, a womon who was dating my sister, was a nurse, and she explained to the officer that she could assist. We were hoping if everything got calmer, he would release her to us. He allowed Ka to get into the squad car to try to talk the sister down. Ka covered her with a blanket because she truly was butt naked, except for some creative body paint. Just as this happened and the police were becoming a little less tense, a pack of five women approached the car. Coming from some sort of ritual, they had painted their faces and were robed in about a thousand flowing scarves each. Their eyes were wild and somewhat rolling in their heads. The wildest of them came forward and told the officer that she was an MD, and that she would take responsibility for the womon in the back seat.

"Lady, unless you want me to book a double in Traverse City, I suggest you move away from the vehicle," he replied, still unimpressed.

With all the confusion outside the car, things suddenly got wild in the back seat. The woman, now wrapped in a blanket, ripped Ka's glasses off her face, popped one of the lenses out, and before anyone could see what was happening, popped it up her cooch. Ka really couldn't see without her glasses, so she put the remaining Coke-bottle-thick monocle right back on her face.

Clearly, they were going to Traverse City after this move. We couldn't leave her alone, we knew this much, so Kristie, along with Ka sporting her single lens, went with them in the squad car. Since the womon was found naked without ID, we had no idea who she was, where she was from, and if she had come with anyone. Almost everyone was gone from the Festival site by this time except a handful of workers, the womyn doing the scarf ritual, and the drifters hanging around to see what they could steal. Uh, borrow. Permanently.

For some reason the authorities released the womon into Kristie and Ka's custody later that day. She gave us the name Trish, which we weren't sure was real, and we started to call anyone we knew in different cities. Madison, did you lose someone? Boston — we have a womon named Trish, anyone there know her? Lansing, are you missing a sister?

Meanwhile, we were cleaning up the Festival site with a single rented U-Haul truck. After the trip to Traverse City, Trish was back on site with us and had already run off once, getting herself naked and heading for the road, so we thought it was safest if we kept her inside the U-Haul. We would pack and load boxes in and she would promptly throw them out.

We had no clue how to handle this.

We had all read *The Bell Jar* and *Women and Madness*, and passed around books by Anne Sexton and Sylvia Plath. We knew we couldn't let a sister go to a psych ward. In our quest to reach a radical feminist understanding of mental health for womyn under Patriarchy, we knew it was a thin line between what was considered sane and insane, and many of us lived on a continuum that defied that line. The crushing confinement of Patriarchy was an entrapment we were working to break free from, and not all of us would make it. We believed that Trish was better off with us. We would wait it out until she came down from the expanded space she was in, and meanwhile, somehow, we would find out where she was from.

At night, post-Festival, we returned to the little house we had rented for an office base. We took turns being on Trish duty, so she couldn't run off down the road or hurt herself. Each hour revealed how deeply she was outside of any realm of safety in herself. She vacillated from making sexual attacks on random womyn in the house to trying to stick her head in the toilet while flushing, or making a run for the door.

It was the '70s. We were well-versed in weird, and actively celebrated unusual behaviors. How were we to know what was "normal" outside of the constraints of Patriarchy? Any number of sisters who had found their way to Festival by year two were survivors of psychiatric institutions, talked about it freely, and were part of pushing on what we all considered normal behaviors. We questioned everything.

So, was it wrong to run naked down the road? Who says? Was her latest move a sexual attack or a hot advance? Who decides?

Our world was one big question mark.

The second night Trish was back from Traverse City, we were making dinner with the obligatory quart jar of bulk safflower oil from the Co-op on the kitchen counter. Pam Lynn, who had hopped freight trains from Oregon to Michigan to get to the Festival, was making stir fry. With superhuman speed, Trish jumped off the couch, made a run for the safflower oil, and started chugging it like an ice-cold beer at a softball game. It leaked out the sides of her mouth and ran down her naked chest.

"Now you've done it — look at yourself! It's all over you. You gotta rub it in," chastised Pam Lynn as she roughly spread the oil over Trish's body, seemingly not at all concerned that this person had just drunk almost a quart of oil, only that she rub the oil that landed on her body into her skin. "It's good for you."

We were done with Festival strike, and it was time to return to Mt. Pleasant, which meant there would be an even smaller handful of us left. We were exhausted from the Festival. We were so damn tired from packing everything up and managing Trish day and night. She never seemed to sleep, and of course, with no sleep she got wilder each day. We brought her back to Mt. Pleasant and then realized that we couldn't keep this up. We were starting to understand that as much as we wanted to help her, and as deeply as we didn't want to turn her over to a hospital, she was getting worse, not better.

There was a smaller psych unit in Alma, a town just north of Mt. Pleasant, and we decided to take her there. Ka and Kristie would stay there the first night as she got settled. They fell asleep outside of her room in the middle of the night as extreme exhaustion overtook them. As they slept, Trish snuck out, chucked her clothes, and was found hitchhiking naked down the nearby highway. She was picked up by the police just as a tractor-trailer stopped to give her a ride.

After a few days in the hospital and some medicated rest, Trish started to come back to herself. She remembered who she was and where she was from, and within the week was on her way home. She stayed in touch for a few years with Kristie. She was able to stabilize with medication and eventually became a counselor herself, helping other womyn going through difficult times.

Trish was the first but not the last woman we found on the Land at the end of the Festival with no ID, no memory of who she was, and with her mind in an expanded and wild state. We realized that the freedom and uncharted territory the Festival offered often inspired womyn to stop taking their meds or to take extra-special meds. Especially in the early years, it was not uncommon to find a sister hiding in a tree for days at the end of the Festival, or walking over hot coals unsuccessfully, or howling into the night air for hours on end.

We all walked into a heightened state on that Land, drenched in the massive energy of community, alive with the reawakened memories of Amazon pride. It rearranged our very molecules, mostly for the better. We all took risks, and for most of us those risks made our lives bigger, our minds more open, our hearts more deeply fulfilled. But nothing works for everyone, and Trish was one of our first teachers in this complicated lesson. It was a lesson we would have many more opportunities to work on in the years to come.

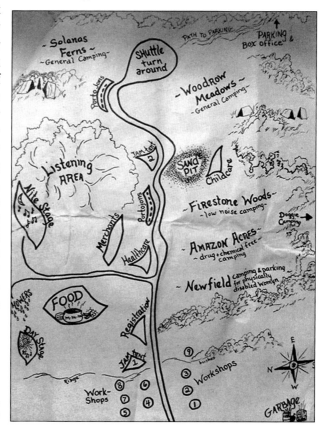

Map of the Old Land, 1979

CHAPTER 6

BERNICE

It was a pretty big deal for us that Sweet Honey in the Rock were coming to the Festival, and honestly, we were a little intimidated. We thought of them as being more a part of the Black Left than the feminist movement, and though there was a clear political and cultural affinity — and their music was fabulous — they were the first group we booked that wasn't primarily part of the womyn's music scene.

We had produced one Festival and were heading into our second, still pretty much a rag-tag group of mostly white, mostly working-class dykes.

In 1977, we didn't yet provide hotel rooms for artists, but we did rent a little house about a mile and a half away from the Festival site to install a phone and provide a crash pad for the trips back and forth from our office in Mt. Pleasant. It was an old but not terribly rundown country house, with an awesome backyard featuring a majestic weeping willow tree. Even though we had a phone, it was a party line, which meant we shared it with several other people in the area. That's what happened in the country before there was enough phone cable for everyone to have their own dedicated line. If you picked up the phone and Gladys was talking, you had to wait until she was done. Or likewise, if George picked up his phone and you were on a business call, his clicking and scrabbling would be the background soundtrack throughout your call.

We had moved in some beds, a few pots and pans, a coffee pot, and a table to spread out our papers. It was your basic dyke crash pad minus 20%, meant to cover us for a month and then disappear.

We offered to have Sweet Honey in the Rock stay at the house during Festival, given the reality that they did not camp. We provided air transportation and shuttles to the Land for artists, but it didn't occur to us to rent vehicles to do this, so our vehicles were as rag-tag as we were. When it came time to pick up Sweet Honey, Laura went to Grand Rapids in a borrowed cargo van, with some pillows to soften the ride back.

Unbeknownst to her, in the van there was a garbage bag of shake, the stems and bits of marijuana that were left over from cleaning bulk grass after the tops and leaf went into baggies to make lids. (A lid, by the way, is an ancient form of measurement, also known as three-fingers, the common portion of pot sold at the time.) Evelyn Harris from Sweet Honey sat on the bag, realized what it was, and wasn't having it.

"What makes you think you can drive a van full of Black women into the deep country of Michigan with a garbage bag of marijuana?" she asked. "This isn't happening."

Still at the airport, Laura grabbed the bag and ran over to some sisters who had rented a vehicle to make their way to the Festival. "Do you have room in your car to take something to the Land for the collective? Just drop it off at the little trailer by the front gate."

Writing this now, I don't imagine that this was cool, or smart, or respectful — but it was perfectly normal for the time.

The day that Sweet Honey arrived was at the end of a two-day rain, so while we were working on the Land and Laura was picking them up, a whole bunch of things had moved over to the house to take shelter. There were musicians rehearsing. The funky amateur silk-screening of that year's T-shirt design was being squeegeed upstairs, the smell of the ink everywhere. And I was waiting for the septic company to come and pump the septic system, which had decided that on this day — our third week in the house — it would back up. That year's T-shirt art turned into a perfect image for that day: Womyn going up in flames, the red flames over on one side of the shirt, the yellow womyn figures kinda crooked and on the right, the two rarely centered on top of each other but somehow eventually making a meaningful design.

I remember Sweet Honey's arrival into all of this, and my fumbling to try to explain how the pandemonium they had walked into really wasn't intentional. I was so sorry, but one thing had led to another and now here we were in a house full of people, no working toilet, the smell of septic tank and ink covering the country air.

They had been in the van for over two hours. Bernice looked about and asked me, "Where do you go to the bathroom?"

"Personally, I like to pee on the far side of the willow tree," I told her. And without shade, she turned on her heels and left, walking through the tall grass toward the willow.

Sweet Honey did not stay in the house that night. They rented a few motel rooms nearby and gave me the bill, which I accepted the next morning without comment or negotiation.

I didn't know Bernice Johnson Reagon's history at that time, that she was one of the founding members of SNCC (Student Nonviolent Coordinating Committee) and influential through her musical career with the Freedom Singers, weaving communal song as a powerful force for social change in the Civil Rights Movement of the '60s. I knew her music from the first Sweet Honey record, which was out by 1977. Now I was learning what it was to be in her presence as she skillfully navigated me and this Festival she had landed in. She was steady, alive, and had a slow and solid power in her personality.

I had a question at some point about their group's setup. I approached Bernice and with abandon, sat on her lap, put my arm around her shoulder and started to discuss. This was a thing in the '70s for some of us more gregarious types — our freedom of expression had been released by feminism, but a healthy set of social boundaries had yet to be developed. I recall their manager at the time starting to approach, I'm sure to slap me upside the head, but Bernice nodded and said, "We're fine."

I think that first year was why Bernice and I always had an ease between us, then and for decades to come. Though I grew to know all the ways she earned the respect and reverence that people held for her, respect that was well deserved, I got to know her first as a sister on the land.

The last time Bernice performed on the land, she returned to do a Bernice Johnson Reagon Songbook set with her daughter, Toshi Reagon, in 2011, seven years after leaving Sweet Honey. I sat down next to her in Central Heating and revisited that first year.

"Bernice," I said, "you and I have never discussed that first year that Sweet Honey performed at Festival, and that crazy setup when you arrived at the house where we had arranged for you to stay. I'm kinda surprised you ever came back. I just want to say after all these years that I hope you realize we meant no disrespect. We literally didn't know any better. None of us had ever stayed in a hotel, and honestly, had little understanding of how complicated it was for us to expect Black womyn to come camp in the rural woods of Michigan."

She responded, "I realized how much you were doing to accommodate us, and to stretch, and it was right that we meet you where you were, just as much as you were working to meet us where we were. We were meeting each other, and we both stretched. And from that first year forward there was never a show where someone didn't come up and say they had first heard our music at the Festival. It helped us a great deal. I'd like to think we helped you."

In so many ways, Sweet Honey's commitment to the Festival — in particular, Bernice's steady participation in all of the ways for almost 35 years — helped the community grow stronger, expand in diversity, and answer the political call she brought to each performance.

One of the deepest learning experiences I had during any Festival was that second year, during Sweet Honey's first performance. It involved a womon who went by Shen, who by then was well known to us, her van left in the parking lot full of barking dogs while she roamed the land very drunk, day and night. During Sweet Honey's set, Shen rolled up on stage. She was shit-faced drunk, swaying and staggering, her long blond hair stringy and her clothes completely disheveled. She, too, had found the liberty of self-expression but had yet to learn the boundaries a society needs to be cool with everyone. We didn't have "stage security" yet, but when she somehow got herself up on the stage, you could just see the entire crew standing around the edges start to lean toward her, ready to move her out of the show.

Bernice was singing and didn't miss a beat. She held her hand up to stop the crew starting to come onto the stage. She walked over to Shen, who was stagger-dancing around, gave her the shekere she was playing, and invited her into the semicircle of singers. Shen took the beaded gourd, calming down just a little, and started playing the instrument with her full heart. I watched as Bernice held her in the group, all the while none of them missing a damn note. When the song ended, Bernice turned to her, bowed ever so slightly, showed her to the side of the stage, and continued their set.

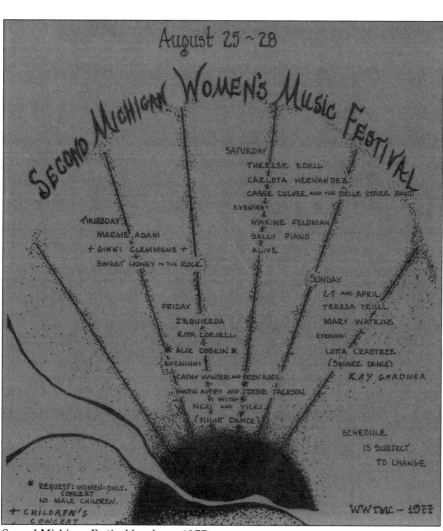

Second Michigan Festival brochure, 1977

1st row: *Stage, 1976* photo by Debra Hirshberg; 2nd row: *Camping, 1976* photo by Debra Hirshberg; *Stage, 1979* photo by Barb Graves; 3rd row: *Camping (Old Land), 1980* photo by Carol Vitelli; 4th row: *Day/ Open Mic stage, 1977* photo by Susan Baylies

1st row: *Holly Near, 1976* photo by Debra Hirshberg; *Holly Near, 2015* photo by Desdemona Burgin; 2nd row: *Teresa Trull, 1976* photo by Debra Hirshberg; *Teresa Trull, 2015* photo by Desdemona Burgin; 3rd row: *Kitchen, 1976* photo by Debra Hirshberg; *Lisa turning feral*; 4th row: *Jan Walsh's VW Bus pulled by donkeys arriving to the Land, 1977* photo by Jan Walsh

CHAPTER 7

ROSE RESTO STARTED DART

I was answering the phone one day at the Festival office. That sounds a little official, but it was two desks lifted after-hours from the local university that were pushed into a living room alongside a huge wooden electrical spool covered in candle wax, roach butts, and dust; a massive stereo system with a wall of LPs; and two funky couches repurposed from a Thursday trash pickup. Our office had a single phone line, which doubled as the only phone for the entire household that I and four other lesbians called home. 1501 Lyons Street was the Festival office's address, and the mailing address for around 20 lesbians who had laid their heads down for a spell and so had mailing rights. I didn't know anyone who used a post office box.

It was some weeks before the third Fest. We had grown from 2,000 womyn the first year to 3,500 the second, and our single-line phone was ringing off the hook day and night come July. I took a call from a womon who asked if we could pick someone up from the bus station in Shelby, a little town 20 miles away from the Festival site. It was 1978 and we didn't have anything like a formal shuttle from Grand Rapids, the nearest airport, but if we were there to pick up an artist when you arrived, we always gave a sister a lift.

"Sure, we can get someone to come and pick you up. There's no bus station there, the bus just drops passengers off at a four-corner's gas station, but the bus does stop, and we can scoop you up."

"What kind of vehicle would the person come in?"

I had no idea what kind of vehicle or who would be driving it, and in our world of running by the seat of our pants in all things, I thought it was a peculiar question.

"I'll be in a wheelchair," she continued. "I want to make sure I can get into the vehicle."

Oh, shit. There hadn't been anyone using a wheelchair at the first two Festivals, and at that point in time, I had never known a single person who used a chair except the people from the Center for Human Development, where I had worked as an aide. Before that job, my only exposure was the guy who sold me firecrackers when I was a kid. I had been so scared of that guy. When I look back, I can see it was partially because I was going to a strange man's house to buy contraband, but the unfamiliarity and otherness I experienced when he rolled up to his screen door in a wheelchair heightened the experience. I was frightened by his disability. I feared any disability that I ran across, and there was no one to talk to about the people who moved through the world with physical differences. No one in my world growing up talked about it, ever.

The job I had taken at the Center put me right in the middle of dozens of people who lived with what was termed "multiple physical impairments and severe mental disorders." I worked there during a time when de-institutionalization was new, so the folks I supported there had mostly been living in institutions for their entire lives. Group homes were becoming the cultural shift, with people with disabilities living more integrated in communities, but my employer was still old school, the last to go in the state of Michigan. I quickly realized that not everyone there had a severe mental disorder, but their physical disabilities and differences landed them in the mix.

I didn't last long at the Center. I got in trouble for taking folks off campus, for sneaking in and reading files to understand the history of some of the people, for laughing too much, being inappropriately familiar with the clients, and for teaching Robyn to take a few steps, after years and years of being strapped to a wheelchair. Part of my job was learning to transfer folks in wheelchairs to easy chairs, or beds, or toilets, so I learned a little about the mechanics of wheelchairs.

And now here was Rose Resto. A dyke calling to say she was traveling from New York City on a Greyhound bus, by herself, to go to a camping music festival, and could we pick her up at a gas station in Shelby Fucking Michigan.

"We can make sure we get you to the Festival, but honestly, that's just the beginning," I told her. "You're going to be kinda fucked at the Festival in a wheelchair. The event is on 120 acres. It is sandy and unlevel, and very spread out." I remembered getting Robyn's wheelchair stuck in the sand the time I snuck her out of the Center to take her to see the river.

Everything we did in that first decade we made up as we went along. When we began the Festival, we thought we were just throwing a good party that we wouldn't have to drive across the country to attend. But our third year in, we realized that we were creating something that had to hold thousands of womyn for four days and have it make sense, have it be safe, and make sure it had a beating heart and a soul. That meant learning not just how to throw a concert, but how to create infrastructure that a large group needed to survive, things like a rural water system, electricity, first aid and health care, food, security, and sewage. We felt pretty damn bold and willing to take on things we had no idea how to do. But the courage of this womon, at this time, to jump on a bus and fling herself into the woods was beyond anything we were trying to accomplish.

I told everyone in the office about my call from this dyke from New York, who was so fierce she was coming by herself in a wheelchair to the Festival. We sat around and talked about it. Whoa — what the fuck is she going to do? How is she going to handle this? We started to brainstorm about the things that would be a problem for her. How the hell is she going to pee? At that time yes, we rented portable toilets for the Festival. For the workers, we would arrive early and dig a few shitter holes, and most of us just peed in the woods. Maybe we could build her an enclosure over a shitter hole, like we make for crew but with a cover and a seat. Ding Forest told us that it needed to have handrails so she could transfer herself from the chair to the toilet. Excellent idea.

We thought the packed dirt road that went through the Festival was good enough to be passable in a chair, but she needed to be able to move in and out of the field to her tent and back to the road. A wheelchair needed traction. At that time, snow fencing was made from 4-foot-long, 1 1/2-by-3/8 slats held together with twisted wire. There were rolls and rolls of it outside the Feed & Supply Farm Store in White Cloud. We were sure they wouldn't miss a couple that disappeared in the middle of the night.

I don't really know how that first year went for Rose. I don't remember ever talking with her about that specifically. But I know she came back the next year, and I suspect that her first trip started the ripple into what grew to a steady network of political disabled dykes coming to Michigan. And with each new wave of womyn, those beginning efforts of accessibility grew. There was now a small network of snow fence wheel-ways around the land, womyn clackety-clack-clacking along on the bumpy path.

We started to have some of the concerts interpreted in American Sign Language for the deaf sisters, and we could hook you up with an interpreter if you wanted to go to a meeting or a workshop. We had one crew person, then two, whose job was to check in and see if any of the womyn camping in the disabled area needed any support. In 1980, there was a growing community of disabled dykes at the Festival.

As minimal as our services were at that point, they felt enough support from and connection to the Festival that we were asked if we would welcome a one-day meeting of disabled dykes on the land on the Monday after the 1981 Festival. There still wasn't much we could offer at that time, but sure — we'll keep the porta-potties near you on the land for an extra day and there's always leftover food available. Do your thing. We would be striking the Festival because we had to get everything off the rented land by Thursday.

By the time the seventh festival happened in 1982, there were 8,000 womyn as we moved to a new and unfamiliar Festival site. The Dykes with Disabilities conference that happened post-Festival the year before had put us on a map in the disabled womyn's communities, and so many more womyn with disabilities came to that year's Fest. On the old Land, everything was on top of everything else, with everyone complaining there was not enough room. But this new site was spread out, and everyone was lost and exhausted. We located the disabled camping area at the curve in the road, right in the middle of all the services and between the two stages, nestled under the powerful mature white oak trees. We called it Mother Oak. But still, this was going to take a shit-ton of snow fencing for these sisters to get anywhere.

We were totally unprepared for the Festival that year on many levels, but the most critical was the failure to provide support systems and services to the large number of disabled womyn who came, easily twice as many womyn as the year before. They had heard that the Festival was a safe place where womyn with disabilities could go into the wilderness and camp among a community of womyn. It was a revolutionary idea in a revolutionary time. In a world that didn't make room yet for these sisters to move about off the city tracks, they took the risk and came into the deep woods of rural Michigan. Between the numbers and needs, our inexperience and unpreparedness, there was an explosion of growing pains that rippled around the country.

Mother Oak was referred to as "The Hill," driving home that unless you actually use or are sensitive to wheelchairs, you don't begin to know what it's like to get around on a constant grade. The snow fencing that was a pain in the ass but functional on the old land was now something like mobility torture: Traversing 50 feet was doable, but the jiggling and jostling over 300 feet of clickety-clack was not possible for the womyn managing multiple disabilities. We didn't have enough accessible Porta-Janes. There wasn't enough support crew.

There wasn't electricity available for the medical devices some womyn needed to use daily, and this was before CPAP machines for sleep apnea were even available. We hadn't even thought of medical devices. Who would go into the woods to camp if their life depended on a medical device? A certain kind of brave and determined Amazon, for sure. The goodwill and community vibe that had led to the Festival feeling like a safe and supportive place for disabled dykes to have a conference disappeared in the overwhelming trauma and drama that covered that first year on the new Land.

Then, so many letters. To our mailbox throughout the winter. To *Lesbian Connection, Off Our Backs, Sojourner*, and just about every lesbian periodical that ever covered the Festival. Articulate letters. Angry letters. Insanely blaming letters. Letters to the editor calling for a boycott. It was so hard to not be defensive and get all tied up in all the ways we tried. To want to find a way to talk about our good intentions, like our good intentions should be the subject, rather than the hard time any of the sisters had camping on The Hill.

It is true, we tried. But some things you try and if you fail it is inconvenient, or you look bad. Other things, if you fail it seriously impacts someone's health and well-being. These are important learning curves, lessons to learn with your eyes, mind, and heart wide open.

CHAPTER 8

SETH AND THE WILD RIDE

Seth eased into the gate in a classic, old-ass Chevy truck pulling a wooden wagon — made from old barn wood sitting on a pair of rickety axles — that carried the horses we had rented. I breathed some relief when he came rolling in. This was not a fancy equestrian situation. For the price he quoted to bring four horses over to the land for the day, I guessed it was going to be a low-to-the-ground situation, but I hadn't quite imagined Seth Barker.

He climbed out of the truck, all legs that were tied to his scrawny torso by a pair of coveralls that had certainly seen more life than I had. Seth was as old as dirt. Layers upon layers of creases covered his face, his hands, his overalls — extending to the little old pony he rode — all connecting him to the ground he shuffled over as he untied the gate, then the horses, still not looking at us.

Seth Barker, his rig and horses, 1985   *Susan Alborell and Lisa Vogel, 1985*

It was early July 1982, and in mid-June we had lost the land we had rented for the Festival. The guy we had rented our site from for the prior five Festivals had become increasingly provoked to drive up to the gate in his Ford LTD to demand to come inside mid-Festival. Sorry, that wasn't going to happen. Apparently emasculated to the max by renting his property to lesbians, he pulled out at the last minute. We were in deep trouble.

We had looked at this new Land the past fall in a dream state of hopefulness, but what a tall order! We couldn't possibly do this. The Festival had grown on the old Land. We had to rent an additional back field for parking, then another field across the road, and we were aching to be in one place without the guy in the LTD harassing us.

We had been lucky enough to find his property in the first place. I sat at the Mt. Pleasant library for hours and hours looking at phone books and writing down Realtor's names and addresses, and I sent well over 100 letters to real estate agents in all of Michigan's rural areas where we could possibly have privacy. This is how we did it before the internet. One response had come, and it was Mr. LTD.

But now that had run itself out, and it was six weeks before the Festival. We called the Brindeck family, who owned this new property, to ask if we could rent the land. They had moved off the property back in the '30s when the old homestead had burned down, and had lived in Ohio ever since.

No. No rental.

We came back and proposed to rent it with an offer to buy: If we didn't make the first payment in October, we would lose the rent and the earnest money we put up. That sealed the deal. The land was enormous, 651 acres, a little more than a full section. It was confusing — no, downright terrifying — to try to figure out in a little more than a month how to make a Festival in this space: how to get electricity there, how to get water, where the stages and childcare and the kitchen could go — all of it.

We had walked and walked around the property and gotten ourselves lost in the woods, and our directions were screwed around so many times we could barely find our own feet. Let's do this on horseback, we thought — we'll have a higher perspective. At the very least we'd be able to find all the boundaries, which wasn't easy since it abutted National Forest almost all the way around. It was wilderness. Riding the property with the horses was our desperate attempt to make sense of it all.

That day with Seth, we rode through the woods, cross-country through the grasses and over the logs, long before the miles of woodchip paths and the feet of thousands of sisters would create the woodland webs we came to rely on. It was hot and buggy, and we were getting into some wetlands again, but we continued because we really needed to see where the southeastern corner of the property was. We started to see some wire fence, mostly submerged in the earth, ferns, and grass. It was old and covered in downed limbs. "Cool, it looks like we found the boundary!"

Seth was talking to himself most of the time, in that very faint whistling and crackling sound that very old men often have, like something is stuck in the upper part of their throat. I hadn't been paying much attention to him. To be honest, I was annoyed that he hadn't just let us take the horses while he napped under a tree. When he insisted that he ride with us, I decided I would just ignore him. But when we came upon a part of the fence that was still somewhat vertical, I heard Seth say to himself, "That held up pretty good. Yes, it did, damn good job."

"Seth, what did you say?" I asked him.

"That fence looks pretty good after all these years. Just saying — I do good work."

"Wait. Did you say you put up this fence we're looking at?!"

It turned out that Seth had lived on the Brindeck farm as a young man, in the barn with the inside animals, which was fairly common for a poor farmhand at the time. He hadn't been back since the family moved in the '30s, and with them the girl who had captured his heart so many years before.

"She was really something, she was," he told us. "But I was a farmhand, and she was the farmer's daughter, and all I could do was work hard and feel lucky when I was around her here and there."

I couldn't believe the deeply kismet moment we were having, suddenly understanding that we were riding our horses around on land that Seth had worked for years, long before I was even alive.

Our asses were sore from being on horses for hours and it was time for a snack break and a review of our newfound wealth of knowledge. Just then a Cadillac pulled into the two-track drive out near the front of the property, where we had left our snacks in the car. Since the property had been empty after the Brindecks left, most of the locals treated it like it was National Forest; they thought nothing of cutting through or hunting or doing whatever they liked. We knew we would have to turn this around gently. At every turn we would have to go up and have a conversation, explaining that the land was being sold, that we were the new buyers, and thank you for understanding that this was now private land, not National Forest.

I swaggered over to the Caddy, which had four people in it. A middle-aged man got out first, then a man with a white beard down to his belly slowly eased out of the car.

"Andy? Andy Brindeck?" Seth's whistling voice was louder than I had heard it all day. "Andy?!"

"Well, I'll be!" said the other old-timer.

The two men looked at each other for a very long time. They slowly approached, shook hands, then patted each other on the back. It was July 1982. These two men hadn't seen each other or spoken for 50 years. Twice the amount of time I had lived at this point. Andy's son and grandson drove him up to visit the land that they had just agreed to sell. He wanted to see it one last time.

There was a magic to this moment that stays with me, always. I often see those two men at the Front Gate on my way into the Land. And Seth on his own, too, leaning up against his old rig. The true passing of a baton had happened that day, and I knew it. I didn't know how we were going to keep this beautiful piece of land, but I knew we would.

I was aware at the time that Seth seeing Andy was likely to be one of the few moments in my life when I would witness two humans reuniting after 50 years, and now that I'm in my 60s myself, it remains true.

After the intense reunion, it was time for us to head back out. My ass was killing me from riding on the huge horse Seth had assigned to me, and he suggested that I try Pokey, his horse. I had only seen Pokey shuffle around through the woods much like Seth, looking old and tired, and I assumed his name fit him just perfectly, but I didn't want to offend. My friend Susan and I thought we'd give it a try, and off we went down the two-track. Once we reached the rise in the hill, and were somewhat out of Seth's sight, I suggested we take them to a canter, and did just a little click in my throat.

Pokey reared up on his back legs and took off like lightning, bobbing and weaving off the road and into the woods. I tried my damnedest to pull on his reins and get his head back, but I was useless against the power of this horse. His head was down, and he was plowing fast. Diving through the brush and riding under tree limbs, I was sure he meant to hit me off his back with any of the low branches that could have knocked me out cold, if not decapitate me as a sacrificial lamb of the land. I reached up to grab the hair on top of the horse's head and pulled up with all my might, at the same time pulling on the reins, and it just pissed him off. He kept running at full speed and my hands were bleeding from the force of the reins. By the time we hit the fork in the road that formed a triangle, I knew if he headed out into the deep woods through the fire trail, I would never stay on his back. My arms were shaking with exhaustion, I was soaking wet with stress, and it was only a matter of time before a tree took me out. I knew I was going to have to jump.

We hit a small opening in the area that would become the Meditation Circle, and somehow, I got Pokey circling, still fast, then slower, and then finally walking. I jumped down, reins in my bloodied hands, my legs barely able to hold me up. It was everything I could do not to fall apart on the ground crying. I started walking in front of the horse, leading him with the reins — my legs shaking, my heart beating, and my confidence in the toilet. Midway back, I thought I would never ride a horse again — ever — if I didn't get back on him now. He let me up, he walked slowly, and was perfectly behaved as we came around the hill and approached Seth.

"Oh, hmm, by golly, you're the first one that's come back on him in a long time," he squeaked as we came within hearing distance.

It turned out Pokey was short for Poco Loco, or a little crazy. He was just the first of a long series of unknown, dangerous rides I would jump onto in search of making a stable homeland for our lesbian nation of magnificent misfits on this square mile of goddess-given earth, but he was one helluva memorable ride.

CHAPTER 9

HOW WE BOUGHT THE LAND

Whenever the conversation turns to Festival herstory, online or in circles, I try to stay out of it. Even though so many statements don't match how things went in my own very hands-on experience, I believe in my heart that each womon's herstory is true and right for her. I deeply know there are tens of thousands of stories in that naked city, and mine is just one. One with a particular inside view, for sure, but it's still just one view. Even when my name is scattered throughout someone's story, I generally try to stay out of it, because once you engage in fact-checking a story, then you're heading down the slippery slope of attempting to edit someone's memory. Or a meaning that they've created from their unique experience.

One story in particular that I've (mostly) stayed out of for years — decades now — is how the Land was purchased. It's become the stuff of myth, legend, innuendo, and accusation. Here is how it actually happened.

We had rented two different Festival sites until June of 1982, when the owner of what became known as "the old Land" pulled out at the last minute. We had been hoping and dreaming of not being on land owned by this defensive, Ford LTD-driving asshat, who would come to the gate almost daily demanding to see me or Kristie.

In one of those dream states we looked at a beautiful piece of land, a full section surrounded by National Forest. It was extremely unusual to find a property this large that wasn't farmed, half swamp, or mostly hill tangled with brush. It was so completely perfect for the privacy and the energy of our community, a gorgeous mix of woods and fields, and meadows. But owning our own space just simply didn't seem possible.

By the time we lost our lease in 1982, we were no longer a collective. My sister, Kristie, and I, both part of the original collective, were now business partners. After five years of shouldering most of the responsibility and 100% of the loan risk, we had decided we had to get real. Prior to that, we had been in different formats of three or five, or even seven collective members. Anyone who has worked in a collective knows that what almost always happens is painfully different from the political ideal. As much as everyone wants to manifest the collective's chosen purpose, a much smaller subset carries the heaviest part of the load. Everyone else shows up for the decision-making meetings, and of course for the Festival, but picks and chooses what else fits in around their lives, their loves, and their jobs.

Kris and I were the ones taking out the rotating loans that kept us afloat and changing our entire lives to fit around Festival. We couldn't begin to get bank loans at that time, with zero collateral and credit, so we went out on a personal limb to borrow money from individuals, paying high interest — upwards of 20% — and most often borrowing from Peta to pay Paula.

When June 1982 found us needing to find a home for the Festival in less than two months, we called the owners of that gorgeous square mile, who now lived in Ohio, to ask if we could rent it. The answer: "NO." Could we rent with a down payment toward an option to buy? Eventually their answer was "yes." Great news! But …

Preparing this site for a Festival with upwards of 7,000-8,000 womyn would mean bringing primary electricity in from more than a mile away, installing electric transformers, and putting down water wells, on top of all the standard Festival expenses. Almost nothing that we had accumulated in the previous six years of producing the Festival would be useful in this huge new space. We were already hemorrhaging money as we prepared the site for that seventh Festival.

So, we went to the community and asked for help in making that first Land payment that would follow the 1982 Festival. Womyn literally went through the audience with garbage bags to collect cash. I know some of you were there and added what was in your pocket. A handful of sisters sent checks after the Festival. All those generous donations helped us meet that first $50,000 payment, which was due October 15. Even so, we had to borrow a little more than half of the $50,000, loans Kris and I knew we would have the bottom-line responsibility for paying back.

Every time I hear about how the community bought the Land, it feels complicated. I never want to dishonor how the community was part of this effort in 1982. I am so deeply grateful for this. I know how much we all wanted to be there, and that desire was carried fiercely in everyone's heart. But through all the hoopla and drama of that year, we raised something like $19,000 in donations. That is a lot of money, for sure, yet for the huge figures we were looking at to buy, insure, pay taxes, and install utilities, it was a significant but still small part of a very big lift.

Through the years, that on-Land fundraising action in 1982 became something that for some felt less like groovy community caring and more like a bad-will vibe of entitlement and resentment. I was deeply saddened that even once the Festival came to its end after the 40th and I prepared to sell the Land, some sisters talked online in a way that still felt bitter 34 years later. "We already paid for the Land years ago — why are we buying it again?" appeared on threads discussing who would buy the Land in 2016, when there were several groups of Festival womyn looking to make this happen.

After that first Festival on the new Land in 1982, I could feel how complicated this straight-up ask for donations was in our community. We were not a nonprofit and didn't want to become one, with a board, nonstop fundraising, government overview, and all the complications that go with that. We had already tried being a collective for six years, and just couldn't handle the concept that a board would oversee our work and make decisions while we did the actual hands-on work. I knew it couldn't work for me. After that, I never went to the community for financial donations without something to offer in exchange until the final two years, when the boycotts were so financially crushing.

So, if the garbage bags of cash were not how the Land was paid for, how was it paid for?

In 1983 and 1984, we sold lifetime tickets to the Festival for $1,000. We sold 82 of those tickets, and although $1,000 was a lot of money then, those sisters received the option to attend 32 Festivals without an additional dollar spent, and many did.

We took out loans of $1,000-20,000 from individuals, paying interest of 10-20%. I borrowed money from my male drug dealer (I'm longtime clean and sober now, sisters). We did everything imaginable to keep those payments happening. Of course, we put every penny of any profit back into the Festival and paid ourselves very little. All of this happened in a time before the internet and Facebook, so it involved one-hour (or four-hour) phone calls, one after another, for each Lifetime ticket or personal loan, day in and week out, for years.

We also leased the Land's gas rights to Shell Oil for $85,000 in the late '80s. We were one of the only holdouts in the county during the crazed natural gas speculation of that decade. Every time they knocked on our door, I kept saying "no, no, and no." Finally, a crusty oil lady with Western boots and jeans flew to our winter office in California to negotiate, and I walked out of that meeting with $85,000 and an agreement that they could not set one foot on our property. They had to drill off-site to come in under our property. No dynamite testing. No touching the earth of our home.

In a field north of the Land and just a little west, they set up a huge rig that drilled over a mile deep and across at an angle to get under our property, utilizing National Forest land. The federal government grants permits all the time for these exploration wells, along with permission to clear the brush and scrub trees, requiring that the land be reseeded when they are done. It grew back quite nicely and became the field where eventually Camp Trans was held for several years.

The deed for the purchase of the Land was originally in the names of Kristie and Lisa Vogel. After Kristie and I dissolved our partnership in the winter of 1983, for a few years the deed was in my name alone. Once I became business partners with Barbara Price in 1985, the Land was held in both of our names until 1995, when I bought her out of the business and the Land. After that, it was held in an LLC in my name alone. Although I knew that I would receive the money if I were ever to sell the property, over all these years I have understood my relationship to the Land as one of trustee, held with all the tremendous love and respect I have for Her and the sisters who call her home.

That beautiful piece of Land is now being purchased through a multiyear contract by WWTLC, the We Want the Land Coalition, a nonprofit formed with the vision of securing the Land "for women, for girls, forever." Before the sale I entered into an agreement — with the support of WWTLC — with the Land Conservancy of West Michigan to establish a conservation easement that protects the Land from development except the minimal improvements needed for WWTLC to host the smaller gatherings that are a part of its mission.

It is the best of all possible worlds. The Land has stayed with sisters, and will, in perpetuity. And out of all of this, I have a livable retirement after my 40 years of producing the Festival. It could have gone a lot of different ways. I never had to face the prospect of having to sell the Land to the most obvious buyers, rock-and-roll event promoters who could have used the considerable underground infrastructure that we installed over the years, or hunters who were already calling when they heard the Festival was done. But the Mother had a vision for that sacred space, and she found the next group of womyn who could carry out Her plan.

More fun in the mud, circa 1986-87

CHAPTER 10

MEN

When we started the Festival in the '70s, I would say I was pretty much a man-hating lesbian separatist. I completely seethed with anger. My entire ecosystem was shaped by layer upon layer of realizations about the complex oppression of womyn delivered by the tools of Patriarchy. Once the blinders were removed from my eyes, I could no longer unsee how Patriarchy served every single man and oppressed every single woman. I was baffled by the complete mind-fuck that females lived in, that we supported, perpetuated, and lived in this world of men — mostly without protest. That most of us slept with and cared for men. That we raised sons and then were relegated as inferior to the very being that we birthed, raised, and cared for. That most of us would die without true agency in our lives. I so deeply wanted to know a world where this was not true, a world where womyn were free.

In the creation of our Amazon camp that became a 40-year Festival, we taught ourselves to do so many things and relied on our ingenuity and willingness to do it the long way in order to do it the independent way. In this leap of faith, thousands of womyn found a freedom and power we had yet to imagine.

It's also true that there were a few very good men along the way.

I first met Clay Carter after the second Festival, when his sons were riding around the Land on their dirt bikes and we were running them off. When he first showed up, I thought he was going to go heavy on us for yelling at his boys. Instead, he acknowledged that they shouldn't have been on our site with their dirt bikes, but, fair enough, considering it had been an empty space for a long time. They lived about half a mile away, down the road and around the corner on a little lake. He welcomed us to come and take a swim in the lake anytime.

We took him up on that swim the following year and found out that he drank cheap beer, just like us. As a matter of fact, he liked his beer so cheap that he made runs down to Ohio to buy a whole truckful of cases, because he felt ripped off having to pay the deposit that the Michigan bottle bill added to each can in 1977. It takes someone really committed to rock-bottom beer to do that. He ran Hesperia Steel Fabrication and had more weird tools and cool shit at his disposal than we had ever seen. Somehow — in this county that was so completely reactive and frightened of this band of lesbians taking over their town for a week each year — he was welcoming, interested, and supportive.

He gave us a key to his house in case we had an emergency so we could let ourselves in to use the phone if they weren't home. His wife was super cool, too, and the two sons we ran off the Land weren't bad either. "Don't go all the way into town to make a phone call, just stop by and we'll let you use it anytime," they told us.

We took them up on it the night of THE storm, a storm so intense that our whole town woke up crying. I can still picture the scene — womyn frantically running in the flashes of lightning that crackled through the sky, just seconds apart from the last one. Michigan summers have always brought some epic thunderstorms, but it seems they were bigger back then. Or maybe we had less gear to protect us or just weren't used to living in the woods with all its chaotic ways.

After the storm passed, we needed to deal with our soaking wet sound and light equipment. Susan and I headed over to Clay's house at about 3 o'clock in the morning. We thought a hair blow dryer would do it, but of course no one took a blow dryer into the woods. We bet there was at least one at their house. We arrived cold and completely drenched, two shivering drowned mice knocking at their back door until they answered. "We need to borrow a blow dryer, we're in trouble on the Land with wet equipment everywhere, if we are going to have concerts, we have to dry this stuff out."

"Come on in, sit down," he said. "I'll put on some coffee — you look like you could use it."

We stayed at the kitchen table making sure our soggy selves didn't drip all over their nice country kitchen.

I had been waiting forever to pee. "Could I please use your bathroom? I'm sure the only thing dry on me right now is my asshole, and I just don't want that last piece of me to get wet."

He didn't blink at that. For a couple of decades, no matter what he saw or heard, or what we brought to him, he didn't blink.

When we started to collect big things in our inventory that we needed to store from one Festival to the next, we didn't have room in our crowded little house at 1501 Lyons St. Clay offered to let us store lumber, pallets, barrels, shovels, and coolers on a hill on his property, covered with big tarps. We named it Outdoor Inventory, or Outventory.

All the Weird Things

The first few years of the Festival, we used 55-gallon drums to cook in, procured from the back lot of the Gerber baby foods plant. Fremont was just 20 minutes away from the old Land, and being so close to their processing plant was like 55-gallon drum paydirt, because what they stored in their drums was baby food, not toxic chemicals, and we needed a shit-ton of barrels for both cooking and garbage, and a few for holding rakes and shovels. At first, we planned stealth barrel heists after dark, until we realized that we could just pull in during the day, and if there were barrels out back, they would just let us take them.

Our kitchen technology at that time was rustic, but functional. We dug a few pits, laid metal fence posts across them, set the 55-gallon barrels on the posts, and cooked the food in the barrels. We quickly realized that since the soil in that area was sandy loam, the pits would start to collapse, so to hold the sand back we lined them with sheet metal, and more fence posts to support the metal sheet. The 55-gallon barrels are 3 feet high, which made reaching over the rim to get to the food, well, dangerous. In the early years, it could be a kitchen worker or it could be you that would reach into the barrels to get an ear of steaming hot corn or a serving of vegetables cooked in foil packets.

We took a few barrels to Clay and asked if he could cut them down, and maybe put a hole on either side so we could put a piece of rebar through each end to move the pots on and off the fire, leaving more of our proud body hair in place. This worked great for a while, but it was still a bit wonky, and the metal of the barrels was rough and not really the right thickness for cooking.

I remembered the time I had seen maple syrup being cooked down over an open fire, gallons and gallons of maple sap being stirred with a long wooden paddle in a big steel pot that was just the ridiculously large size we wanted. I took a six-pack to Clay's and described this pot and together we sketched out an idea. Then, he made a prototype. He made four pots that first year, and four more the year after that. These pots were substantial pieces of the Festival mothership: 120 gallons large, much heavier than the Gerber barrels, impossible to lift out of the fire, and very difficult to drag over the fence posts. Clay was always thinking about our projects, and he came up with the idea of a steel rack that would fit into the fire pits, which by now had grown to three, 20-foot-long infernos of kitchen love.

He also helped us achieve Kim's ambition of making pasta for thousands. You can imagine trying to pour huge vats of pasta and boiling water into a strainer of any kind — impossible, if not deadly. It also took forever for pots that large to come to a boil; starting over on a fresh boil during a dinner shift just wasn't conceivable. We had to keep the water hot. It was Kim's idea that we could do this with a big basket with long handles that could be set inside the pot of boiling water, then removed when the pasta was cooked, the water staying at a low boil for the next lot of pasta. Clay made us six huge, beautiful custom baskets, and we were ready to rock some pasta.

Clay liked all the weird things we brought him to make, and he felt our sincere appreciation for his creativity and his skill. He understood that what we needed to create our town just didn't exist in the world in many cases. If we could imagine it, he was our partner in shaping it out of steel.

In the third year of the Festival, we realized for the safety of the numbers coming, we couldn't let sisters park near their tents or tent next to their cars. We knew we needed to have a shuttle. At first, shuttling was done by sisters who arrived in trucks, and either volunteered to drive them nonstop, loaded with womyn and gear, or allowed other womyn to drive when they needed a break. If you arrived at the Festival driving a truck or a van, you would be asked if it could be used for shuttle. Or if your car had a CB in it, by chance, could it be used for security?

We soon moved from borrowed trucks and vans to a tractor, rented from the local farmer, that pulled a hay wagon. Instead of hay it was piled high with sisters and their growing amount of stuff. The hay wagons were cool and could carry a lot of womyn and gear, but it only worked well for younger, more able-bodied sisters; everyone else's bodies were at risk. I had mostly given up on my childhood — and adult — fantasy of having a train with cars for people and camping gear and luggage that would go chug-chug-chugging through the woods on round trips from Treeline to Triangle. But I was still always daydreaming about different ways to shuttle the sisters from the parking area into the campgrounds that were more functional and fun than cramming into the back of a long line of vans or bouncing along on a hay wagon.

Once again, I went to Clay. We needed to come up with something with seats, something that you could step up into, not hurl yourself up on, and it would be awesome if it had a frame to hold a removable cover for those opening days with torrential rain or blazing sun. We sketched out an idea in the crowded office that ran alongside his shop, surrounded by unidentified pieces of metal, cases of Budweiser beer stacked tall, and dust so deep you could practically plant asparagus. We made pencil scratches on the back of a piece of cardboard ripped off a box. He fabricated one surrey then another. I remember when he drove the first one over. He was so excited because he had wired the surrey with interior ceiling lights, something I hadn't thought of, but it was such a sweet touch. He was so proud of his overall contribution, the extra special things that never ended up on his modest bills.

He did the same thing with our first bus. Letting go of the train idea, I described the fantasy of taking a full-size school bus, cutting the sides right off, removing some of the seats so there was gear storage, and adding step-up runners. He jumped at it. A few weeks later I was out bushwhacking at the front gate — trimming trees for a path for the new wire fence — when he arrived with the bus. He had the biggest grin on his face as he rolled up the county road. He was so excited for us to see our new chariot of the goddesses! He had made a backlit WWTMC sign for the header of the bus we would lovingly call Bodacious. WWTMC — so official! Just another example of the little something extra he always added to show his love and respect.

One year a sister setting up the Kitchen fire pits slipped in the porous sand alongside a pit, slicing her thigh open as she fell against the sheet metal lining. It was a horrible accident, the worst we'd had on the Land up until that time. It drove home that the fire pit setup was dangerous and that we were lucky that this was the first time a major cut had happened on that steel. I told Clay we had to figure out another way to hold the pits together.

He called me that winter to say he'd seen some folks disassembling a water tower and taking down the big tank that sat at the top. "What are you going to do with that water tank?" he'd asked. They told him they planned to cut it apart and sell it for scrap. Cheap. He bought it.

"Lisa, this steel is a quarter-inch thick. I'll bring my boom truck, drop it in sections in the pits, weld the seams together, put in some spreader bars that will keep the pits at a constant distance across, and you'll never have to worry about it again."

And pretty much, we didn't – because of Clay, who was always thinking about us, always thinking about a better way. In that way, he was just like every womon on the Land, always trying to find a better way to build our piece of heaven.

Russ the Rain Man

I had met Russ before the second Festival, when we knew we couldn't run on a generator again like we had the first year. I had called contractor after contractor. They had each asked me what I needed an electrical panel for, and offered one version after another of stupid suggestions and comments:

"You can just run it off my car battery."

"I don't know why you're even having a music festival — there's already one in Remus."

"You can't possibly need 200 amps of electricity, little lady. Do you know how much power that is??"

Exhausted by the process and pretty well drunk, I had dialed one last number, a contractor named Russ. I told him I was looking for a 200-amp service panel to connect with a drop from the power company.

"What are you going to use this for, Toot Sweet?" he replied.

Toot Sweet?! "That's none of your fucking business!" I shot back. "The only thing you have to know is if I have the money in the bank to pay you and the answer is yes, I do."

Silence.

"O-K," he said. "Let's start over." By the end of the afternoon, I was in his warehouse, 12-pack of beer in tow, climbing around looking at electrical panels, learning the difference between one-pole and two-pole breakers, what a main and sub-panel were, how much voltage was lost over what length of linear feet of distance, what you could and couldn't do. We had broken out electrical schematic manuals, and he was testing me on how to add up amps needed for each location. I was so his Toot Sweet.

He witnessed our growth over the years and was an integral part of our expanding town. No one-year leap was larger than when we moved to the new Land and had our largest attendance by far — more than 8,000 womyn. We went with our initial idea of how the Festival service areas should be laid out for a few years, made a change here and there every year, and then in 1988 and 1989, decided to make significant changes.

Throwing all the areas up in the air and reconfiguring them made sense to us and ended up being the ongoing design of our Festival site, but of course it meant a complete reconfiguring of all our utilities. Russ had a Rain Man type thing he would do whenever someone was stalled looking at our hand-drawn schematics and contemplating where a panel would go. He would start in:

> *"Well, this is the old panel we used at the Witch's Kitchen, but now it goes to Sober Support, which of course is the old Womb location. The Womb location is now where the Movies used to be, and well, we had to add more electricity there for the Womb because of all the tea-making and we dug in a sub-panel. That was the same year we grabbed a new feed off the Home Base transformer when the Saints moved across the road — with all those coffee pots we had to have a lot more electricity. Of course, that was back when the transformer sat above ground, before those numbnuts got ahold of it with their truck that one year."*

On and on he would go as he scrolled through every electrical box swap and Festival area location change since we hit the new Land. At any random moment something would spark his reverie, and he would start from one point on the Land and begin the list of names of the different panel locations, which transformer they came off of, and if they had sub-panels, just kinda murmuring it to himself, sometimes drawing it out for someone who he thought maybe didn't know. Most of us didn't. But he did. And well, I did. And that was our very deep bond.

Every foot of that cable, every breaker in a panel box — for me and Russ, that was our love story.

He was the first of so many men who stepped through the distance between straight men and lesbian feminist separatists to see the good in what we were doing and decided to contribute, knowing he would never be included.

We built the Festival to live in a world of womyn, and to have a break from breathing the air and mindset of men. I often joked that I was "taking one for the team" when I got off the phone with some guy here, or had a meeting with some guy there, or went walking in front of a bulldozer guiding the good old boy in the rig as we shaped our town. I didn't really like men, that was true. But because of the Festival, I learned to love some very special men so much.

CHAPTER 11

GROWING PAINS ON THE NEW LAND

The Festival had been growing every year since 1976, some years doubling from one August to the next. Year two saw 3,500 attending. In year three, there were 4,700, and 5,900 came in year four. By year five we were 7,000 strong, bumping up to 7,500 in year six.

In 1982, we took the huge leap and immeasurable risk of buying land — along with all the enormous setup expenses — to hold a first-time event in untouched wilderness. This would be a property that no one could make us move from, no matter how dykey we were, unless of course we missed a land contract payment. We fully realized that the chances were good that we would pay the initial $50,000 payment on October 15 and never be able to make another one, making it an excruciatingly expensive one-year rental. But these were the risks we took at that time to have space, to have some autonomy, to create community. We were hard-headed and big-hearted lesbians making the world up as we went.

The growing lore of the Festival, passed largely by word of mouth around the world, meant upwards of 8,000 womyn attended that first year on the new Land. And then the following year — boom — 3,000 fewer womyn attended.

I fully realize, even now as I write it, that 5,000 womyn attending an event was a big number. It was a huge number. In the last two decades of the Festival, I would have been so happy if that had been our steady number. But it was a shocking change after the steady increase we had experienced since the first year. We were completely unprepared. We did not have a business model of any kind, other than our deepest commitment to charge as low a price as we feasibly could so as many womyn as possible, from every economic reality, could attend.

At that time, the Festival cost $68 for four days, including all meals, two stages, all services. Our goal was that you would not have to spend another dollar once you arrived. We offered reduced rates that started at 50% off the ticket price. That often morphed into sending a ticket without charge to a sister in need: "Take a load off sister and have a good time." We subsidized buses by giving eight full Festival tickets per bus if the organizers matched the commitment by subsidizing some of the bus seats for low-income womyn.

Our aspiration did not include having a prudent reserve (that concept was still unknown) or paying ourselves a wage above poverty level. We had so many ways we wanted to make the Festival better, to serve more womyn, to pay sisters for their work. We spent the money generated from each year's increased attendance on the next year's expansion and improvements. There were always dozens of great ideas waiting in the wings to put the dollars to use in our town. In those dreaming, scheming, expansive early years we were totally ill-equipped for the downturn in attendance of 1983.

1982, the first year on the new Land, was challenging for everyone. Everyone bore the brunt of the logistical nightmare that was our hurried entrance on to the new Festival site, but some womyn carried more than others. Our growing pains were suddenly less exciting and more excruciating. As funky and free-flowing as the Festival was in its first six years, I knew that one thing was critical: Sisters could handle Festival being primitive, with just a few conveniences, and move with a form that was super-simple as long there was a container holding the whole thing in a net of community trust. We all enjoyed that trust those first years, and the Festival community flourished. Of course, we always faced issues and every year had its hot topic, but nothing that lodged that razor-sharp wedge of us-them. The problems we faced in 1982 were serious, though, and they formed a wedge we would live with for some years. That showed in how many fewer womyn returned in 1983.

The bursting size of the 1982 Festival, compounded by searing logistical problems at every corner, destabilized everything and everyone. Our funky party in the woods was now the size of a town, and it wasn't sexy or sisterly when the generator that ran the well pump out near RV broke down, leaving no showers or drinking water on half of the Land, or a hard rain washed out the back road so you literally could not leave, or the Gordon Foods delivery was late and we ran out of dinner mid-service. The shuttles we ran to get womyn from the Front Gate into the Festival campgrounds and around town (flatbeds pulled by tractors, along with cargo vans and pickups to assist) ran on a dusty two-track dirt road that hadn't been driven in decades, creating clouds of dust that mushroomed 50 feet on either side of the road, leaving everyone choking, coughing, and spitting.

Sisterhood is powerful — and super powerful when it is pissed off.

The Beginning of Oasis

During that 1982 Festival, a womon started acting out in various places around town. The womon — I'll call her Carolyn — was having bursts of aggression alternating with weird antagonistic sexual behavior with random womyn. She started stalking one of the singers from Chevere, a Latin Jazz band from San Francisco, literally jumping up and grabbing her ankle to try to pull her off the stage mid-soundcheck. We had womyn shadowing her to make sure she wasn't going to do injury to herself or anyone else. The womyn of the Womb, who doubled as health care and emotional support back then, decided to take her off the Land and to the hospital.

Over the prior six years, when the Land thinned out post-Festival and most of the workers were on their way home, we often discovered that we had someone on the Land, someone we didn't know, who was in a full-blown episode of disconnection from any shared reality. The story of our journey with Trish that I told earlier was the first and longest experience we'd had, but every summer for many years there was a sister in need of serious help, right when there were so few of us to be of service. We had learned to ask womyn not to take the freedom of the Festival as a cue to go off their meds for the week or to experiment with psychoactive drugs. But the very expansive energy of the Land put even the most level of us into an altered state, so it was understandable how the sisters who lived outside of the lines day-to-day would burst from the page after a few days of Amazon freedom camp.

The Womb workers did not want to leave us in that position again that year and decided to act before the Festival was over. They felt that the hospital was the most likely place for this sister to end up, so they decided they would do the hard thing and take her to the local hospital to be checked out. After they left the hospital, they made a stop in town before returning to the Land. Meanwhile, Carolyn had talked her way out of the hospital, stuck out her thumb, and was back on the Land before the Womb workers had even returned, telling everyone how the Festival had turned her over to the man. It blew up like crazy all over town. The community was fractured. Furious.

In true form, Festival came and went, and there we were, a handful of us taking down the last of it, with this sister still among us, screaming into the night, jumping out at unwitting womyn in the woods, throwing food at womyn one moment and making an inappropriate sexual advance the next. She said she didn't have the money to leave. She was looking for a ride, but no one was willing to let her into their car by this time, and forget it, she wasn't going to help with any of the work needed to close out this Festival that had taken her to the hospital.

By then we were totally over her. When she jumped in a van to go to the beach one evening, a couple of womyn went to pack up her tent and leave it outside the gate. We couldn't physically make her leave — we were unwilling to involve the county sheriff to have her evicted in the only legal way possible — but we could physically remove her things. Inside her tent, as they packed up her gear, they found thousands of dollars of cash balled up in the corners of the tent. Who knows if she came with it or where it had come from.

This is the origin story of how we started Oasis, an area that existed to provide emotional support distinct from the Womb. We understood we had to have a solid, loving, and predictable way to support and work with sisters who were living in a range of emotional and cognitive realities. The first few years of Oasis, in response to this painful experience that first year on the new Land, we tried having Oasis be co-coordinated by one counselor/ therapist person and one survivor of psychiatric institutions. In theory it was an awesome and even radical idea, but we couldn't pull it off. After four years of trying, we admitted that this type of mix was not something we could make work in a weeklong experience of an ad hoc emotional health care.

Oasis eventually evolved to include various support groups, a place to have a cup of tea and sit with someone if you were having a hard time, 12-step meetings, a chill-out space — and periodic crisis intervention. It was a beautiful part of our Festival community, a haven to provide peer support for sisters on the Land, with womyn on crew who were experienced in being with sisters if they landed in an expanded state, in our most expansive universe.

DART on the New Land

All of our failings in 1982 and our earnest but inept attempts to solve them kept piling on, but none cut more deeply than the severe shortcomings in the area that would become known as DART. Our earlier efforts to make the old Land accessible were lauded as groundbreaking and had brought more womyn with disabilities to the Festival, but we were woefully unprepared. The huge increase of disabled womyn attending that 7th Festival — combined with the new, much larger site — was a logistical nightmare for the sisters who had come to the Land. They trusted that they were included, that it would be a safer space, a space where it was challenging but possible for womyn to camp with support, to navigate the environment, and to be part of the community. We had selected what we thought was the perfect campground location, only to realize that the disabled sisters referred to it as The Hill, or Crip Mountain. The work we had done in the past was now inadequate for the number of womyn attending and the stages and services spread out on the larger site. We had serious work to do, and we had no idea on how many levels.

We started with our best efforts at some physical solutions. After that year we started by putting a new and larger crew to work in the DART campground. We bought a small used bus with a wheelchair lift, the first of a rickety fleet, and named her Doris. Later in the '80s we bought a second larger bus, Demming; still later came Dottie, then Dusty. We rented wheelchairs for the sisters whose chairs broke or for the person who might become injured or disabled while at Festival. The 80-page program was translated into Braille and we installed guide ropes for independent navigation within the DART area for sisters with vision impairment. As it became clear how many womyn depended on medical devices for daily living, we doubled the electricity in that campground.

After attempting to cover the distances needed with snow fencing for wheelchair traction that first year, we built a wooden wheel-way in Central DART in 1983. But it was logistically impossible to build wooden wheel-ways everywhere womyn needed to travel. We discovered that carpet, cut into 4-foot-wide strips and laid with the hemp side up for grip and the carpet side down in the dirt, provided enough traction to roll a wheelchair over the sandy ground, and it made it much easier for sisters with any mobility challenge to navigate the Land.

We accumulated every piece of used carpet we could find from Salvation Army, Goodwill, thrift stores, and from dumpster diving backlot throw-away bins of carpet retailers in all of western Michigan. We became experts at cutting 4-foot-wide carpet strips with utility knives and taping them with duct tape to make long runs. We used wood chips to smooth out the dips and stretched the carpet with stretchers to stop the carpet from bunching up. Finally, the carpet was secured with 10-inch nails into the sandy loam.

On the big push days, upwards of 100 workers would be on rug duty — International Rug Rat Day! You earned your worker stripes by showing the hemp burns on your breasts from carrying roll after roll of carpet to their eventual locations.

Every year we bought anywhere from one to two thousand yards of carpet, runners, and area rugs, covering our ever-expanding reach of carpet paths and replacing carpets that had worn out from use. By now we were carpeting the inside of most of the 50 large service tents and the paths that ran between them and snaked between every event and meeting area.

It was functional but still not great. If anyone really wanted to cover some distance at the Festival with a manual wheelchair, they needed assistance. Few at this time had the electric scooters that would become so common. We researched what golf courses did to make paths to and from their putting greens, and talked to road builders and driveway pavers. Our first blacktop path went from the Main Kitchen, past the entrance to the Night Stage, and then all the way around the horseshoe past the Community Center to the Womyn of Color Tent, with a 300-foot spoke into the back of the Day Stage bowl. We also replaced the boardwalk that intersected the DART campground with blacktop and made a blacktop pad at the DART eating tent near Main Kitchen. It was a little more than a third of a mile in blacktop. It was a start, but not enough.

Two years after that first blacktop, a womon who had been on crew for a couple of years came up to me and asked me to use her chair to get from the Belly Bowl, where the crew ate, to DART, where she worked. "Try any of the three paths," she dared me. "Try all three of them." I was in my 30s, working out at the gym regularly, and felt myself to be strong, but I failed on the second path. I could not do it. The next year we put down another thousand feet of blacktop through the worker area, up to the worker showers and out to DART. Several years later a path was added all the way down to workshops, and out to the farthest workshop area, with a spoke added down to the Night Stage, for a cumulative total of nearly a mile of blacktop.

Looking back, I would say there was at least a solid decade where we were in a periodic adversarial dynamic with the community of campers in

DART. Despite expanding crew and budget in DART every year, we were in a downward spiral of being unable to resolve all the accessibility issues presented on a square mile of wilderness. We had segued from our initial earnest desire to make it more possible for womyn with disabilities to be part of this community, to ping-ponging between dozens and hundreds of requests for special accommodations, with no true north of what was reasonable or even possible.

There were those who felt appreciative for accessibility efforts that were continually being added to, particularly first-time womyn to the Festival. And some womyn felt that anything that happened anywhere on the Land needed to be independently accessible to everyone. As much as we felt willing, we could not imagine 650 acres of forest becoming totally accessible. We had made our desire to make the Festival more accessible known, and now there was a powerful group of womyn telling us how to do just that. We wanted to build a Festival that would be fully human, and that meant learning how to do this.

It was the decade before the Americans with Disabilities Act (ADA) went into effect in 1990, and there was a new and fierce political movement peaking in the Disability rights community. Festival was now full of disability activists who had a whole different level of expectation and organization than the womyn who had started coming to the Festival in the '70s. The overall energy of DART had shifted to political activism, lesbians and feminists always being at the vanguard of so many new radical movements. The Disabled Lesbian Alliance, formed in NYC in 1978 by Connie Panzarino, was on the frontline of this work and in the forefront of the Michigan community. With the growing radicalism in the disability community, more and more people were rising to demand what was needed and to speak to the full experience of people living and loving with disabilities. For every DART camper who came and was thrilled to have the support to camp in the woods, there were two womyn threatening to chain themselves to the speaker stacks unless the DART seating area was moved. All of us had so much to learn about what it really takes to live in a community with diverse needs and abilities, and once we started down the path of that learning, it was a long and bumpy road.

On the Land, I was often asked to sit in on meetings about one issue or another, but I had a firm pass on meeting with any group during the actual days of the Festival. I knew once that had started, it would be what I would do all day, every day. I did agree to go to a meeting at DART in the early '90s, and I sat in a circle with a couple hundred womyn as they shared with me what it was like to manage their day-to-day at the Festival. It was epic. There sat Rose Resto, the first disabled woman who'd come to the Festival, red in her face with anger. Connie Panzarino spoke quietly and firmly as she described how she had to bring two attendants to be at the Festival. "If you mean that you want to include disabled womyn in this community — and I believe you do — things need to change."

Mary Jane P was also at this meeting, someone who I knew would never give me any slack. She was the first person I can remember who had a motorized scooter on the Land, and she was infamous for running down womyn who were in her way. It was so damn hard to try to talk with her and communicate that she could not drive so fast and make womyn jump out of the way. She was a womon who had a powerful personality and carried a lot of anger. She would spend hours on the phone with our office, arguing about every detail of everything from the workshops to demanding that she go to the front of the line when she arrived to insisting food be delivered to her at her campsite.

After a particularly aggro conversation when the phone had been passed to three different office workers (the hold button is always your best friend in a hard conversation), I realized that the relatively easy part of the work in committing to a community inclusive of disabled sisters was dealing with the physical solutions like carpet paths, electricity, or helping put up someone's tent. The more challenging commitment was being willing to listen and experience firsthand someone's anger about what they had to deal with in the world. What they had to deal with to be in community at Festival. If you were someone who was going to listen, finally, you would likely be the recipient of a backlog of unwitnessed anger and frustration that would often come right out the side of the neck instead of in a clear, clean sharing of thoughts and feelings. This was the real work. This was real life.

We worked as a community through the '80s into the '90s until eventually, slowly, the pieces were knitted together, and our systems and services were fine-tuned and predictable, led by love but accomplished through years of struggle. We did a lot of things wrong, we stayed in conversation, and we transformed.

The entire Festival community held the value system of making space for sisters with different abilities as one of our most holy agreements. No longer was it only a DART womon asking a person not to stand in front of the wheelchairs at a concert, but the entire audience was as likely to applaud with their hands shaking in the air in appreciation as clap and yell. The three old DART buses putted around the Festival, and though they were old and repaired thousands of times, Demming, Dottie, and Doris were beloved chariots. The drivers of those buses became iconic stylists, loved by the DART campers as much as the drivers loved their DART sisters.

DART community and culture thrived with the leadership resting in the capable hands of disabled sisters and beloved allies, and the DART area itself became a gorgeous center of Festival events and celebration. Workshops ran there all day, and the DART fire pit was known to be a gathering place late into the night. DART Special Olympics were infamous — the dildo relay passed chin to chin as wheelchairs and scooters raced along the blacktop path to the finish. At the final Festival there were more than 500 womyn registered for DART. Many of these sisters, who first came to Festival with able bodies, now needed this support to make their final trip to the Motherland. There were still great holes in our accessibility, but we kept talking, kept making incremental changes that would make someone's Festival more possible, safer, even more comfortable — all of us more wisely knowing that perfection in those woods would never happen, but real life would always be ours.

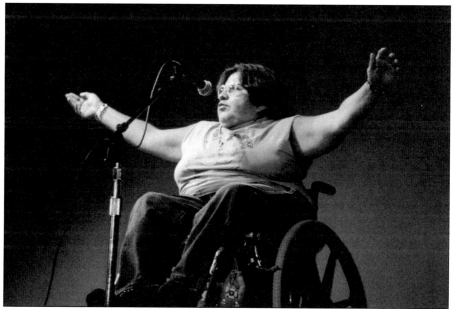

Roseannah, 1988 photo by Toni Armstrong Jr.

Workers laying rug runners
photo by Desdemona Burgin

The DART fleet

CHAPTER 12

LOST & FOUND

I don't remember wearing jewelry growing up. It wasn't a thing many kids from my side of town did at the time. Plus, this baby butch was happy keeping it simple. When I came out as a lesbian, the month I turned 18, I started noticing the cool things that some sisters wore around their necks. These were pieces of nature — a rough stone in a ring, maybe a feather wrapped with colored yarn — not necessarily pretty things like the charm bracelets or petite crosses on dainty silver chains that I saw teenagers wearing on TV. When I finally decided to sport a necklace, it was a silver-colored jumping dolphin, no doubt made of pewter, with a stainless chain. I had never seen a dolphin, or the ocean for that matter, but someday I knew I would.

I wore that dolphin day and night, and it made me feel strong, grounded, free. It wasn't really a piece of jewelry; it was a totem that rode with me, or sometimes I rode with it. An amulet that gave me strength and kept the Patriarchy at bay as my newly forming matriarchal heart found its pulse.

So, when I realized that I had left it at the dock after taking a swim before the long drive home from the Midwest Womyn's Festival, I exited the highway around St. Louis to find a payphone to call their office. No one answered, so I left a message. I got home and called and left another message. I reached someone the following day, described exactly where I had left it, said a whiny bit about what it meant to me, and asked them to please look in lost & found. Had anyone picked up things from the dock area?

When I called back a couple of days later, they said they would call me if it turned up, but I knew it was gone forever. This was 1977.

The first year on the new Land, 1982, a friend came backstage and said someone was asking for me. "She says you don't know her, but she needs to speak with you directly, that she has something for you." I went out and a tall, kind-looking sister was waiting just beyond security. She explained that she volunteered at the Midwest Womyn's Festival. She'd been cleaning out a storage closet and came across an envelope with my name on it, which she recognized from coming to Michigan.

"Is this yours?"

My little dolphin had lived for five years in an envelope in a closet. It took this womon with the big smile and kind eyes, whom I was meeting for the first time that day, to bring her back to me. This sister, Sara Deerheart, felt the pull to connect what was lost, then found, to its home.

I can't say that I remember Lost & Found being a thing during the first few Festivals, and I'm sure the same was true for the Midwest Festival crew who had stored my dolphin for five years. But as our little Festival mushroomed and expanded in every direction in size, complexity, and difficulty, of course so did the stuff that was left on the Land when the sisters departed.

Every worker has a story about realizing that the tent on her path no longer had someone in it, and that another tent nearby had been empty for days since the campers had left Monday. Could it belong to a worker who had hooked up with another worker and was still on the Land, but had never made it back to her own tent? Announcements were made at the evening dinner meetings and notes were left on tent zippers: "If this is your tent, let Set Up Strike know, because otherwise it's coming down the next sunny day."

We found whole backpacks at Triangle, complete rucksacks at One World, elaborate toiletry bags tied to a tree up at the showers. The years with big rainstorms on Sunday would find the campgrounds covered in wet tarps, some in trees, some in bundles that had been so close to making their way home. Whenever there was a rain toward the end of Festival, a steady part of the coming days involved workers laying out tens of thousands of square feet of tarps in the late morning sun, returning to turn them over in the midday heat, then dutifully folding the dry tarps and delivering them to Inventory, where workers would mark the size on two corners and box them up with like sizes to become part of our backstock. We were a town of tarps, and during the years of BIG rains, even our deep back stock could be called out of storage.

There were plenty of dramatic stories from the Front Gate, where the crew might witness a car pulling over 30 feet from the county road, a sister opening her trunk and then dumping a bunch of luggage before roaring off the Land, her tires spitting gravel. "I am NOT taking your shit home!" This crazy-ass thing was reported more than once, the bold exclamation mark at the end of a nasty Land breakup.

There were numerous sweeps of the woods. The first wave was womoned by a Set Up Strike crew leader with Cling-on sisters, our affectionate name for campers who stayed a day or two to help clean up. The next big sweep was just after Short Crew left, and there was yet another toward the end of Long Crew, but there were also plenty in between. The campers left a lot of things, intentionally or not, and the hundreds of workers who left in stages over a period of 10 days did pretty much the same thing.

As soon as Short Crew left, a corner of the Flamingo Room (the eating tent in the worker area where smoking was allowed) was commandeered for the beginning of the massive sorting operation. Boxes of every imaginable type of water bottle. Shoes over here. Coolers stacked there. Full suitcases and backpacks heaped on pallets. Sleeping bags piled here. Children's clothing tucked over this way. Jackets and sweatshirts, pants and T-shirts, and underwear — well, if the underwear was found on its own, it was considered permanently lost. Wallets and watches and jewelry were cataloged and stored in the Accounting trailer. Tents were stacked on the end table. But the tarps, the tarps went straight to Inventory. If you left it wet or in a tree, it was ours.

Our public phone lines rang off the hook from June until mid-August, and then quieted down completely during the week of Festival. Post-Fest, pretty much the only calls were from girlfriends looking for their partners on crew who had not called in for way too long, and for our Lost & Found. Stacks of Lost & Found forms were by each phone, ready to take the pertinent information to see if we could find a match. Once a match was made, we would calculate shipping, call you back, get a credit card, and then away it would go back to the house that served as our off-Land office, to be picked up in the garage by the friendly UPS driver, Cindy, who in her snappy brown shorts had an uncanny way of looking more and more like Susan Sarandon the longer we were sequestered in Walhalla.

One year I was part of sweeping the woods behind the Belly Bowl, and a tent that had had a note on it for days was now considered left. Not lost, just left. I undid the zipper and peeked inside, where I found nine pairs of shoes with other sundry items. Nine pairs of shoes! Who would leave a tent behind with nine pairs of shoes?! And then I realized that I knew that one pair of boots very well.

Our beloved Impy Simms featured these boots from time to time when she did her roving reporter persona. Once she had interviewed me in something that was reminiscent of a nurse's uniform, complete with white cap, but accented with these big stacked black boots. Her interview questions were usually quite bizarre, and the experience was less an interview and more a window into Impy's mind. It was performance art, and Impy was the director, producer, and the lead.

We lost so many inhibitions in that beloved forest and found a freedom that was wild and rough. Some of that freedom expressed itself in the incredible array of stuff sisters brought to the woods to reveal a part of themselves that was held back in Area 51. Sisters costumed themselves elaborately, bedazzled their campsites, and put up every imaginable kind of art installation around the Land. Hobbit homes. Intricate altars. Body-sized mobiles created from branches, feathers, and ferns. Barbie Doll sex scenes with absolutely no Ken. Magical fairy lights exploding on Easy Street. Beautiful signs and paintings popping up everywhere, as womyn added beauty to their shared home.

One year a sister brought full-size paintings on canvas to exhibit at the Triangle, complicated paintings featuring rather tortured imaginings, including blood imagery, and distorted pained faces, lanced bodies that were exorcism-like in their intensity. Some sisters were triggered by the graphicness of the visuals and didn't like it one bit that they had to walk by this imagery as they went to and from One World and Triangle. This artist reportedly would roam the paths at night wearing a mask painted with blood red accents on a penetrating vulture face. Long conversations happened at One World, where the installation was placed, and these conversations traveled to the Trailer Park outside of Staff Services, and eventually included One World, Security, Oasis, and me. The freedom to express your art, whatever your art might be, was critical to our community. And the freedom to move about on this sacred and healing womyn's Land and not be horrified and confronted face-to-face with your own past injuries was also important. Coexistence in a diverse community comes with a price, and we took turns paying that price to be together.

We negotiated where the paintings were to be, off the beaten path, but in the night they were strategically moved back to the previous, well-trafficked location. We had talked to this sister about her mask and paintings, and how they frightened sisters, and yet she was passionate that it was part of her identity. Once again, we were up against the tension of difference, and our job was to keep talking — to offer support to the sisters who were tripped out by the mask or the paintings, to express compassion to the sister who needed her community to see this dark side of her spirit, and to try to find a balance where all can exist.

There is always a price.

Each one of us has our own vulture mask that emerged in those woods, and there was no tidy way to keep it hidden once it was witnessed in the light. I learned over and over that the process was the point. For all the things that were solved and resolved, there were just as many that remained always a process.

After a lifetime of not being seen, here we could begin to find ourselves, bring our spirits out into the open, discover parts of our very essence that had been long covered by the restrictive suppression and oppressions of Patriarchy. This is what living and working together gave us. This is the offering we made to each other, year after year, a gift so deep that it lives in us now, though we are separated by time and space. Our very identities shook up, lost, and then found.

And through all the tremendous transformations happening in each womon, we worked. Our very essence was as a working community. Whether you were ever on crew or not, our community was what it was because of the commitment we had to each other to be a part of making a life we wanted to live. We worked for each other. Embedded in every piece of what we did in the creation of our town was the care and consideration we felt in our hearts for our sisterhood. Which included handling all your stuff left on the Land.

After the first initial rush of matches from the first four days of phone calls were loaded in vans and shipped out UPS, a team of sisters would head to town in another van or two and launder loose items: towels left hanging in the trees by the showers, sweatshirts found under a bush, little T-shirts left unclaimed at Sprouts. From the laundromat in town the clothing went directly to the Pole Barn and got married with the stacks and stacks of keepables, and the full bags and suitcases that we didn't unpack to wash. The Flamingo Room tent would soon be coming down, and we would pick up this task again after we were off the Land, while continuing to take calls from campers, artists, and workers who realized they had left their favorite hat, or somehow forgot their tent at shuttle base — and now I'm back in Philadelphia!

Back at the house, we waited until the cutoff day, when we would no longer look for your stuff, to make our final round of matches. After that, if the thing could be used in a Festival area eventually, it went to Backstock. If it could be used by the womyn's shelter in Ludington, it would go there. Everything else landed at the Goodwill, replenishing what scores of Festival sisters had wiped out on their way to the Land in early August.

I was clearing the phone message machine a few days after we were off the Land, and a sister was describing a knapsack she had left, detailing what was left inside. "There's a red flashlight, a brown T-shirt with cutoff arms, a pocketknife, a notebook, and most importantly, a vulture mask inside a brown leather pouch." Her beloved mask, a talisman it seemed, that had caused such a stir. As much as it was a pain in the ass at Festival, I was sorry we didn't have it to return to her.

From the Community Center womyn to Shuttle Crew, to the sweeps by Cling-ons and Set Up Strike, to the dozens of sisters folding tarps, the organizers grouping things together by type, the clean-machine Amazons who loved to do huge piles of laundry, the shipping sisters who would weigh and tag and ship, the trucks and vans that moved it about, and the final sisters from the office who re-sorted it again in the pole barn, this stuff was touched, lovingly, by so many womyn. We knew that we could never tell which stone was someone's amulet, which pair of ripped-up denim was someone's power shorts, or who had given you that faded T-shirt, possibly a someone who didn't walk this earth anymore, but their shirt did, on your back, in the woods of August.

We all have pieces that we carry, or that carry us, and it's sometimes impossible for another person to grasp what this shirt, this leather bracelet, this bowl means to another sister. Every picture tells a story, every shred of clothing, every rain poncho adorned in stickers, each concert blanket covered in dried grass and melted bits of ice cream from the Cuntree Store had herstory, and identity, and meaning. It lived a life with someone on the Land. Someone who came to a forest in Michigan to hear a concert, and what she found was so much more.

CHAPTER 13

LET'S TALK ABOUT SEX

Over time I became more accepting that the image of the Festival community projected into the wider world by the gay or straight press didn't match the reality of the community. More often it was closer to the upside-down world of complete fabrication, portraying our community as the direct opposite of what anyone on the Land experienced.

Granola-cookie, Birkenstock- and flannel-shirt-wearing dykes, unshaved pits, and legs. Shaved heads. Man-haters.

So many stereotypes that diminished and patronized lesbians were used on the womyn who composed the Michigan community from the very beginning. But we know who we are, and we knew it then. And so, yes, we were all these stereotypes they hurled at us as insults. We claimed them. But we were — and are — so much more.

One of the most bizarre stereotypes that landed in the '80s and persisted for more than two decades was that the Festival was anti-sex.

Before the cautionary years of AIDS, the lesbian community of the '70s was all about sex. The Festival for many was one big tent swap of connecting intensely with a sister you met at a Kitchen shift or maybe someone you pulled an all-nighter with at Front Gate security. More relationships, long or short, began and ended in that week than the whole rest of the year. If we added up the miles that sisters traveled to keep those new relationships going off the Land, we could circle the globe many times, a trail of lesbian hope and tears.

The sexual freedom that lesbians felt in the huge wave of coming out in the '70s included liberation from all the heterosexual labels and constrictions. No more danger of pregnancy from casual sex. If you were sexual with many partners, the labels of "slut" and "whore" just didn't apply to the ever-loving connection of sexual exploration with your sisters. Loving and sexing with other womyn was an act of self-love. It was a revolutionary act. It was political. We were building our community through consciousness-raising groups, food co-ops, printing presses, and one fuckbuddy at a time.

But sexuality at the Festival evolved to be so much more than having sex with other womyn. Away from the harsh gaze of Patriarchy, time revealed how constricted so many of us felt as we moved about in the outside world, and how free in our bodies we felt away from the oppressive energy of constant interactions with men, even after just one day. Our self-images were no longer clouded by the nonstop messages about female sexuality and sensuality that seeped into our consciousness from television images and song lyrics. There was a quick and easy freedom as we felt ourselves liberated from the limitations we had internalized our entire lives. We walked more in our bodies, in our sensual selves, and felt more sexy, sensual, and alive. Older bodies in corsets, fat bodies in G-strings and fishnets, butch bodies in a tool belt and boots but nothing else, young bodies in a loincloth or tutu, single-breasted cancer survivors' chests proudly bare in the sun — all expressions were beautifully open and celebrated. And of course, we also wore flannel shirts and Birkenstocks.

In the '80s and into the '90s, when the explosion of BDSM (bondage, discipline, sadism/masochism) burned through the lesbian community like wildfire, it brought a complexity to a communal living environment like Michigan. In the earlier years, even though everyone mouthed "safe, sane, consensual" as the defining rules of the road, it was up to each person to decide how to respect this universal guideline.

Leather dykes started to have scenes and play parties in and around general campgrounds, freaking out their next-door neighbors.

The tents gave a false impression of privacy. What seemed like a wall was really a tiny fraction of an inch of very flimsy nylon. It was like your neighbor was in bed with you, but not.

The Twilight Zone had already been set aside as the anything-goes campground for those who wanted to party all night. Now we designated it as the go-to for kinky sex parties. This meant a group of party-hardy jocks might end up next to the raunchy sex scene of a Stations of the Cross, with nothing more in common than being asked to be in a safety zone away from anyone who hoped to get some sleep.

We soon came to understand that there was a pretty good contingent of people who were discovering the exhibitionistic side of their sexual identities. Part of what interested them was having folks hear them, see them, walk past them as they had sex. The whole thing morphed very fast in a few years. Soon we were dealing with womyn being freaked out because of a cutting happening in the shower, a flogging at the back of the Day Stage bowl, or blood left on the Acoustic Stage to be cleaned up by the stage crew in the morning before a sound check.

In the heat of all of this it was considered very uncool to attempt to put any kind of container on someone's sexual expression. Conversation after conversation — "Hey, remember? Safe, sane and consensual includes your sisters who do not want to see the flogging when they are at the concert, or who totally freak out walking through Fest with their kids when you're walking down the same path wearing nothing but a butt plug with a horse tail and you're on a leash" — fell on ears that could only hear the call to this new version of a sexual revolution. Let the Vanilla Dykes be damned!

The gay press loved jumping on the idea of puritanical lesbian separatists, and story after story appeared, reporting as fact that the Festival was anti-sex and anti-S/M. It was part of the narrative of the larger sex wars of the

'80s that became another thread in a long-evolving storyline that diminished lesbians. No doubt, some in our community had a difficult time with the entire concept of S/M sexual practices, but the issue from the Festival's point of view was always one of consent. Consent, and the question of how do we, as a community, live together respectfully in shared space?

The issue articulated by some of the S/M community was that they didn't have a place to play, and that Festival was pushing them out of the central spaces of the Festival into spaces that weren't accessible to everyone. They wanted to play and have their scenes wherever they camped or wanted to go. They focused a big portion of their anti-establishment energy on Festival's ongoing demand that they not make their scenes public or involve womyn who did not want to be included. And, hello — there were children in the community.

During the height of these conflicts, someone made a flyer about S/M and sexual freedom that was handed out at the gate. On Friday late afternoon during the Acoustic Stage, a plane approached, flying low. This was not unusual because local prop planes made trips over Festival from time to time. Suddenly papers started floating down — those same S/M flyers — some into the audience, most into the nearby swamp, but others down to Howard's asparagus field 2 miles away. Some peppered the county road. It was thought to be a triumph of S/M activism by those who arranged the drop. I thought it was an expression of a myopic point of view. What was to be gained by making this sexual dialogue available to the local men, who were now discussing the flyer in the corner pub? A prized possession those flyers became! Freedom of expression came at a price, paid by the next womon who met these men, not 5,000 to one, but as a single womon from Festival who walked into a store, bar, or gas station, to find five men joking about the lesbian S/M flyer. Couldn't we keep our complicated laundry to ourselves?

One year some womyn put flyers up in the Porta-Janes, requesting models for their new pornography magazine. That excited the leather dykes, the exhibitionists, and the anti-porn sisters equally. I caught wind that there was a planned disruption of the meet-up announced in the flyer. I understood how sharp feelings were on all sides. I headed down to the Triangle on my bike, intending to talk the magazine womyn out of staging their photo shoot then and there. In those days, years before the internet, I could be incognito. Hanging out on a hay bale, I watched as groups, duos, and singles arrived in leather chaps, strap-ons, whips on hips. It was a colorful group of dykes. I kept hoping I would be able to pick out the pornographer in the crowd, but so far, I could not tell. There also happened to be a very intense volleyball game taking place at the Triangle volleyball net, six to eight womyn on each side, playing fiercely in the trampled ferns. Shuttles came and went with children hanging off the seats, as Triangle was where shuttles made their turnaround to go back to the Front Gate.

From a distance I started to hear a sound, almost like at a football game.
"Rah rah-rah! Rah rah-rah!"

I couldn't understand what was being said, but it was getting louder as it got closer and the energy around the whole Triangle kept rising to a new pitch.
"Rah rah-rah! Rah rah-rah!"

Now I could see the beginning of the march, complete with signs (where did they get the supplies?!) and dust rising from the marching feet.
"Rah rah-rah! No More Porn! No More Porn!"

The leather dykes started to gather as an opposition force, to meet the opposition force that was the march.
"No More Porn! No More Porn!"

I was keeping my eye out for the pornographer in the crowd, who either hadn't appeared or was now in hiding.
"No More Porn!"

This was getting dicey. The leather dykes didn't want anyone messing with their opportunity to be photographed for this book, and the anti-porn sisters were set to close this down.
"No More Porn! No More Porn!"

The volleyball game came to a sudden stop. A 6-foot Amazon with the ball spiked it fiercely into the ground.
"WHAT?!! No more corn?! Goddammit, I hate it when they run out of corn!!!"

Triangle volleyball game, 1982 photo by Bonnie Morris   *Not out of corn!* photo by Bev Cicolello

CHAPTER 14

EDIE IN THE '80s

My father died in December 1988, a little over two years after retiring from The Shop. Saginaw Steering Gear, a division of General Motors, Plant No. 2, banged out steering gear parts around the clock for decades. Harold had worked the line and walked the cement floors for a little over 20 years, losing his hearing and his knees, but gaining health insurance for life. Auto factories were where working-class people in Michigan hoped to land, believing the United Auto Workers would always be there, always be strong. I was dumbfounded when he took early retirement at 63 instead of 65, because this was the man who had worked every extra inventory shift, every holiday, every 12-hour change-over schedule, and any weekend they would give him. But in the end, he took 20 and out.

He was so fucking ready. No more pulling on those shiny charcoal work pants and that matching short-sleeved, button-down shirt laid out and ready on the bedroom chair, preloaded with his wallet and coins, the plastic pencil holder that resided in the upper left pocket, "Saginaw Steering Gear" displayed across the top in red. For 20 years, these only came off on weekends, when the gray outfit would get its once-a-week washing in the basement. He was over it, and I figured he knew his time was running out.

His death only two years later changed every single thing for Edith. Harold had been her conduit to humanity. I'm sure that wasn't true when she was younger, when she quit high school and worked to help support her family and buy her younger sisters' clothes and food for the family table. But in her middle years, he drove her where she needed to go, did the grocery shopping, and basically interfaced with the world for both of them. When Harold died, Edith had to start over. Completely.

She was 63 when Harold died, younger than I am now, but her life with Harold had gotten so small, their agreement so complete, that she had become agoraphobic, leaving the house for only two exceptions. At just under 5 feet tall, she had brittle silver-gray hair that got washed and combed out once a week by the gay homosexual that ran a little shop in the neighborhood, who would dutifully let her know when her perm needed updating. She was fond of saying, "Don't break my hair!" It was such a helmet-head, created by the fresh layer of Aqua Net applied daily from the aerosol can. She also went to church across the street, and eventually, Harold was known to drive her those couple hundred feet to Mass.

Otherwise, she was the queen of her kitchen table. Never left. She listened to talk radio in the morning and segued over to her kitchen TV to watch Phil Donahue, Sally Jessy Raphael, and later Rosie O'Donnell. "Oh Lisa, you think everyone is a lesbian," she said when I told her that her beloved talk show host was a lesbian.

That was true. I TOTALLY did.

When Harold was dying, I taught Edie to drive, to balance a checkbook, and where to go to grocery shop. On one trip to the grocery store, I found her glazed over in front of the battery section. She looked at me, at the batteries, then back to me. With so much overwhelm and vulnerability in her voice she asked, "How do you know which one to buy?"

She had never bought a battery. My life was filled with D cells, C cells, 6-volt batteries, car batteries, FM batteries, drill batteries, and AAs. And my mother had never bought a single battery. It was so simple and yet so profound, her level of starting over.

Her skin was in a constant tremble for months and years after his passing, and yet the light in her eyes pushed forward. Though I feared she would, she never completely crumbled. When she called me on the Land in August 1989, less than nine months after we had lowered Harold into the ground, to say that she and Donna, my brother Greg's wife, were coming to the Festival for a day, I was silent for more than a few beats.

"Uh, Mom, it's been a while since you've been to the Festival, and I'm not sure it's such a good idea."

She had been to the second Festival in 1977, and then came again in 1984 with Donna and Judy, my brothers' partners. The three couples had rented a cabin up in Walhalla, and the boys would drive their spouses down to the Festival and drop them off at the Front Gate, returning to pick them up at the end of the day. The Security Crew showered them with a lot of attention on their arrival, and for years afterwards my dad or one of my brothers would boast, "Well I've been inside the Festival!" This because Security would allow them to come in the Gate and turn around to head back north.

But now we were in the late '80s, and knee-deep in the public sex conflicts that rolled over our Festival community. We had heard that there would be demos at that year's Festival — larger public sex scenes, confrontative actions to push back against the demand by Festival that sisters engaging in BDSM sex honor the "safe, sane, and consensual" agreement and not engage in public sex where others were non-consensually involved. Some members of the BDSM community had been railing against this, and it seemed obvious that part of their program was to have sex, intentionally, in public, and the raunchier the better.

While strolling through the Crafts Area in 1984, Edie had unwittingly paused before the sex toy shop with a whole table of vibrators in different shapes and styles buzzing away on battery power.

She wasn't that tripped out by nudity in general, but her body issues and sizeism got a workout on the Land. "Lisa, I just don't get why those really fat womyn run around with nothing on."

"Mom, do you think only skinny womyn get to be naked? It doesn't really work like that here."

"But Lisa, she only has a G-string on! And flip-flops!"

But now she was thinking of coming when there was a big BDSM demo planned. My sister Kristie wouldn't be here to share oversight of Edith, and I wasn't all that into managing my feelings about what she might see on the Land.

"I am going to fucking kill whoever starts to flog their partner in front of Edith."

I thought back to the year before, as I looked over the Night Stage audience at 7:55, pacing at my habitual location on the ground by stage right. There had been a large group of leather dykes standing just behind the DART seating, and their costumes were elaborate. Most were things you'd see here and there on the Land: body harnesses, whips on hips, leather collars, some chainmail clothing, and a smattering of leather chaps and vests.

But one image in particular endured from that night. A tall Amazonian womon came into view, the evening sun bouncing off her metalwork. She was over 6 feet tall and featured 8-inch spike heels on her thigh-high patent leather boots. The rest of her bare body was crossed with leather straps adorned with metal studs. Her shoulders had gladiator-like leather plates that came out 6 inches from either side of her robust shoulders, shiny spikes reaching for the sky. On her face she had a leather mask open only to her eyes and mouth. Her big red hair fell out from below the leather and rested on her shoulders.

This was getting so heavy-duty.

I didn't feel frightened of her or the group she was with. But I felt full-body anxiety when I tried to hold that image in my mind with the sisters settling onto their blankets, comfy in their jeans and flannels. Families rolling out their tarps and setting up their chairs for the first show, kids in their PJ's, licking their ice cream from the Cuntree Store. How do you have this conversation with your 7-year-old? YOU KNOW their eyes have already found this group.

How do we make a space for the wildest, most expressive parts of who we are, and at the same time consider what these images bring up for other womyn and young girls?

"You know Mom, the Festival has always been a place for all kinds of womyn. And there's some edgy stuff happening these days. I'm not sure you want to be in that mix right now."

"Oh, I've seen a lot at that Festival. Like that one womon in the Crafts area the last time we were there. She was big and fat and had nothing on but a nail through her tit and a bullwhip on her hip. She really freaked Judy out!"

Maybe she was more prepared to be at Festival than I was for her to be on the Land.

When she showed up that year, she walked through the Land a bit fragile — she had lost so much weight over my father's illness and death — but head high. Nydia's mother Nina, who was always at the Festival, always dancing to the conga jams and staying up later than most, greeted her as another elder, but clearly was too entrenched in the happenings on the Land for much connection. Edith and Donna wandered through the day, and as Night Stage started to take shape, I set two chairs in front of the mixing stack for them. I visited them at the change of sets, and my mother motioned for me to come close to her mouth so she could whisper in my ear.

"Christ, Lisa, someone just came up to me and asked if I was Edith Vogel! She said she saw the chairs come out and wondered who would sit in them, and then when Donna and I sat down she recognized me. She said she always wondered if the Vogel name was connected to her. She's your dad's cousin from Detroit and was even at your dad's funeral. I can't believe this happened. I am so embarrassed!"

"Why are you embarrassed, Mom?"

"Because she saw me at THE FESTIVAL."

"But Mom, do you get it? She is here too."

This was the heart of it. She balanced pride and revulsion at the same time. She would glance around the stage area, her eyes going up the lengths of scaffolding, scanning the enormousness of the Night Stage, and mutter to herself, "Womyn did all of this?" Yet in the next breath, she would worry about someone recognizing her, and maybe worse, recognizing me as the organizer.

When I came out to her as a lesbian, she said things like, "Maybe that's OK for all of your fancy friends, Lisa, but real people are not OK with this." She was forever taunted at weddings: "When are we going to your daughter's wedding, Edith?" Working-class folks in the '70s and '80s didn't feel the least bit like they had to be cool with this.

One year the *Detroit Free Press* ran a big cover article headlined "LESBIAN WOODSTOCK," where they waxed poetically about the Festival. Everything was positive, but they used my name. Right there in the Sunday paper.

"What am I supposed to tell Gramma when she reads this?"

"You could tell her, 'Some of my best friends are lesbians.' "

CHAPTER 15

CILANTRO

As dynamic human beings, we gravitate toward harmony and commonality, even though our world is alive with differences. Growing as a person and expanding as a clan of people involves learning to live with difference — exploring how living with dissimilarities makes us personally and communally stronger, and how learning to challenge our fear of difference is a profoundly good thing. Embracing our differences allows us to grow in unexpected ways, to expand our view of the world and experience the multiverse that is the planet we inhabit. We had many opportunities within the Festival community to grow through exploring differences. I think most of us would say that we were willing to try more there on the Land because our hearts were so incredibly open.

One area where we were never able to make much progress, however, was cilantro.

I didn't grow up eating cilantro or hardly anything green except canned green beans at holidays. When I started to buy and cook my own food around the age of 13, I quickly became a freak for fruits and vegetables, learning by trial and error all the things. Like that the avocado looks like a vegetable but is actually a fruit and has to be slightly soft to eat, and that the cucumber looks like a fruit but is actually a vegetable and has to be eaten before it's soft. When I was 14 and waiting tables at the Texan Restaurant, on my breaks I would walk across the four-lane street to the produce stand to explore the new world of fruits and vegetables with my tip money. I loved all of it!

A big part of my summer as a child was biking into forbidden neighborhoods and climbing cherry trees, apple trees, pear and plum trees, and eating away until my belly was sore, or I was run off by the owner. I always asked for a watermelon instead of cake for my birthday, the one day of the year I got to choose, and I usually won the Fourth of July watermelon-eating contest at the public playground. I knew something about fruits.

I became a vegetarian when I was 16, freaking out from the size of the breasts compared to the size of the legs of the chickens I was cutting up every day at my job at the Char House, where I cooked 60 hours a week. Forty-pound box after 40-pound box, I saw a lot of chicken, and I started to worry about how those chickens could possibly hold up those huge breasts on those little legs. I knew something was not right. I stumbled across an article about industrial farming — it must have been in 1973 — and that was it. I became a vegetarian for political reasons rather than health concerns, because I didn't really know anything about treating my body right at that time. I just didn't want to be part of treating chickens that way.

I was what you could call a rabid vegetarian. I would throw out someone else's meat if it came into the house, leave the table if you ordered a burger at a restaurant, and refuse to eat with my family at holiday meals because they ate meat. I knew zero about anything but the most basic, functional vegetarian cooking, but I was teachable.

The first couple of years preparing menus for the Festival was very basic: cooked corn and potatoes, bread, cheese, salad, nut butters. We expanded to simple things like steamed foil dinners and boiled eggs. We were learning how to cook over open fire and prepare food for thousands at the same time. Soon we were attempting recipes. I remember that burritos were one of our first. Sloppy Josephines made with tempeh came soon after.

As we entered the '80s, both the Main Kitchen and Worker Kitchen needed to have their menus enlivened. I met with two dykes who were sous chefs at Greens Restaurant in San Francisco, an upscale vegetarian restaurant in the Marina district. Most of what they suggested we couldn't consider for one reason or another, but one idea for the Main Kitchen was an exciting addition: Southern Rio Stew. It was new and different and had ingredients we hadn't used before like hominy and butternut squash. It would be such a hit with the sisters!

By the '80s we were now a major customer of Gordon Food Service, who sold us all our produce and disposables like toilet paper, paper towels, and so on. During Festival week they delivered two 44-foot trailers of food to the Main Kitchen between Monday and Tuesday, and then on Friday morning at dawn, swapped a third full trailer for one that was now empty. The People's Federation of Food Co-ops delivered yogurt, granola, grains, beans, and nuts; Rosewood Farms provided hundreds of pounds of tofu and tempeh; and, local bakeries kept their ovens working overtime for all of our bread. Even with these other suppliers, by the late '80s our food need was so great that for the week of the Festival we were Gordon Foods' single largest customer (and Gordon Foods was the single largest distributor of food in the Midwest).

I was still working with our Gordon's rep Dan Robertson — who was by then the head of the sales department — when we had these menu changes. With all things, but especially this Southern Rio Stew, I impressed upon him how much I relied on having all the ingredients confirmed and delivered.

"Dan, it's not like I can run out and just buy 400 pounds of zucchini on Sunday morning. We are way up north, and some of our ingredients — people haven't even heard of them around here."

He understood. He wasn't servicing individual accounts anymore, but he kept ours because it was so large, complicated, and just a little fun for him, a pleasurable challenge. The hominy, butternut squash, and fresh herbs were all things that would be difficult to source elsewhere, and I repeated to the point of high annoyance how critical it was to have these items on the Friday truck.

The delivery was made, and everything was there. Excellent. But when the Kitchen pulled the ingredients to start making the Rio Stew on Sunday, they discovered that the 15 boxes of cilantro they were about to clean did not contain cilantro. They contained flat parsley. Kim, the head Kitchen coordinator, was personally in my trailer within three minutes. Cilantro was critical to the taste and success of this new menu item.

I left a message on Dan's work phone, but it was Sunday. I called his home number, which I had squeezed out of him promising to only use in an emergency. I was having an emergency. I felt like I could hear him shit his pants over the phone.

"What's the latest you need to add the cilantro to the dish?"

"If we have it by 4:30, it can be cleaned, chopped, and stirred into the dish as it goes out on the line."

"Trust me. I won't let you down."

The day went forward, and I knew this would signal the end of trying to do unique ingredient cooking in the Main Kitchen. Too much risk. Kim, Claire, and the crew went through all the stages of preparing and cooking the new meal. Around 4 p.m., a message came from the gate:

> *"Lisa, there's a guy here driving a Cadillac dressed in a suit.*
> *He says he's making a food delivery, but he looks more like FBI to*
> *me."*

It was Dan Robertson. He couldn't find the amount of cilantro we needed in all of Grand Rapids, so he took off in his Cadillac DeVille and drove to Lansing, buying cases of stock from food distributors and clearing out grocery shelves. His backseat and trunk were both full of cilantro, just in time for dinner.

The story became part of the sales force training at Gordon's, the legend of the guy who would go to any length to meet his customers' needs. Dan had a real commitment to our Festival, and he and I had a jovial and very real friendship over the phone. Even through his growth as a salesperson and eventually his ascent to high management at Gordon's, he always kept an eye on our account, and I always had that number that rang in his kitchen.

The Southern Rio Stew was made that year and that year only, because we had yet to learn that cilantro, a little green herb that can easily be confused with flat parsley, was an utter delight to some, but caused others to run down the road crying with loathing. Harmony and commonality. Aversion and abhorrence. Side by side at the same table.

72

1st row: *Feeding the Amazons who changed the world, 1978*; *Still feeding them through 2015*; 2nd row: *The hearth, 2011* photo by Anna Campbell; *Greenbeans, 2012* photo by Desdemona Burgin; 3rd row: *International Board, 1986* photo by Bonnie Morris

CHAPTER 16

WE BUILT THIS CITY

We called it a city built by womyn. It was constructed each and every July and taken apart every single August, year after year, for four decades. It began with put-in week, when womyn put in the electrical and plumbing on the Land and slept dormitory-style at the office house in Walhalla, 15 miles away. Toward the end of that week, we would install a small 20x20 tent for what we called the Belly Button, the baby sister of the Belly Bowl, and load it with boxes filled with frying pans, toasters, coffee pots, and 40-quart stock pots. Camp Kitchen.

On Friday of put-in week, at 1 p.m., a lineman from Oceana Electric would climb the pole just off the southwest corner of our Land to reinstall the fuse on the transformer that energized the underground primary running onto our property. A little lamp sitting in the dirt was plugged into a duplex receptacle on an electrical panel standing alone in a field. When it flickered on, a round of applause erupted from the handful of us. We were grateful that there had been no big boom signaling a failure of one of our 11 underground transformers. Instead, we marveled at a little lightbulb shimmering in the August sun.

Our electric line being energized meant the water pumps could be started. Shortly afterward, our Plumbers powered up the 4-inch well for the Worker Area to flush the pipe that had sat quiet for more than 10 months. Naked sisters jumped into the inaugural cold gush of Land water. Seven more wells scattered throughout the Land were opened and flushed that day, and then sterilized overnight before being run for hours the next day again, blowing water into the open forest and fields.

That morning we received a food delivery from Gordon Foods for the Worker Kitchen, as we did every Tuesday and Friday for the next 5 1/2 weeks. This first order was then cross loaded into a van and parked in the shade, allowing time for the electricity to come on and cool down the walk-in coolers we had trailered over from a storage barn earlier in the week. At 2 p.m. ice was delivered, along with a two-door ice freezer to house the first 300 of the more than 6,000 bags that were used on the Land in an average year.

On Saturday, four early members of the Lace Crew and two cooks were the next to arrive, sequenced so Lace could go into the storage barns and truck over the plywood and framing lumber for the Worker Kitchen and Belly Bowl floors that the Carpenters would start to build on Monday. The four initial Carpenters arrived Sunday, and later that evening, everyone made one last trip to the Walhalla house for our yearly welcome dinner signaling the annual move to the Land. Thirty womyn sat on the floor in the living room, lounged on the grass or in Adirondack chairs in the yard, or gathered at the

8-foot library table we used as a dining room table. The menu was always lasagna (one white vegetarian, one red with meat) that had been made three weeks before and frozen for that moment. Traditionally I put out the dinner that night, unfreezing the lasagnas, baking them off in the afternoon, setting out a big-ass bowl of Caesar salad, some grilled broccoli, a couple of pies, ice cream, coffee, and sweet tea once TL was on the year-round staff. Literally the same meal for almost two decades. And we liked it like that.

On Monday morning, all eight wells were tested by the Plumbers, who filled two little bottles per well after thoroughly heating the ball-valve faucet with a propane torch to make sure no organic materials from the forest or animals remained. They handed these off to a driver, who took the bottles in a little cooler to the McDonald's in Hart, where they were passed off to the manager of the water testing lab in Muskegon, who drove past Hart at 8:30 a.m. on his way to work from his home in Ludington, 45 minutes away. The samples were cultured and tested for coliform. Three days later the test results were faxed back to the Office Trailer, which by then had been set up with computers, many multi-line phones (that had to be rewired into the rental trailers every year), the fax machine, rows of file cabinets, desks, and

Opening a Land well

Electrical put-in

most importantly, the coffee station.

If all tests were clear we faxed the reports to the Health Department, but if we got a positive, the process was started over. We flushed the well, burned off the tap. We knew that human error was more likely than our actual underground water source being bad. This water — that many of us carried home in cars, planes, on motorcycles, and trains — was water that we revered and trusted.

Home Is Where the Hearth Is

The Carps built the 40x40 floor for the Worker Kitchen on Monday and reinstalled the Galz dishwash platform so the Plumbers could install the large sinks and scrunge area, where food waste was scraped from pots and pans. Once the kitchen floor was down, Lace erected the 40x40 tent over it, and the Carpenters followed behind them to install four pairs of saloon-type swinging screen doors, one on each 40-foot side of the tent, placed exactly where the most flow happened in the kitchen. One set was oriented toward the Belly Bowl, where they'd run big pots and trays of hot food to what would eventually be hundreds of workers. One went toward the three walk-in coolers and the eventual 40-foot refrigerated trailer. One led to the food storage tent, which was lined with cages constructed by the Carps to keep the raccoons out of the plethora of tempting dry goods. The last one led to the dishwash. The raccoons had been awaiting our return, anticipating the tasty 25-pound bags of granola and those salty Ak-Mak lezzie crackers. If they were lucky, they'd get to bury their heads in a 5-pound bag of coffee.

By that point, we had one of the three 24-foot trucks we rented to supplement our two 1-ton farm trucks and multiple old pickups. The Lace Crew would drive up to the Pole Barn, where we stored all our "indoor" equipment, to meet Lorraine, and from there load two commercial six-shelf convection ovens, one stovetop oven, another grill/oven combo, one behemoth of a reach-in refrigerator for Galz, another one for the Belly Bowl, and all the startup inventory for Galz and the Office that they could safely fit around the kitchen equipment. All of it was old and ugly, bought at country diner auctions or from the bowels of used restaurant equipment warehouses, but we rebuilt and nursed and loved these for years and years. The large items had to go into the Worker Kitchen before the screen was installed at Galz Diner and after enough of the floor was down at the Belly Bowl.

Inventory Barn photo by Angela Jimenez

Since truck time was precious, the timing was practiced, and teamwork was proficient. While the Lace Crew was off getting that load, the Carpentry Crew was rolling out the stored linoleum on the Galz floor and taping the seams with trusty duct tape. Rough plywood was damn near impossible to wash clean of kitchen spills, but even well-used linoleum worked great.

After the doors were hung a group of womyn from Flex Crew created screen walls for the 160-foot-long and 7-foot-high perimeter of the Galz tent. They attached the four-foot-wide screen to the frame of the saloon doors, sewed the pieces together with fishing line, and safety-pinned the top to the rope that ran all along the bottom of the tent roof. A slightly different technique was used every year, but it always involved at least one tall sister, long enough in her legs and arms to reach those top connections.

While all of this was happening, other womyn from Flex Crew bleached down all the Galz and Belly Bowl tables and shelves that had been stored for the winter in barns that had not been — and never could be — rodent-proofed. Howard's Barn was one we had been renting since 1982 from a crusty asparagus farmer who lived 2 miles south of Gate 6. Eventually we rented two other structures from Howard, the top of another big barn, and the bottom of another for lumber.

Our pole barn, which we bought in the '90s after losing our two other storage rentals, was a 10,000-square-foot steel building that had previously been the Pepsi distribution center for that part of the state. It was huge, and very tall, with three powered roll-up doors that were tall enough for tractor trailers to drive in and load up with hundreds of cases of Pepsi. Plus, it had two loading docks, which we rarely used, but we all agreed were super cool. We lined the entire perimeter with 8-foot-high, 4-foot-deep shelves, with additional shelving sections in the center, and there was still room to store our motley fleet of vehicles if they were packed bumper to bumper.

The pole barn was stacked floor-to-ceiling with boxes, each marked on three sides with its work area, box number, and total number of boxes for that area: Gaia Girls, 18 of 32, or Womb, 7 of 58. For years we bought skids of standardized boxes, 20x20x10, which could fit two-high on our wooden shelves, and 20x20x22 to store the bulkier items. In the leaner last dozen years, we saved and used hundreds of boxes from food deliveries. Among our favorites were the cartons that 15 dozen eggs came in (they had nifty hand holes), 25-pound tomato boxes with their fabulous rigid lids, and the more petite 10-pound green bean boxes, which were great for office supplies.

A Rite of Passage

Each day, a large tent or two was installed by the Lace Crew, along with anyone else who was itching to wrap their hands in white medical tape and reacquaint themselves with sledgehammering. The Office Tent, Inventory

Tent, the 30x50 Lace Tent, Worker Health, Massage, Belly Bowl, Galz, and Signz Tents all went up before Long Crew arrived, providing coverage for all the materials and equipment that would start rolling out of storage and populating the core of Workerville.

Erecting the big tents was a mixture of a carny rite of passage and witchy sacred dance, rolled into a grueling lurch of team physicality. First, the awkward and very heavy tent top was carried by two to three womyn to the right location, unfolded and then stretched, one woman on each corner rope pulling tight, tighter, as the heavy vinyl billowed and then — one-two-

Sledging ballet photos by Tessa Millesse

three — dropped all at once. We used old-school 3-foot-long, tree-branch type wooden stakes that were tooled to a rough point on one end and had a metal cuff around the flat end to prevent the wood from splitting as it took the recurring beating from the sledgehammer. The tent companies these days use gas-powered metal stake drivers with 1 1/2-inch-wide metal stakes, only using sledgehammers to set the stakes in place. Our desire was to have the tent company on the Land for as short a time as possible, and save as much money as feasible, so our contract specified that we would install and remove most of the tents, and they'd provide old-school wooden stakes because we didn't own or desire a big, loud stake driver.

We did possess dozens of sledgehammers, ranging from 8-pound lighter hammers used by new sledgers, up to the beefy 16-pound mamas fitting for our female Thor sisters who were strong enough to swing them repeatedly around their heads, and experienced enough to not hurt themselves or others. Learning to sledge was a skill that was passed down each year, and photographing womyn sledging was a very well-honed skill as well.

Especially popular were images and then later video of the three-way sledge ballet used when putting pegs into very dense and hard ground, a process that could break an individual sister down.

Three womyn steadied their sledge heads, stacked one on top of the other, made eye contact, dropped into energetic connection, and then sledged in a rhythmic synchronicity on the same peg. I go, you go, now you — one sledge hitting the peg while another was rounding the next shoulder, while another was being brought back away from the peg, creating a circular motion with three constantly moving sledgehammers. It was so beautiful, like a graceful ballroom dance or the perfect three-way basketball assist. I admit that though I was one of the first to learn to sledge a peg and lace the large canvases together, I was never one of the strongest or the most gifted sledgers. Still, I did put in at least a peg or two most years. Everyone ....who could pick up a sledge.......did, at least once a summer.

All the Walhalla Office Crew had now moved to the Land and were joined by the monthlong Office workers and the two Long Crew Drivers who made airport runs, shuttling crew to the Land and prowling the big box stores for supplies. Together, with whatever Flex Crew members were available, we took on all the miscellaneous tasks falling between the other crews like laying rug in the Massage, Worker Health, Signz, and Inventory tents, pulling the grass out of the pea stone in the Worker Showers, escorting deliveries, cleaning the Porta-Janes and sinks so they were ready to greet our sisters, and pumping up the tires of the 32 garden carts that were going to be in high demand when crew members unpacked their trunks and lugged their tents, beds, and gear into the woods.

There were as many as 175 womyn on Long Crew in the middle years, and in the final 15 years, a hearty 115. The total number of womyn on the crew for Festival week was around 450. Each womon had a Polaroid photo taken of her, which was posted along with her name on a board that ran along the inside wall of the Office Tent, organized by crew, with cross-reference notes for those who had moved from Long Crew to Short Crew. This way, new womyn on crew or anyone who forgot someone's name, could go to the photo board — "Oh, that's Bruno, NOT Frances. I'm so glad I didn't call her Frances!"

The only problem was, because we didn't want to be wasteful, we didn't use color photo printing when that became possible, so we reused those Polaroids, for years. Forever. Anyone who had been around for a decade or two or three now looked only remotely like who they were when the photo was taken. Time was slowed down, or sped up, or it had a wrinkle in it, or we lived in a vortex, and even those photos showed this to be true.

Pyramid once said, "It is a Festival of letting go." Nothing truer was ever said about the experience of building our city each year and taking it apart afterward. Our small early-summer crew loved working and living together in the office house in Walhalla, talking with sisters on the phone to sell tickets, registering sisters for DART and Childcare, and coordinating last-minute crew changes. The week before put-in we were never ready for the change, we really didn't want to move to the Land yet, and we were good with our mighty little office crew. And then the week before put-in was so magical and kinda primitive. By the time we were there, everyone in the office wanted to get off her desk and go out and erect electric panels or carry heavy water tanks into the woods, stoned with the wild scents of the fields and forest, as lighthearted as the crickets jumping with every step we took across the fields.

Put-in week, when we moved to the Land, felt like the sweetest time of all, and we often wished just this little crew could do the whole Festival, eating in a small circle on stumps, sand chairs, or simply in the dirt, a milk crate to hold your plate. The air felt sweet against your skin and the wind so gentle in the quiet of the night with only 30 womyn sleeping on the whole of the Land. But then Long Crew arrival was completely joyous — HELLO PAGE! HELLO NORA! It's been too long since I've seen you, my friends! — the air crackling with energy.

Just a little over 100 of us on Long Crew felt like the perfect number, and surely, we had what was needed to take it all the way to the Festival. We never wanted it to change. Giggling in the Night Stage field, evening runs over to swim at the 'Ake, long walks with friends in the morning before work. And so much hard work, all day every day. The work flowed with everyone in synchronicity, watermelon juice on our chins or dripping onto our grungy cut-off T-shirts and funky tank-tops, dirt under our nails and between our toes. How could this be so fleeting? Only 10 days before Short Crew arrives and it's going way too fast — we wish this could last forever!

Short Crew arrived blaring fresh energy and excited love all over town. How could we have wanted to delay their arrival, by even a day? The quiet evenings were turning into a solid rhythm of activities, while in the day the village exploded with work to prepare for the arrival of the Craftswomyn, Artists, and Festies.

And this is how it was. It was a city that we would build and let go of, every step its own work of art and wonder. Every part of it was something we had to let go of, for the love of what would come next.

CHAPTER 17

THE LONG DAYS AND NIGHTS OF LONG CREW

I don't know how many years it rained on the day Long Crew would arrive, but I know it was many. The week preceding that drenching day was typically a stretch of blissfully sunny days, a light wind rustling the tall grasses not yet bent by the many feet that would soon be stomping about in work boots. I swear I would have endured a week of driving rain to allow these womyn to unpack their vehicles, cart their things to their campsites, and set up on a dry bed of leaves for a soft cushion on the forest floor. But instead, it rained three out of four Long Crew arrival Sundays. The sisters who would be here for a month ended up wetter on the inside of their raingear from the sweaty effort of their load-in than on the outside from the pouring rain as they dragged their abundance of camping gear deep into the woods in search of privacy in the night of the forest, at least until the week of Festival.

If you'd been on crew for four years you were eligible to store things in the barn for a nominal fee, and pretty much everyone, even those who lived in Lansing or Chicago, at least stored a sleeping board and a foam mattress. Short Crew could store four items and Long Crew could store six, and most folks maxed out every year. The typical bed setup for returning crew members, particularly Long Crew, was a 4-by-8-foot piece of half-inch plywood, cut to 6 feet long, set on four to six milk crates with a piece of 4-inch foam for the mattress. After that the options were idiosyncratic and endless. A feather comforter or a mammoth animal skin, even an heirloom homemade quilt was far more likely than a sleeping bag. Though the bottom surface of everyone's tent was tent cloth, colorful rugs, anti-fatigue mats, or even outdoor grass carpet covered where your feet hit in the morning.

Work clothes, evening clothes, clothes for temperatures in the high 90s or oh-my-goddess-it-hit-40-degrees-last-night, dress-up clothes, clothes for parades, clothes for dances and all those choice items that you labeled "Festival" but still took home in case you got the itch to wear them in the real world. And then it had to go back into the forest in the garden cart.

Of the 450 womyn who worked on crew, 115 of those were on the four-week Long Crew. The Short Crew often had as many as a fifth or a quarter new womyn each year, but Long Crew had so many returning, experienced womyn that even Short Crew members had a hard time getting on the one or two Long Crew openings each summer.

The lore of Long Crew ran deep and wide, and the experience of being on the Land for that month was treasured. Leaving a job for more than a month was difficult for many, and a common discussion on the path was the tale of how the job was good, but they wouldn't let me off, so I had to quit. Womyn negotiated big-time jobs with one caveat: I need this month off.

Oh, and I'm not available by phone, text, or email, except one day a week. Still others negotiated lifelong relationships with a similar condition: I disappear for a month every summer, can you handle that?

Long Crew set up the site to be ready for Short Crew, and Short Crew prepared for the Campers and ran the areas that provided systems and

Beloved farm truck photo by Chewy Kane

services during the Festival. During the densely rich 10 days when only Long Crew worked the Land, a steady chain of U-Haul trucks emptied our 10,000-square-foot storage barn up in Branch, 20 miles to the north, while a pair of 1-ton farm trucks and U-hauls vacated the various spaces that we called Howard's Barn, 2 miles to the south. Thousands of pieces of wood, mountains of carpet, rolls of pipes, stacks of 55-gallon barrels for trash and recycling, mountains of wheelbarrows, and a jungle gym of sinks and custom-built furniture were in constant movement from Howard's, one hillbilly load after another, making it down the slow country road 2 miles away. At the same time, a pair of 26-foot trucks filled with thousands of boxes of supplies for all Festival areas, piles of garden carts, mounds of worker storage, stacks of water heaters, and masses of miscellaneous magic made the longer trip down the sandy winding road from the Branch barn, a trail vehicle with crew following behind.

On site, sisters were busy making home for the Festival family. Stage dimensions were measured, levels were shot by transit, cribs were set, frames hammered out, plywood sheets carried and screwed down. Floors were built in the DART tents for smoother accessibility and at the Community Center for dancing and basketball — just 4 inches off the ground, but enough to make it safe and smooth. Deep in the campgrounds and around

Chipping the paths photo by Angela Jimenez

the perimeter of the road, well over a mile of foot paths were brightened, as wheelbarrow after wheelbarrow of oak chips were pushed along in relay, first one womon shoveling from the huge pile, another wheeling the load partway up the path, then yet another wheeling it deep into the woods. Two more sisters then spread the chips along Easy Street, Womb Way, or Old Workshop Walk, enough to find the path through the woods in the moonlight.

Directional signs were set in place, broken trees removed, eye-poking-height branches trimmed, mountains of carpets rolled out and staked. The artists in Signz mixed colors and designed new art, painting into the dark of night when their only distraction was the constant buzz of mosquitoes. Showers reemerged from the pea stone, water heaters were plumbed and fired up, faucets repaired and installed all over town, plus a few water fountains here and there for fun. The Plumbers' motto, "Take No Breaks, Pee in a Jar," was one of the crew T-shirts we all wanted to score — we all shared that tenacity on Long Crew. And morning, noon, and night we would sit together and share the wonderful meals Galz Diner made for us.

It was only 10 days between when Long Crew arrived and Short Crew officially began, but it felt like at least a year. A year to walk in the quiet, at first only a handful of the big tents, then a city ballooning, empty. Waiting. A year to reconnect with your Long Crew family, hear about breakups, hookups, deaths, great jobs gotten and then left to be here, the real job. A year to sink deeply into the rhythm of working in the woods, showering under the sky, growing dirt under your nails and calluses on your hands and feet. A year that goes by in the blink of an eye, yet so much more than a year's worth of experiences packed into the humid last week of July.

In the last decade of the Festival, most of the Coordinators on Long Crew had worked on Festival for at least 20 years. That meant they had two or more cumulative years of living on the Land together, being part of this web of womyn who created the structures that would hold our town. With so many Long Crew members also having many years in, we shared a depth of knowledge and a profound interconnectedness that was visceral and unforced.

It was something that got into your blood, a call to the earth, a walk back in time and a trip into the future, a deep need to be of use in building this thing from the ground up and taking it apart afterwards, making sure the forest was returned to itself. Long Crew was populated by sisters who had an essential desire to not see another tent when they went to bed, to awaken to the calls of the first birds, and to rest their heads to sounds of rustling leaves and tree frogs as the night closed in. The experience was primal, and it fed the most elemental parts of us, the spirit that yearns to be one with the community of the forest. This is what we had for those precious first 10 days on Long Crew.

Certain social community connection traditions for that week were long planned, but other happenings would pop up. Like the Pants-Off Dance-Off that got everyone into the Belly Bowl when it was announced on a paper plate stuck to the dinner serving line (pants being something many were willing to let go of for a twirl — I know I was). Or the year that Ferron came to visit Long Crew, and we all sat in the Belly Bowl, passing the napkin container as we broke down in tears from the deep reveal that is her gift.

On Wednesday evening we would meet for a Community Meeting, a tradition that was almost as long as the Festival, with most everyone from the working community sitting in circle to discuss anything that anyone wanted to discuss, anything that weighed heavy on the heart or curious in your mind. In that circle we discussed everything from womyn brushing their teeth in the shower to budget decisions. The afternoon before the meeting sisters would check-in with each other. Any idea what issues will be at the Community Meeting? We discussed, processed, wept, and laughed over everything:

> *Racism as experienced in Workerville.*

> *Birth order (Oh, THAT's why you act that way. You're the youngest!)*

> *Can we just kill the raccoons?*

> *Why do some womyn use paper plates instead of reusable?*

> *Trans inclusion.*

> *Why did I get on Crew, and she didn't?*

> *How classism influences our working relationships.*

> *Is it appropriate to have sex at the dance — and what about the teenagers being there who could witness this?*

> *How loud is it cool to play music in work areas?*

> *Are sisters really flushing their nose with neti pots in the showers?*

We talked.
We struggled.
We laughed.
We got mad and walked away. But we always came back to that circle.

The days stretched long but the punch lists were always longer, and some imaginative woman or another was constantly coming up with new tasks that would make something a little safer, a little prettier, a little more accessible, a little kinder to the womyn who came next. We took on those tasks, often grumbling a little, but also welcoming the creative ideas that were folded into the work we did and the love with which we approached each task.

Whatever we did in the outside world, each person took on a Long Crew persona. I like to think we each owned our own Land spirit every day we were in those woods.

Like Lorie, longtime Carpentry crew beloved and eventual Coordinator, who arrived at a community meeting once wearing nothing but mud.

Ayla, part of the original group of Mt. Pleasant dykes that birthed the Festival, kept the drumming going on Long Crew and rarely passed by without saying, "Anything I can do to make your day a little easier?" She said that to many womyn, and I knew she always meant it.

Lisa Lisa, the elder of our Long Crew flock, stayed underneath the tree canopy because she was allergic to the sun, with the stinkiest bottle of lotion in her hand, ready to give any and every tired worker a foot rub. "Come sit down lover, take a load off those strong feet."

Or Pyramid, who in response to the Community Meeting question of a flogging happening on the edge of the Night Stage dance (Don't we have an agreement that we do not do this in shared space?) stood up and said, "Perhaps the next time I will juggle with three raw eggs." And then sat back down. The circle sat in silence, and somehow, we understood that to her, flogging was performance art. Just like juggling eggs.

We loved and accepted one another as family does, making room for the deeper person to emerge over time on the Land.

By the end of the first week, the Night Stage was built, most of the barns were unloaded, dozens of large tents were up, and the campgrounds were ready. We marked this feat by having the Long Crew Dance on the empty Night Stage, celebrating all that we accomplished in the week, all the ways we had grown together in those sacred woods. We danced with reckless abandon, spinning madly, throwing ourselves around on the plywood floor, or slowly grooving on the edges of the commotion — ours was a sweeping, inexhaustible joy. They say that dancing like nobody's watching is the way to free your spirit on the dance floor. But at this dance, we danced like everyone's watching — everyone is dancing with you — and we savored the sweetness of being seen.

On Sunday morning after the dance, sisters would come to eat in pajamas instead of work clothes, lie around in the grass, rest their heads on one another's bellies, and tell stories of the night. The sweet sweat of our labor still happened for a few on this day, but most would rest, together, on this rare All Crew Day Off. All day we would revel in the afterglow of Long Crew Dance, our most sacred ritual of Long Crew, and float through the late morning grass on the energy of that union. Nowhere were our bodies more liberated, our smiles bigger, our sweat as pure.

The very last Long Crew Dance, I danced four hours straight, but I still wasn't among the last to leave the floor. I listened from my tent to the final songs, the stomping feet, the howling in the night sky, the anguish, the laughter.

The last Long Crew Dance. I felt the tears of joy and sorrow from my sisters float through the air, as my own wet my pillow. Joy. Sorrow. Intertwined. Not two sides of the coin — just one coin.

CHAPTER 18

WE ARE READY FOR YOU

The arrival of Short Crew always brought a cacophony of energy, both energizing and overwhelming to those of us who had lived the last 10 days on the square mile of Land with only 115 sisters. We quadrupled in size in just a couple of days and yet the energy boost was closer to a hundredfold as our crew sisters set up their camps, unpacked their inventories, prepped their areas, met with staff, and figured out schedules, all to be ready for the Amazon campers soon to arrive. Short Crew hit the ground running, clipboards sparking with life, hugging the many sisters they hadn't seen in 50 weeks as they kept moving and hugging, hugging and moving.

Some crews had as many as 100 boxes of inventory to unpack, breathe life into, and then reformulate into the unique form and function their area contributed to the shared vision of our town.

Games, cribs, dress-up clothes, a tire swing, safety fencing, and arts and crafts for the Childcare areas. Huge rolls of twine for the Parking crew, along with reflector vests, flashlights, and coffeepots. Boxes of herbs and Mason jars that would soon hold teas in the Womb for all that might ail you, including the loved and hated "Ass Tea" that would knock the camp-crud out of even the deepest nonbelievers, even if it did taste completely like ass.

Calculators for Box Office, Coleman lanterns for Shuttle, easels for Workshop presentations, 100-cup coffee urns for the Saints Concession Stands and Community Center. Two-way radios, FM radios, CB radios. Duct tape, masking tape, packing tape, Scotch tape, electrical tape, spiking tape, and seven colors of flagging tape, which isn't really a tape at all. Poster boards, white boards, cork boards. Pieces of lace, twinkle lights, Green Tara tapestries, multicolored string lights in the shape of animals or flying saucers, paper globes, beautifully painted Signz, funky fabric covers for hay bales, ferns attached to tree branches to create a privacy screen — these were our adornments. Simple. Basic. Beloved. Somewhere, someone needed just about all the things, and through the frenzied few days of Short Crew setup, all the things were popping out of boxes and being put to good use.

Coordinator Coffees at 8 a.m. were now two large circles deep.

"Anyone have a 3-by-4-foot purple table with an ornate labrys painted on it delivered to their area by mistake?"

"We could use all the womyn you have to spare to stack wood at the Main Kitchen this afternoon."

"Festie-wear will go on sale for staff at 1 p.m. on Sunday — assuming we get some of those spare workers to help us fold."

"What do we know about the numbers — is Shirley running the betting pool again this year?"

The meeting was 15 minutes long, period. We all had long and dense days in front of us so there would be no sidetracking (unless you were clever enough to slide a joke in sideways).

Every night there was a dinner meeting, hosted by various crews, where womyn new on the Land introduced themselves and communitywide announcements were made.

"I'm Sparky, I'm from Jamesville, I'm working in Oasis. This is my fifth year working, my 10th Festival."

"I'm Tatiana, I'm from Austin, I'm working in Brother Sun. This is my first year working, my third Festival."

"I'm Lyn, I'm from B.C., come on over to the Saints and I'll toast you a bagel. This is my 28th year working, first on Saints, and my 29th Festival."

On big arrival days this ritual took a long-ass time, but it was important that each woman be seen and heard on her first day on the Land. We followed this tradition with nightly announcements, party invitations, and often a Festival story by some longtime Festival worker.

"The raising of the Goddess ritual at the back of the Night Stage is happening at 9 p.m. tonight."

"Please leave the Plain Foods Table food for those who really need it. If you can happily and healthily eat from the standard line, please do."

"The Sano party is happening Friday night and all who dare are invited."

Wednesday night was always the large Community Meeting. Thursday night there was often a Community Workshop, each year with a different focus. As part of our process of determining our shared values and priorities, and respecting and understanding our differences and similarities, we sat together to do the hard work of building community. We chose to push ourselves and each other to work on the difficult issues that can sit silently, patiently, and eventually painfully within a community that is intentionally not made up of homogeneous humans. We chose to say out loud the things that separate us, the things that bind us.

We had anti-racism and white privilege workshops, we explored our anti-Semitism and internalized misogyny, we examined classism and ableism. We had an Allies in Understanding night to discuss our varying perspectives on womyn-born womyn space and trans inclusion. On the 30th anniversary, there was a workshop about the herstory of the Festival, told by different longtime members of the community. On the 40th, we came together to grieve the end of the life cycle of the current physical manifestation of our community.

I had to choose carefully how to spend my time during those precious few days before the Festival opened, as my waking hours numbered close to 20 out of every 24 by then. I always attended the Community Meeting on Wednesday, and I never missed one of the Community Workshops. I remember going to the hospital one year when I was hemorrhaging so badly from fibroids. The doctor said she could do a D&C on the night shift in the operating room, since she was on call that night. "Great. Can I come back at midnight? That way I can go to the Community Meeting and be back here in time for the operation." I was gray and gaunt and exhausted from having only three-quarters of the blood a body is supposed to contain, but it was one of my most sacred commitments.

In the openings between all the scheduled gatherings, there were creative parties, some that lasted just one summer, and others that had staying power. The year after shigella, when we started the Sanitation department, I asked Ellen to coordinate the area, because if anyone could make the job of cleaning the toilets, showers, and sinks fun, surely it was her. "Make a purse out of a sow's ear!" I challenged her. Her brainchild was the infamous Sano Parade, with floats, costumes, and mayhem that made everyone want to be on that crew. Louise, the coordinator of Garbage, rode on the back of a borrowed two-seater convertible, wearing a long cape of black garbage bags, doing the figure-eight wave while wearing big-ass, elbow-length black rubber gloves. It's an image forever burned into my heart. The Sano Parade continued for years, with different departments arriving with plans for their elaborate floats, everyone lining up to cheer and laugh along the blacktop path through the Worker Area.

Sometimes our ideas exceeded our available time or energy. The Downtown Open House — with tours of the Trailers, poker in Accounting, and a pie-eating contest at the Worker Kitchen — got combined with a Downtown Carnival that included three-legged races, celebrative foods and a dunking booth rented from town. It was so fun, but totally exhausting, and we gave that extravaganza a go just one year.

Friday night was the Shabbat dinner for Jewish sisters and friends, with fresh challah baked in the kitchen. That night after Shabbat, the Goddess statue was raised, with drumming, chanting, and deep lez community woo. I never joined that circle, though I often stopped on a trip to the porta-potties and sunk into the vibe from a distance. I had to choose to continue the work that sat in my hands — my work in the trailer was my sacred ritual, to be ready for the sisters soon to arrive.

On Saturday, MJ Audio would roll in with a 24-foot box truck full of equipment for Night, Day, Acoustic, and August Nite stages, as well as gear for our rehearsal tent. Myrna Johnston had provided sound equipment for the Festival since 1982, every year making the trek from Boston to the woods of Michigan. Their truck slowly made the rounds, unloading gear at each stage in the morning. By the end of day, music, first from one sound system then the next, rolled across the fields. I got a run of excitement down my back every single year when I first heard Myrna's voice: "Testing, one-two-three."

The Short Crew Dance kicked off at dusk that night on the Day Stage, as the larger Night Stage was now fully occupied by the Lighting Crew working late into the early morning focusing lights. I have vivid memories of walking to my tent as the lighting crew worked through the chill of the late night, floods of color here then there. The condensation from their breath in the cold air took on bits of color as their water vapor gave the color something extra to reflect upon.

Sunday, the Craftswomyn arrived to set up their elaborate booths, marking yet another shift as the Crafts area blossomed with awnings and tables offering pottery, music, tie-dye, jewelry, books, massage, leatherwork, and every imaginable form of handmade clothing. As the Craftswomyn assembled their spaces, workers couldn't help but float through, planning to return as soon as they opened to add even more decoration, adornment, and fun to their Festival costumes and tents, or to shop for that special gift for the sisters back home. So many memories tied to this space: the cup you bought your first year; the bracelets you gave each other the year you fell in love; that sexy skirt you bought to feel more fly when she left you for another; your first dildo strap, handmade by a dyke in Toronto. The Crafts Area pumped up the volume of creativity and magic on the Land, while providing a little shopping therapy away from home.

Later that night, the Community Center hosted the No Talent Talent Show, another window into the playful and imaginative beating heart of Workerville. The long tradition began back in the '70s, when after finishing the stage one year, workers spontaneously jumped up and performed for one another. I remember Mary Gemini, performing naked except for her black chaps, accompanying herself with a stick sliding across a wire refrigerator shelf, singing "I Hate Men."

"I hate men, except my father and my brother and a few selective others.

"I. Hate. Men."

One of my favorite songs coined for the evening was when Porp from Tucson sang "I Can't Love No Dork."

> *"She did weird things to me like when she loved me with her feet."*

> *"But I can't love no dork!"*

Monday morning broke early, and the city buzzed with anticipation. This day at 10 a.m., the annual health inspection was scheduled, and after this, the gates would open at 1 p.m. Galz served only a cold breakfast to workers that morning as they were busy shining all the surfaces. The town got quiet, with workers staying in their areas or home tents, out of sight of the health inspector. I awaited the radio transmission that Susan was starting down the interior road, riding in the car with the inspector, led by Lisa in one of our Security/Communications vehicles and followed by another. I knew I had about 20 minutes before I needed to jump on my bike and ride over to the Main Kitchen, 20 precious minutes that I could fill with last-minute work on this Opening Day. I would arrive just as the inspector was pulling into the Main Kitchen, the primary place of focus, to shake hands, comment on the weather, and do what Susan and I did best together, talk about anything and everything but health department concerns.

The inspector, wearing a crisp summer shirt and khakis, entered both rented 40-foot refrigerated trailers and aimed a testing gun to check the temperatures of the towers of 5-gallon yogurt containers, stacks of boxes each containing 40 pounds of cheese, a mountain of bread, or the wall of egg cases. She walked over to the Outland Food Tent to review how we were storing fruit, washed her hands at our sink, dried her hands with our paper towels, and read the signs directing womyn how to test dish water. Wash, rinse, sanitize.

Into the Prep Tent, she looked to see that the tubs containing dozens and dozens of serving spoons and tongs were sparkling clean, and then ran her hands over the massive polyethylene chopping blocks on the 4-by-8-foot custom tables where scores of womyn would soon be chopping vegetables. She always expressed a little amazement at the raccoon cages, where the 35-pound bags of granola, nuts, and stacks of pasta were safely kept. I knew she was unnerved by the grass floor, and just as I saw her gazing about at our unusualness, I would shift focus and motion over to the Night Stage, towering in the distance, and say, "Is this the year we're going to get you to come out for a concert?"

I knew this had a good chance of inspiring her to direct her official clipboard toward the table and hurry that permit-signing along so she could get the hell out of there before she was glamoured into coming back for a concert.

I knew she wanted to.

I knew she never would.

On her way out I radioed downtown, reporting that the inspector was exiting the Land. I could hear the celebratory dinner bell ring, then a little cheer, followed by a big wave of relief. Not much could close a Festival down, but the health department could do it.

There were many years when sisters would park along the road waiting for days for the gates to open, and when someone left the Land and returned to Workerville they would share, "The line has started!" A day later, "The line is halfway to the back gate!" On Monday morning, "The line is almost to Madison Road!" That meant 3 miles from our Front Gate, which meant we were about to get a call from the sheriff requesting that we open the gates early.

The Line photo by Desdemona Burgin

Sisters in the line set up campsites, laid out cookstoves, and swung in hammocks. They walked the line in fabulous outfits and chatted with one another, starting their Festival right there on the county road. Security/ Communications and the Satellite Crew worked their way up and down the road, reminding womyn that they were in fact on a county road, not in the Festival, so to please keep their clothes on and stay out of the actual road. Locals came and sold hot dogs, hot coffee, doughnuts, and stalks of gladiolus, and passed out cards for their restaurants. "Crystal Valley Tavern Welcomes the Womyn's Music Festival." They used our "y."

Meanwhile, in the interior, pickup trucks made last-minute tours of the Land to collect unused rugs, no-longer-needed pallets or scraps of wood left from a build. An Opening Celebration rehearsal would happen on the Night Stage at a time that was negotiated between the sound crew (who'd gotten the bones of the sound gear up the day before) and the stage crew (who were busy painting flat black anything that didn't move — stairs, catwalk, trim). Joanne from Carps would arrive to move the interpreter platform a little to the left, so it wouldn't be blocked by the big stage pole. The Plumbers would make one last check of the idle shower banks that would soon be used continually day and night — ahh, showering under the moon and stars in the forest! One of the greatest gifts!

A last-minute check to all Front Gate areas — Box Office, Shuttle, Orientation, Parking, Security/Communications and Traffic: "Are you ready for us to open?"

As much as we encouraged Downtown staff not to go out to the road and add to the clusterfuck that was about to happen as womyn poured through the Front Gate, the excitement was too much for many to resist. Even though our lives working together each day seemed to be a complete miracle, the experience of the gate opening was the moment we all had worked toward. Everyone had their Front Gate outfits: tutus and parasols, wild wigs and leather chaps, handsome cowboy suits and snappy cop uniforms, bustiers and butterfly wings.

The countdown started, the two double gates swung open, and the loudest cheer erupted:

"WELCOME HOME, SISTERS!

WELCOME HOME!"

Front Gate sparkle
photo by Desdemona Burgin

CHAPTER 19

A BIRD'S EYE VIEW

The Front Gate was always a swarm of activity. It was part wild frenzy, with sisters grinning and sweating in the August sun, rushing about, so happy to have arrived. It was also part finely tuned orchestra, all the pieces moving in perfect harmony to accomplish the arrival process of thousands of sisters at once.

Workers would be directing cars into the temporary parking chutes at the Shuttle Drop, while they explained how you would unload all your gear, park your car, pass through Orientation, and then return to travel on a Shuttle into the campgrounds.

"Remember to look at the letter on the top of the pole in the row where you park! Between now and Monday is a lifetime, and in this field, it's easy to lose your car."

Approaching Orientation, you'd hear, "Welcome sisters, right this way!" and be swept into the darkened tent where a video playing on a loop imparted everything from camping tips to cultural mores in seven minutes. If you were new on the Land, there was a Festie Virgin chat room with experienced Festivalgoers who were there to embarrass you by loudly calling out "FESTIE VIRGIN!," and then patiently answer all your questions, while sharing things they wish they had known before they got on that first Shuttle.

Another tent had sign-up sheets for workshifts and colorful signs explaining what the work in each area included. If you were attending an entire week of Festival, part of your contribution to the community was to work two four-hour workshifts in one of the 45 Festival workshift areas. We built and ran this village together, and everyone participated.

It Takes a Village to Build a Village

The Festival was loaded with systems, services, and events designed over the years by what the community most wanted — a collective vision that reflected the shared priorities of a deeply feminist space. The only way all the details could work, for all the considerations to be in play, was with everyone contributing time, labor, energy, and love.

Yes, you paid for the Festival, but the entirety of what it had grown to be was not something that could simply be bought. It was something that each woman helped to create, in part by her workshift, and in whole by each woman's commitment to participating with her full intention in the creation of our village.

Every day needed hundreds of workshifts to be filled to keep the village operating. You could do anything from hauling garbage to rocking babies to chopping onions or making herbal teas. Some womyn tried different workshifts every Festival; others knew that making Nutloaf on Tuesday at the Main Kitchen was always one of their picks. I invariably recognized the sister who did the Stage Security shift on Sunday at the Acoustic Stage each year — it seemed like it was always her, always there. She was low-key, did her thing, seemed steady sitting on her folding chair, the orange polyester security vest disappearing into the forest as she sat along the edge. It was a comfort to see her, and though we rarely spoke, the familiarity we each had was sweet. We would nod and smile. Here we both are again.

We got our inspiration for the workshift idea from the Midwest Womyn's Festival in Missouri, where they used volunteer workshifts for kitchen duty and cleanup. I think at the first Festival our workshifts were Food, Childcare, and Healthcare — those were pretty much the only areas we had identified. There was a parking area, but cars came in and parked in a patchwork of directions, mixed with tents and coolers and bedrolls on the ground. This was in the olden times, before there were portable chairs, screen tents or awnings, when the tents you crawled into were mostly made from heavy, stinky canvas. Only the occasional family tent was peppered around in the distance, with a lumbering, oversized awning extending in front of the zipper, always in some state of soggy collapse.

There was no Shuttle, because we assumed everyone was young and able-bodied, like most of us were in the '70s. A Healthcare shift meant supplying band-aids and passing out salt pills to counteract the 100-degree temperatures. In Childcare there were a few coloring books and a sister to watch the pre-lesbian-baby-boom handful of kids as they tried to figure out what to do with themselves in that old, stinky army tent.

Over time, our city of sisterhood bloomed in complexity and care, and even though we had upwards of 600 crew members at our height, it took thousands of womon-hours to make the entire town work.

> *Seventy-five womyn were needed to prepare dinner on Saturday.*

> *Fifteen womyn for the 2-4 p.m. shift at Sprouts Camp.*

> *Eight for the Womb and 12 for Security/Communications.*

> *Ten to empty recycling barrels and sort cans.*

Not everyone loved doing their workshift, and not everyone did their workshifts, but I know in my heart it was one of the key decisions we made that fed the soul of the Festival, allowed it to be owned by all of us, and put us each in charge of caring for what we created together.

Sisters would ask — often — if they could pay extra and not have to do their workshifts. "It's my vacation, I don't want to work." That came up more and more as a suggestion for how to generate more money when the Festival faced difficult financial times. We would patiently respond that the workshifts were not an economic exchange, though they had an economic component, so thank you but no, you could not buy your way out of this shared expectation. Workshifts were the hands-on part of being part of something bigger than your individual needs and directly taking care of something beyond your own campsite or yourself. It was a path to building community, an active way to provide a service to your sisters, and a beautiful avenue of learning how the village worked from the inside. It taught us the power of being of use to your community and gave us all ownership of how things flowed. Besides, I wish I had kept track of how many womyn let us know they had met their lover, life partner, or best friends during a workshift. Thousands of beginnings were sparked while chopping onions, overnighting at the Front Gate, or parking cars.

It was the lesbian OK Cupid before the internet, but live, unfiltered, no photo needed.

Eight sisters to haul garbage at 6 a.m.

Sixty-five womyn to prep lunch and 20 for dishes at the Kitchen.

Twelve to do Stage Security at the Night Stage.

Six sisters to work at Brother Sun.

On Opening Day load-in and Closing Day load-out, the Shuttle Crew needed vehicle drivers, luggage loaders, workers to direct sisters as they arrived, and others to manage the nonstop flow of sisters, so tired of travel and so eager to get on a Shuttle and back into the Festival grounds to set up home. If you had previously done a tractor training session and had a Festival tractor driving license (a literal license card) you could fill one of those sexy tractor-driving shifts. More than likely, you were helping sisters load gear and get themselves into a surrey, up onto Bo Bus — an old school bus painted white, with the sides cut off so you could enter all along the perimeter — or into the back of a pickup or van. Some sisters arrived with big carts for their gear and could hike into the woods without a shuttle, but probably 90% of the thousands of womyn who attended each year had themselves and their gear shuttled into the Land. It was a huge undertaking that took all the extra crew members from around the Land that day, as well as just about everyone's patience.

Some "owner-operators" used their own vehicles for Opening and Closing days, but the main Shuttle vehicles were the two custom canopied surreys pulled by tractors, Bo Bus, plus every single pickup or van the Festival had in its 28-vehicle stable.

The Visual Ride Into Festival

For those who couldn't just climb into a surrey or up into the truck beds, there were three buses with wheelchair lifts to take sisters to DART, while other vehicles went to Family Camping, and still others that went to Over-

Surrey ride photo by Diane Butler

50s. But most went back and forth to the Triangle, putting along at 5 mph, with Shuttle stops along the way. If you knew where you wanted to camp, you were ahead of the game and could get off at Tree Line or Midway then hike along one of the wood-chipped paths into the canopy of the forest. Coming down the road, you would see paths leading into campgrounds, an occasional large Community Sleep Tent for those who didn't have their own, banks of Porta-Janes along the road, and banners hanging from trees. At the Triangle, the Shuttle stopped, and sister Amazons would unload all that gear — tents, coolers, awnings, cookstoves, backpacks, and campsite décor — in a well-orchestrated chain, handing one item to the next womon, then the next, and the next until the huge pile of gear was unloaded and the Shuttle started back to the Front Gate to pick up more sisters.

The Triangle was a hub of activity, with sisters lugging gear to the north, east, and south. The One World Area was laid out and ready for hundreds of workshops, some in large fields for popular topics, others tucked in under trees for quieter conversations, with media presentations in the darkened Media Tent. It was usually quiet here on Opening Day, but the next day, Intensive Workshops would start. At night, the large field would be filled with sand chairs and blankets for films projected onto a large screen against the backdrop of the forest — Movies Under the Stars, with free popcorn and the promise of womyn-identified cinema, where you would be surrounded by an audience that thought more than a little like you.

At Triangle you'd find an old-school Message Board, with slots labeled alphabetically so you could leave a note for a friend. With the Land only a square mile, it was amazing how many sisters you could see in an afternoon, unless of course you were looking for someone in particular, and then you could wander around for days, most likely 100 yards away from where she had just passed by.

Ernie — I'm camping in Jupiter Jump Off in a big red tent — meet you there at 7 p.m.

Jane — if you want a ride back to Madison on Sunday, meet me at Triangle at 4 p.m.

Barrie — I hope you have my tent, wandering around looking for you! I'll be at the Main Kitchen at 5 p.m.!

From the Triangle, heading toward Downtown, Family Camping for mothers with toddlers occupied the fields and woods between One World and the Main Showers. I remember one night, I had ridden my bike down to One World to try to find Lia and sit with her for 15 minutes during a movie. Returning on that path, walking my bike in the dim moonlight, it was very dark, probably close to 11 p.m. I could see mothers carrying their babies and gear into the woods to set up their tents. What fucking Amazons! I was so humbled by their determination to be in the woods with their families,

Movies Under the Stars
photo by Desdemona Burgin

and so grateful that they felt that these woods were safe for a mother and a baby in the dark. There were organized Helping Hands to assist mothers with babies to unload, haul their gear in and set up, but this late into the night, no doubt help was hard to find.

Across from Sprouts was Over-50s camping, which started as Over-40s. As the Festival matured, and many of us with it, we had to bump the age limit up to make sure there was space for elders. Of course, in the early years of Festival, womyn over 40 were the elders, but after four decades, our age spread was wide, and elder Amazons were determined to return each August, flying their freak flags high. Over-50s flowed into DART, a great location if you didn't need full DART services but could use some help now and then. Helping Hands were organized for Over-50s load-in and load-out, as well as DART, with specific Shuttles coming to each campground drop.

Sometimes if a sister just needed to chill out, she would go to Sprouts to be in the gentle energy the area created for babies and toddlers. Some years there were as many as 250 children under 4 years old registered, a mix of wobblers, sleepers, and toddlers. The Set-Up Crew would move through that area during Long Crew, raking sticks, clearing branches, and making the ground as smooth and safe for babies as possible. The new area carpets always went to Sprouts (along with DART and the Womb), so the babies crawling around on carpet, under the canopy of beech trees, were not resting

their little heads on rugs that had been stored at Howard's barn over the winter. It was so peaceful there, womyn rocking babies, little ones napping in the sleep tent, games and artwork happening in the activity tent. Mothering. The whole area had the biggest wash of energy of nurturing and kindness.

Gaia Girls Camp was another story. It was full of kinetic activity and games and raucous energy, girls swinging on tree swings, playing dress-up, and doing talent shows. If your mother said when you signed in that you could be a "wanderer," then you could check yourself in

On our own… photo by Anna Campbell

and out of Gaia at will, roaming the Festival with your friends, safe among the family of womyn. Some girls rode the Shuttle all day long, some sold painted wood chips along the paths, but on Saturday, all the girls jumped into the annual Gaia Parade, which went from Gaia, through Downtown, and into the back of the Night Stage. Girls on stilts, girls wearing wigs, maybe drawing on sideburns and featuring flowing scarves. Womyn would line the road and cheer, and the girls would blow bubbles and dance feverishly to the drummers, running wild and free, reveling in their moment to be the absolute center of the celebrations.

Everything Is Art

The Femme Parade was dress-up time for adults, with the femme sisters taking the lead to feature the beauty and breadth of femme presentation. Dominatrixes in full leather. Sporty femmes in cut-offs and T-shirts. Tutus and corsets, naughty nurses, glamour models, nightgowns, slips, and so much fishnet.

Femme Parade photo by Gigi Nicolas

The Butch Strut, which happened another evening, was the energetic opposite, with cowboys and chainsaws, lots of leather chaps, vests, and hats, muscle tees and straps around the arm, or simply strap-ons.

Everyone was celebrated, in whatever way they wanted to present themselves. We cheer you. We see you. We love you.

The pop-ups were the most fun for me, because I would be sitting at my perch at the Day Stage, and from the distance

Scouting for Femmes photo by Gigi Nicolas

you could hear laughing, or see some commotion, and then from the back of the bowl would come the Redhead Parade — all redheads, all naked, red hair and ginger bushes proudly running through the crowd. Or the Pudding Parade, where the sisters would cover themselves and each other's naked bodies with pudding and then parade around the Land. Or the rainy years, when the sisters would wrestle in mud, covering each other completely —

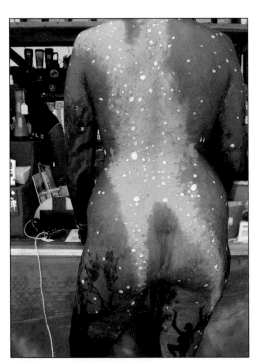

Night sky photo by Chewy Kane

you couldn't get close unless you wanted to go in the mud! It happened to me once. I didn't not like it.

A large group or an organized thing was not required to pull off some performance art. I always really loved that couple who would dress identically at the Day Stage in very distinct outfits. Plaid skirts and suspenders. Cheerleading outfits. Matching socks. They had a plan, and they worked their plan, and we all appreciated them for it. I never met them, but I always recognized them.

Body painting doubled as performance and visual art, with painted bodies floating through the Land. Jayne and Pamela, the two most prolific body painters, must have painted more than a thousand womyn over the years, some with swirls, some with intricate forest scenes or full-body nightscapes, or possibly just some adornment to the face. A single dot for some. A full body wash in blues for others. It changed something inside the wearer, and at the same time changed something in the sisters who gazed upon the body art. The full body could be a canvas to move about the Land all day long, with hundreds smiling at the sun setting gently across a sister's shoulders.

Past Gaia Girls, just around the bend, was the Womyn of Color Tent, a space for WOC and their guests. There were three neighborhoods within the Womyn of Color space: The Living Room, which at times welcomed all womyn to participate in certain workshops or celebrations; the Sanctuary and Firepit, located behind a brush wall woven with ferns, at all times a haven for Womyn of Color only; and the Patio, the front porch that was open to all womyn, always.

Sometimes I would be passing by the Community Center on my bike just as a dance class was happening, and I couldn't help but jump off and get in a quick Salsa with Maryasha or tag someone for a Two-Step. The dance floor doubled as a basketball court, surrounded by tables and chairs with sisters relaxing with their morning coffee from the Saints, maybe eating a bagel or meeting a friend. The mornings there morphed from Hip Hop lessons to Ballroom, over to African Dance and back to basketball, all sharing the single plywood floor built for these activities.

In the early morning, I worked in my trailer and once the town was moving, I rode my bike from stage to stage, helping to call whether there was time or interest for an encore, welcoming and thanking artists backstage, talking on the radio in the ferns, making sure I saw at least part of every set on the Land. From 8 a.m. to midnight there was something happening on one of the stages, sequenced to never compete with each other's sound or audience. It was an overload of the senses if you tried to do all of it, which many of us did, and then the quiet of the night would ease us back into the forests. I rarely could handle being in the buzz of the Belly Bowl for Midnight Meal, though I always got a plate from Lia, or snuck in the side door of Galz Diner. I would sit outside on a stump on the edge of the Flamingo Room Tent, or at a table in the dark, releasing everything that had happened from 5 a.m. until now, some Pad Thai on my plate under the midnight moon. I would count how many days remained. There were never enough, and there were always too many to imagine getting through. Filled up and exhausted from the saturation of life packed into a day, I walked on the dark familiar path to my tent, found the zipper by feel, and crawled into bed. Electric shocks ran through my body until I fell asleep and dreamt of the Amazons of Festival.

1st row: *2009* photos by Diane Butler; 2nd row: *2010* photos by Chewy Kane; 3rd row: *2012* photo by Desdemona Burgin; *2009* photo by Diane Butler

1st row: *2014* photo by Desdemona Burgin; *2007* photo by Chewy Kane; 2nd row: *2011* photo by Chewy Kane; *2013* photo by Brynna Fish; 3rd row: *2013* photo by Brynna Fish; *2008* photo by Angela Jiminez

CHAPTER 20

COBRA

I had never made a call to China before, but without an email address, I had to give it a try. I prayed that the person who answered the phone spoke a little English, because I spoke no Mandarin. I called twice during what would be early evening there, with no answer. I was pretty sure I got the time change right, so I tried again the next day. Someone answered.

"Wei."

I was ready for this, as I had looked up one word and that was how to say "hello."

"Wei. I am sorry, I do not speak Mandarin. I am looking for the band Cobra. Can you help me?"

"Cobra? I give you number. Better English."

The name of the person I was to call was Xiao, who I later found out was the guitar player. I reached her on the next call.

"Hi — I'm Lisa from the Michigan Womyn's Music Festival. I heard of your group and saw a video. I would like to talk about you coming to our Festival."

Cobra was the first womyn's rock-and-roll band from mainland China. I had found out about them when I got a call from a man who had heard them play in Beijing and was committed to helping them get to the United States. Randomly, he had heard about our Festival and thought maybe we would be interested. He sent me a link to a scratchy video. It blew my mind. Everything I knew about Chinese culture at that time was folkloric or traditional music. Chinese American artists had performed at the Festival in the past with traditional instruments, as had the Asian American Dance Theatre. I hadn't imagined a female rock-and-roll band that played something like a mix of punk and metal. Now I could imagine it, and I was on fire to bring them to our Festival in the woods.

We were always looking for more diverse artists and forms of music, and wanted to include womyn who came from different countries and cultures. Early on, womyn's music and culture was thought of as mostly white singer-songwriters. Just as it was true that the lesbian feminist movement wasn't all white and middle class (though it was most often represented by womyn with those privileges), we knew womyn making music and art were far more diverse than it had appeared in the early years. Singer-songwriters had the advantage of being able to travel by themselves with a guitar, they had less overhead, and needed just two mics. The Girl-with-Guitar segment of the community's musical voice was heard disproportionately because of this. As a Festival producer I wanted to include the groups that couldn't afford to go out on the road but played in the clubs and streets of New York, Chicago,

San Francisco, Boston, and Toronto. From early on we booked rock-and-roll, jazz, funk, Afro-Cuban drumming, and even had a Big Band come in from San Francisco.

We had no sponsors to help us achieve this goal, but we were committed and creative. For the Jerene Jackson Big Band in 1978, we couldn't begin to afford to buy 14 plane tickets for one set, so we booked the entire Green Tortoise, an old-school hippy bus that mostly went up and down the West Coast, complete with couches, bunk beds, and a lot of pot smoke. This promised to work well until there was a mutiny early on in Salt Lake. The band leader got thrown off the bus by the rest of the band and she had to book her own flight into Michigan. Shit happens.

We could have booked the Festival with mostly singer-songwriters and had an audience for some time, but I know one of the reasons Michigan lasted for 40 years was because of our diverse programming. We always tried to balance enough artists that everyone knew with styles of music and artists that were completely new, sometimes even challenging. We didn't try to make each set work for everyone in the audience. It was OK if you decided to take a walk, show up late, or hang out in the far back. We trusted that the music would get to each sister in its time, and knew that if the quality was there, all the music would reach a group that deeply wanted to hear it.

We invited Sweet Honey in the Rock to play the second Festival, the year after they had released their first recording. I always felt a little easier reaching out to an artist if I thought she was lesbian. We had no idea if anyone in Sweet Honey was gay, but we knew they were radical and political, and they came. Their taking a risk and saying yes to playing the Festival changed a lot of things in our trajectory, including learning not to assume who would want to play our show, and what the Festival would bring to artists.

In 1979, we booked the Harp Band, a Latin jazz group that included a concert harpist along with two conga/bongo players, a vibraharp player, and band members on saxophone and bass. I can still see the little booklet called *The Harp Guide* that listed harp players from around the country. I worked my way down that list calling harpist after harpist to ask if I could rent their personal concert instrument for a week until I found an elder sister in Lansing who became our go-to harp source. Many of us had never heard a concert harp live, and to hear it in this form was thrilling.

African drumming and dance were brought to the Land through Edwina Lee Tyler and a Piece of the World, Women of the Calabash, Ase Drumming Circle, and later by Ubaka Hill, who taught drumming and coordinated the beloved Drumsong Orchestra for the last 20 years on the Land. Drumming became the heartbeat of the Land, a steady anchor to a dizzying wild ride of a week with thousands of sisters. Edwina's group played on the old Land the second year there was a Day Stage, when we were still finding our way about being real with groups that were new to our fledgling Festival. I wanted them to feel comfortable and was unsure if the naked wild ways of the Land would be off-putting. As life unfolded, Edwina's was the first group to come out on stage topless, and she may have been the first artist to do a whole portion of her set right in the audience, completely breaking down the barriers between artist and audience.

I can still feel, viscerally, the deep impact of the first Night Stage performance by Sawagi Taiko. This group from Canada was in the vanguard of womyn stepping into playing the big Japanese drums historically reserved for men. My heart exploded as everyone in the audience felt the wave of power flow out from these sisters on the drums.

As with all things, men and their contributions were elevated in the musical legacy of so many instruments, while womyn's accomplishments were devalued. Many traditions directly and indirectly excluded womyn from playing countless instruments. The taiko drum, the djembe, the dundun, the electric guitar, and the drum kit were all instruments that mostly fell into the domain of men. But not here.

If we were to create a multicultural and diverse community, this vision had to be represented by the womyn who were upfront on the stages. We believed that if we could all see ourselves there, in all our infinite variety, and in all the ways we express ourselves, the diversity of the womyn who attended the Festival would broaden too.

In 1981, we hired the first lesbian punk band that we were aware of — the Contractions from San Francisco. It was often the punk bands and the grittier rock-and-roll bands that made some sisters question whether they were part of us. But they were, and they inspired each new generation to make their way to the Land, excited to

Tribe 8, 2000 photo by Diane Butler

see Tribe 8, Team Dresch, Bitch and Animal, 7 Year Bitch, and Le Tigre roar from the Night Stage. The mosh pits, frightening at first, became a rite of passage, with audience members calmly rearranging their seats to make way for the stage diving. Although the pit became the domain of the 20- and 30-year-old crew, it always welcomed the crones.

It is difficult now to imagine the Festival without theater, dance, comedy, and spoken word, but up until 1984, the Festival ran only music, with 12 Night

Stage performances between Thursday and Sunday. The Day Stage, which started in 1979, ran just two sets a day on Saturday and Sunday. In 1984, we started the Acoustic Stage, and both stages quickly grew and developed their own flavor of artistry.

Elvira Kurt, 2010
photo by Desdemona Burgin

Kate Clinton was the first nonmusical set we booked. What would the Festival have looked like if we had evolved without comics like Karen Williams, Marga Gomez, Elvira Kurt, Mimi Gonzalez, and all the sisters who made us laugh at ourselves over the years? They became part of the way we understood ourselves. They reflected back to us our shared experiences with all the oddities and complexities we had yet to name, and helped us not take the serious business of creating an Amazon nation too seriously.

Marga also brought six of her plays to the Land, becoming one of the cornerstones of our theatrical presentations that included Reno, Five Lesbian Brothers, Split Britches, Topp Twins, and Sharon Bridgforth's Bull-Jean Stories. Writers and spoken-word artists also had a home at the Acoustic Stage, where we sat riveted listening to Judy Grahn, Alice Walker, Dorothy Allison, Staceyann Chin, Sister Spit's Ramblin' Road Show, and Climbing PoeTree. I don't remember what Alice read that day at Acoustic, but I remember — because it was repeated so often in the years to follow — the impact she had on the audience when she challenged us to think about calling one another "guys." We had challenged so much language and created our own when what we knew failed. We took the "e" out of womyn and used female pronouns. But we still defaulted to the ubiquitous "you guys."

It is also almost impossible to imagine the Festival without the dance troupes.

Staceyann Chin, 2012
photo by Desdemona Burgin

The presence of dance companies started in 1986 when the Dance Brigade came roaring in and won our hearts. They continued to weave throughout the herstory of the Festival, performing 16 times and adding their powerful dance to all the stages. Terry Sendgraff, a pioneer in aerial dance, introduced a new kind of movement when her group, Treelings, brought stilt-walking and trapeze to the woods, beginning 20 years of womyn learning stilt-walking on the Land. The Festival carpenters made dozens of stilts in different sizes, and we bought fanciful fabrics for stilt pants so every parade and gathering had sisters walking tall and proud.

Amy Christian came with Terry that first year, and afterwards returned to teach giant puppet-making and stilt-walking with Wise Fool, adding this magical dimension to the Land. And then there was LAVA. Kay Gardner called me up after seeing the circus arts group up in Maine, and I was so excited that I booked them that very year. The power of this acrobatic movement exploded in everyone's hearts.

Wise Fool owned a large, free-standing, four-legged trapeze rig with 20-foot spans in New Mexico, and though we had gotten very creative about how to do trapeze from scaffolding — and even had huge custom crash pads made for our growing circus arts — we were limited in what could be done without a real rig. In 2004, we rented a truck for them to bring their rig out to Michigan. Sunday afternoon at the Day Stage featured a collaborative circus performance with Wise Fool and LAVA, and the beautiful rig that allowed them to do breath-catching, multi-person trapeze

Circus Sunday, 2004 photo by Diane Butler

tricks, bungee dancing, rope drops, and aerial fabric dancing, along with all the ground acrobatics and clowning we already loved. Their courage and sheer strength made us all feel fiercer. We made Circus Day a big afternoon party with free popcorn and a rented cotton candy machine, handing out spun sugar and working all the children into their own circus act, spinning wildly through the grass.

Cobra made it to the 1996 Festival, the first female rock-and-roll band from mainland China to play in the U.S. It took hiring an immigration attorney to get their visas, and buying Northwest Airlines passes from the back of the newspaper to afford their plane tickets. That was back in the day when people sold their frequent flier coupons on the underground market, and we were not beyond leaning into that. That one set took a lot of energy, expense, and stretching, but it gave us all so much. The womyn from Cobra fucking loved the Festival, happily camping in the woods, stomping around on the Land snapping photos, offering everyone Chinese cigarettes, watching every set, and giving us blazing rock-and-roll during their show. We fell in love.

The culture of Michigan was more than Girl-with-Guitar, though we loved us some singer-songwriters, for sure. But we also loved rock-and-roll, African drumming, Klezmer, Latin, jazz, R&B, Kurdish folk songs, and reggae. We loved dance and circus arts, and poetry and quiet stories. The more our music and art grew into being international and multicultural in its bones, the more our community grew with it — in our hearts and in the reality of who walked on the Land. We never forgot our differences, but we learned to celebrate, together, during that one week, when it was womyn who played all the instruments.

Cobra, 1996 photo by Toni Armstrong Jr.

Cobra and LV

1st row: *Shirley Childress Johnson and Tracy Chapman, 1987* photo by Anna Campbell; *Karen Williams, 2013* photo by Gigi Nicolas; 2nd row: *CocoMama, 2015* photo by Diane Butler; *Lez Zepplin, 2006* photo by Angela Jimenez; 3rd row: *JD Samson, 2010*; *Marga Gomez, 2008*, photos by Desdemona Burgin; 4th row: *Nedra Johnson, 2007* photo by Desdemona Burgin

1st row: *Kay Gardner, Therese Edell, Betsy Lippitt, and Nydia Mata, 1987; Maxine Feldman, 1987,* photos by Jennifer Campbell; 2nd row: *Medusa, 2014; Alex Nolan, 2014,* photos by Desdemona Burgin; 3rd row: *BETTY, 2013; Gina Breedlove and Linda Tillery, 2015,* photos by Desdemona Burgin; 4th row: *Marcelle Davies Lashley and Cris Williamson, 2014; Audrey Lane-Getaz and Judith Casselberry, 2015,* photos by Desdemona Burgin

1st row: *Shelley Nicole, 2011*; *Sia, 2009,* photos by Desdemona Burgin; *Melissa Ferrick, 2011* photo by Anna Campbell; 2nd row: *Allison Miller, 2014* photo by Desdemona Burgin; *Bitch & Animal, 2003* photo by Diane Buttler; 3rd row: *Shelley Doty and Vicki Randle, 2014*; *Ferron, 2015,* photos by Desdemona Burgin; 4th row: *Elvira Kurt and Pam Parham, 2012* photo by Karen Hellyer; *Ubaka Hill, 2011* photo by Desdemona Burgin

1st row: *Dorothy Allison, 1996* photo by Toni Armstrong Jr.; *Krissy Keefer, 2006* photo by Desdemona Burgin; *Julie Wolf, 2007* photo by Desdemona Burgin; 2nd row: *Topp Twins, 2005*; *C.C. Carter, 2015*, photos by Desdemona Burgin; 3rd row: *Cris Williamson & Crew, 2015* photo by Desdemona Burgin

1st row: *Slanty Eyed Mama, 2010; Barbara Higbie, 2005;*
2nd row: *Aleah Long and the One World Inspirational Choir,*
2015; 3rd row: *Alive!, 2015,* photos by Desdemona Burgin

1st row: *Elders; Tina Banchero in flight,* photos by Desdemona Burgin; 2nd row: *Queen and LV; Bitch on top scaffolding with Charlz blowing fire,* photos by Desdemona Burgin; 3rd row: *Opening Ceremony* photo by Desdemona Burgin; *Flaming arrows* photo by Amy Schwarz

CHAPTER 21

GETTING SOBER ON THE LAND

In 1978, I rented a little camper trailer for $100. Even though it was the third Festival by then, I still didn't own a tent. I slept right on the stage during the first Festival, under the piano, so frightened that someone would come and fuck around with any of the gear we had rented on a wing and a prayer. Year two, I slept in my Dodge van. By year three, I'd graduated to a gumdrop pink camper.

Though the Festival still didn't have much in the way of worker food besides a few loaves of bread, a bag of granola, and some hand fruit, we always bought cases and cases of Old Milwaukee beer, 99 cents a 6-pack in the '70s. The little fridge in my camper trailer was continuously stocked with Old Mil, with at least one cabinet holding partial bottles of a mishmash of equally cheap hard liquor. The dinette table that popped up when the middle mattresses of the bed disappeared was put to use for rolling joints or drawing lines of coke. Lots of jokes were made internally and externally about that gumdrop trailer being the Den of Shame.

I retired there most nights after work ended or the show wrapped up, ready to party until passing out with the last one standing. I was 22 years old, and apparently I could live and work with next to no sleep for days at a time. I recall many mornings on the old Land, feeling the acidic dread as the first signs of dawn trickled into my awareness. That sinister sound of the first bird in the morning. The icy drop in temperature that happens just before dawn. And then the horrid glow of sunlight around the top of the trees. I had done it again.

I couldn't stop myself. I didn't think it was visible to anyone but the rotating group of womyn I partied with through the night, that is, if I thought about it all. It might be the members of a rough-and-tumble band I partied with one night. A processing session with the ever-struggling tech crew on another. Or my friends who were on crew who would circle by around midnight. I didn't realize that the only common denominator in this rotating party was me, and that folks on the more normie side of partying did this occasionally, whereas I did this every single night.

We were in the early years of our community, still developing our ways of being with each other, but already integral to our way of creating our own civilization was prioritizing talking in circle with each other and processing everything. Post-Festival that year we huddled in concentric circles in the tall grass up on the hill, exhausted but never too tired to tease out every detail about how things went, enthusiastically airing out criticisms and periodically offering animated praise. We analyzed where to park cars, which meals ran out of food, how to better prepare for rain, and what we learned about just how far we could string extension cords from the two electrical panels before we had zero juice at the end of the cord. We were making things up as we went, learning from every mistake, and if we hoped to have yet another Festival (because each year always looked like the last), we had things to improve and we knew it.

That year, as the bedraggled circle of Amazons spitballed topics, someone (I imagine it was a worker from the Womb) brought up their concern with my drug use. I was pretty sure it stemmed from the night that I had stayed up all night talking and partying with Terry Garthwaite and ended up being quite ill-behaved.

I had discovered Terry and her band, the Joy of Cooking, in a record bin on one of my lazy afternoons searching for female singers at my local record shop. I had been so excited to find my first rock-and-roll band that was led by two womyn, one who played a bad-ass electric guitar. That was Terry. Her co-leader, Toni, played keyboards, and together they shared lead vocals and songwriting. Most importantly, they were the fucking band leaders. Terry wore hippy shawls, leather vests, and short skirts, and sang with a gravelly earthiness that felt almost butch if I could allow myself to think that. This was before what we knew as "womyn's music" had come to be, and I could count on one hand the positions that female musicians played in popular music at the time.

Chick singer.

Piano player, maybe.

Singer-songwriter was really what was most acceptable.

I'd found the Joy of Cooking record in 1973 when I was a junior in high school. Now it was 1979, and I couldn't quite believe I'd booked Terry Garthwaite to play the womyn's music festival I was now producing. We connected after the show Saturday night when we discovered our shared fluency in a variation of Pig Latin where you insert the sound "OB" before each vowel sound in a word. We proceeded to hang out and converse in Ob-Talk, a language neither of us had spoken since junior high, though our junior high tenures were almost 20 years apart. I was thrilled. She wasn't just an artist I had loved since I was a teenager. She was a trailblazer who showed me that things in rock and roll could be different through her pure grit of making it be so.

There were few people awake that night, when over the hill I saw Robin Tyler stomping her way toward the stage. I had hired her that year to be the production manager and it was a terrible fit. So bad a fit that I had to let her go mid-show, and ask her to stay away from the stage, where she was causing a lot of upheaval among the crew. The dim light of morning showed that she wore her omnipresent army togs and safari hat as she rushed down to the stage where Terry and I had been watching the night turn into day.

Robin ripped off her wrist ticket, threw it at me, and stomped away. We sat there quietly for a few moments, turned to each other, and said "wOBow."

I had been in teen heaven, sitting with my feet hanging over the plywood stage, gabbing away in Ob-Talk under the stars for hours with someone whose music was part of my foundation. As the dawn truly started to break, Terry realized she had a shuttle to catch. She had to get to her off-land cabin, pack up her stuff, and get back to the Land to meet the airport driver. I didn't want the night to end so I offered to drive her to get her gear, but my van was solidly parked in by other trucks and couldn't be moved until midmorning. The only vehicles I knew of that had keys were the two Womb vehicles, the vans we kept available in case there were any medical emergencies that needed to get transferred off the Land immediately. They sat there idle most of the time, but they were irreplaceable when they were needed.

I went to the Womb and said I needed to borrow an emergency vehicle for an hour. The person looked a bit dumbfounded, I'm sure because I was there at 6 a.m., clearly without sleep, sporting a purple wig I had somehow picked up along the way, and my eyes were probably rolling in the opposite direction. I was drunk, stoned, and coked up. And I'd be right back with the van, I promised.

I'm pretty sure this was why they were now talking about my drinking and drug use in the circle. That was a fucked-up thing to do, taking the emergency vehicle, but really, did they have to generalize my behavior? Another womon echoed that she felt similarly concerned and that she understood everyone partied a little and that the Festival supplied beer, but she questioned my extreme consumption and the decisions that I made under constant use. I felt agitated and uncomfortable. I sat there listening, trying to disappear into the tall grass.

"Shit. Fuck. I have a problem. I can't believe this is happening. I have a serious problem."

"How did I ever get surrounded by so many fucking squares?"

I didn't think for a minute that my problem was the nights that turned into days without a moment's sleep.

The truth is I was fully an alcoholic before I ever started to produce the Festival. The complexity of doing the Festival work created the perfect vortex of stress, social anxiety, and political pressure that exploded my teenage problem-drinker into a full-blown drunk by the time I was 21. I honestly cannot imagine going through the constant growing pains and stress that learning how to produce the Festival heaped on my young life without substances to blunt the feelings or bolster the bravado needed to fake it until I could make it. I was solidly drunk and stoned for the first seven Festivals.

But the living contradiction was real. As we created this community and formulated our newfound matriarchal feminist values, I was living a parallel life where the primary thing of importance to me was to make sure I had a mix of substances to blunt reality, even if it was a reality I so passionately believed in, and to which I wanted to dedicate my life. We were raising our consciousness of caring for all sisters, sincerely practicing honest engagement, earnest work, active contribution, and love, yet my personal capacity to show up literally and spiritually waxed and waned as my drug and alcohol use grew a tighter and deeper grip on my life. The only thing I had going for me that blunted the growing psychic schism was that despite

LV, circa 1976-77 photo by Laura Munter

my using, I threw 1,000 percent of what I had into the Festival. I wouldn't let a job, a lover, or family come between me and my focus of creating this gathering for womyn. Only drugs and alcohol were between me and that world.

In the '70s and early '80s, mixing recreational drugs and alcohol was so prevalent in the lesbian community that we would literally do a sweep of the Night Stage area after the show to rouse

LV, 1979

the womyn who had passed out, to make sure they could wake up, and to send them on to their tents. There was a popular "drug store" that set up shop in the camping area, and it was so out of control we had an undercover narcotics agent warn us to shut it down or they would. Few sisters had found recovery during this time, and if I heard of an isolated woman or two who had gotten sober, I made sure I gave them a wide berth. We were starting to create more spaces to be together out of the bars, but the bars were where members of our community found each other, and the fallout of that lifestyle was real for many of us.

I got sober after the eighth Festival, at the end of 1982. December 7. Like many, I had no real intention of getting sober at that time, but I had to do something, finally, to get everyone off my back. I headed off to California, where I had spoken to a counselor at the demand of my lover at the time. My lover had said no more cocaine or no more her, and so on that fateful phone call I was trying to talk with this counselor about the cocaine, but she insisted on asking me about my drinking.

"The drinking is not the issue. The girlfriend only has a problem with the cocaine."

But she persisted with her questioning. I remember getting off the phone and thinking, "FUCK — she's going after the booze, too."

I imagined going into a treatment center like Diana Ross in *Lady Sings the Blues*, under a palm tree with a big hat and bigger sunglasses. That was the brand of grandiosity that lived between my alcoholic ears. I ended up instead at the El Cerrito AA Fellowship, and I wondered if I would make it through the week of holding the huge, hairy hands of men while I faked saying the Lord's Prayer in a circle at the end of the meeting.

Surely a week of doing this would get everyone to chill out on me.

But after a few days of not drinking, I started to have real problems. I got the sweats and shakes and was crazy fitful through the night. I could barely physically raise my hand when they asked if there was anyone in their first 30 days of sobriety. I shook so badly driving my car I would pull over and cry, regroup, then make my way again. I couldn't talk on the phone — I was so frightened of every normal interaction.

The phone, the instrument I played so well in the orchestra of Festival.

I stalked the house sleeplessly in the middle of the night and crashed under a blanket on the couch in between AA meetings during the day. I found that the only place I felt the smallest amount of normal was in that room with the hairy hands, and so I would take myself there three or four times a day just to ease the complete disintegration of my nervous system.

I was 26, too young to be an alcoholic, as I always said when someone suggested I had a drinking problem, but now I could look down at the channel of my life and see how it was going to unfold. If it was this bad having my first go at not drinking for a few days since puberty, how was it going to look in another decade? It wasn't my drinking that scared me, it was how these first few days of not drinking disintegrated me that scared me straight. I was truly frightened. I had been drinking very regularly since sixth grade when I started to babysit for members of the Devil's Disciples motorcycle gang, who supplied me with all the wine I could drink and the occasional joint. If I wasn't watching their babies, all I needed was a buck and they would buy me a bottle of 99 cent Boone's Farm apple wine on one of their constant walks down to the liquor store a block away.

My biggest fear once the initial cloud of detox dissipated was whether I would be able to continue to do my work on the Festival. What I realize now is that I could not have continued to do the work had sobriety not entered my life. My life of drinking and using had led me to be internally dishonest, and that fundamental dishonesty with self can only stay contained so long before it would start to bleed steadily into everything I did and affect everyone I loved.

Coming back to the Land sober in 1983 was not smooth. In the Mt. Pleasant office, I wasn't loose and fun — I was scared and stiff. More than once I had a sister tell me she liked me so much better when I was drinking, or even yell at me to go get drunk. I was an asshole when I was drinking. Now I was an unrecognizable boring sonofabitch sober. The whole family system of the Festival production was based on me being Dad the Alcoholic, and all the pieces were on autopilot to pull me back into that role and keep the system as we all knew it.

I remember walking through those early weeks on the Land, my first year sober, tears running down my face, a constant that I couldn't even attempt to hide. There was no skin on my face, no buffer over my nerves, and it showed on every level. My tears were but a symptom of the inner terror that was coursing through my veins. I remember throwing up back by my tent before my first sober Community Meeting, so deeply wretched with my inner fears and knowing I had to move forward. From that day on, my mash-up of the Third and Seventh Step prayers was my mantra that I repeated before every meeting, before every difficult discussion: "Relieve me of the bondage of self that I may serve this community. Take away my difficulties that stand in the way of my usefulness."

I decided not to stop buying the beer that the Festival had always provided for the crew, which by this time was served in old bathtubs we dug into the ground and filled with ice. Bathtubs of Beer were part of the lore of working Festival, and I would be damned if I would change that because I got sober. The little pink teardrop trailer I started with on the old Land had steadily grown, and by the last year of my drinking it had expanded to a 38-foot motor home with a party that never stopped. I gave it up and bought a tent. I didn't want the reminder of all the sleepless nights I'd partied until dawn, and I was finally ready to sleep in a tent on the Land. On the ground. I was getting back to ground zero, and from there all things were once again possible.

CHAPTER 22

WE CAN LIVE LIKE THIS

To make it through my first sober Festival, I had called up the couple of sober sisters I knew and asked them to come work on crew. Kim J became the Night Stage manager and Hillary H came to work in Central Heating. I knew that Nell, who coordinated Sober Support, was clean and sober (I was finally looking forward to talking with her instead of turning away to walk in the other direction as soon as she appeared). And then, as always, at the helm of Performer Support was BE, who by chance was the speaker at the very first speaker meeting I went to — there at the podium, telling my story.

On the Land we met for evening recovery meetings under the magnificent Maple Tree that lived by the side of the Night Stage until a storm many years later split her in two, revealing that the old dame was well over 200 years old and worn out on the inside, yet still so beautiful and strong to our eyes. Other times, we met at the Old Meeting Tree in what would become Over 50s, or behind our tents, sometimes under a lean-to in the rain.

I was starting over, and these sisters were my touchstone — the faces I found in the community meetings, the sisters I followed on the path, literally and figuratively. There were few sober sisters at that time, but our numbers slowly grew. I stopped filling the bathtubs with beer after my first year sober and feared people would say it was because I had stopped drinking. They did, because it was completely true. I was awkward as hell the first couple of Festivals in recovery because no one really knew quite what to do with a sober Lisa. But I wasn't alone. The camaraderie of drinking was one way I broke through the producer stigma that hung over me in the worker community, and now that I was sober, not only did conversations stop as I approached a table, but the pint was now slid under the table and the joint was cuffed instead of passed to me. The isolation I felt in recovery moving through a partying community became an unwanted companion to the growing seclusion I felt in my role as producer.

I got sober December 7, 1982. The explosion of dykes finding recovery all over the country became a hallmark of the '80s. Up until then, the '70s lesbian life was the bar life in cities of any size, or there were always one or two group households that served as the community bar. Mine was one of them. As much as we valued our hearts and minds expanding with our newfound political analysis, this did not extend to our physical and spiritual well-being or influence how we were killing ourselves one bottle at a time.

As recovery grew in the lesbian community, more sober sisters came to Festival and the recovery community on the Land blossomed. Meetings happened 24 hours a day for every type of recovery program on the books, and someone was always at Sober Support if you needed to talk. Each of us suffered from addictions to substances, compulsive ways of being, and attachments to other people or things that threatened to take us down, or at least keep us from our freedom. Sometimes it is easier to face your issues when you hear someone share the truth of their inner challenges. Instead of turning away, your love and respect for them grows, as you witness them survive the reveal. And then you have the gift of realizing that what the sister spoke about was something that got in your way too, and your own opportunity for change grew.

Our small group of sober sisters in the worker community became the foundation of my recovery, allowing me to continue to produce the Festival for another 32 sober years. The principles that recovery brought into my life expanded the integration of feminist values into my work and gave me a deeper understanding of what we were attempting to create. This gave me a vision for my role as a trusted worker who wasn't the boss of other people, or a producer who attempted to drive by mandate. Instead, I strove to do my best, communicate exhaustively, and hope that others would support the vision I was working toward. My recovery gave me the strength to support the vision of other womyn, learning more deeply that my role was to help manifest the hundreds and thousands of visions sisters brought to the Land.

I wanted to be of use to the Festival community, and the clarity that embracing service brought to my identity as the producer was life-changing. The details of creating the town — from how to keep the porta-potties clean to building safer and more fun shuttles to expanding childcare options — were every bit as important as the much more visible performances on the stages. I always included myself in cleaning sinks and toilets, running garbage, cooking for the all-crew day off, and making coffee in the morning, even when I couldn't squeeze any more waking hours out of my body and time ran so short. It was a spiritual understanding that came from recovery: She who is faithful in that which is least, is faithful in most. All our work was an honorable gift we gave to one another, and as someone whose work was often looked at as more special, it was important for me to remember this gift in my hands, my back, my bones.

The values of the program worked in my life in such a way that I internally shifted away from the framework of rules and guidelines, and moved towards intention, realizing that the only thing that mattered was group engagement and a living respect for the community. It was a fantasy that rules and guidelines control people anyway, or that there was anything we could and would do if rules were broken. What was in front of us was to create a world with shared expectations and shared intentionality, knowingly, by choice. This became the foundation that held our world together, more and more each year, a fabric of understanding and love, rather than a set of guidelines and rules.

We were reimagining a living Matriarchy in that beloved forest. We understood analytically that patriarchal systems are about exerting power and control, while we believed matrilineal systems are about inclusion, sharing, and support. But manifesting our matrilineal beliefs in all our relations and actions comes from spirit and heart, more than mind, and this new expansive way to approach our lives was a big shift in our world view. Could we let go of the fear that feeds the need to control and try to practice unconditional regard for all our sisters, whether we connected, loved each other, or even liked one another? Could we extend radical hospitality regardless of our personal differences, believing that all should have an honorable seat in the community?

These principles I learned in the program, which are essentially the same principles that guide most spiritual practices, mixed powerfully with the radical lesbian values of centering womyn and recovering our matriarchal ways of living in community. Lesbian feminist values at the time were not necessarily mixed with a spiritual moral code, but we consciously wove these together. There was also the organic ideology we were germinating on the Land as we lived together for an increasing number of years. The moral code of giving all that you were able to for the betterment of the community. The moral code of challenging yourself to acknowledge and work with privileges and differences, to care about the needs of one individual as well as those shared by the entire group. The moral code to live on the Land with respect for all living things, expanding our connection to the plants and animals we share space with, stepping back from the hyper-human focus and recognizing we were but one group of animals on the planet. Intersectionality wasn't a word or even a concept then, but it was our shared life.

Day after day, week after week, the months turned into years one day at a time. We supported each other to include the principles of recovery in our Festival life together. The expression of that spread through the community, mixing with lesbian feminist values and our feral Land mores. We aspired to bring radical honesty to all our interactions and learned to tell the truth without attempting to change someone else's mind. We learned to listen without planning our next response. We grew patient with ourselves and our sisters, and learned to value integrity above results. We expanded our courage to do the impossible tasks and held steady in the most difficult conversations.

And perhaps most of all, we were learning the principle of humility — the realization that we made mistakes daily, and the acceptance that we would survive them. Learn from them. And keep living. Making new and different mistakes. It just made it all so much easier not to have to be perfect. And at the same time, it made trying to be our best so much less burdensome. It had a back-ass way of making what we did more stable and secure because we were less attached to protecting an image of not making mistakes. This group of lying dopers, sloppy drunks, dishonest scam artists, and manipulative control freaks carved a new way of living together, one step at a time. And we did this by telling each other the truth of who we were, and deciding that together, we could seek a different way and make another path.

Tree of Life, 2014 photo by Desdemona Burgin

CHAPTER 23

BABA AND IRA

When I first met Baba, her name was Carol Vandermolen, and she was a first-year worker on the Carpentry crew. I watched her as she made her way around the first couple of days, looking shy and kinda dweeby. I made a point to go up and introduce myself to her in the Belly Bowl. "Poor thing," I thought, "She's having a hard time." She seemed awkward and nervous, but that's not unusual for a first-time worker in her early days on crew. Everyone else seems to know what they're doing. Everyone else looks like they have a lot of friends. And there you are, new girl on the path, alone and feeling like everyone is looking at you but no one is seeing you. I later found out that the mild trembling I saw in this rugged, muscle-laden Amazon was a medical condition. Over time, I would watch it go from a tremble to an uncontrollable shake that took over her entire body. But that would take a few years to unfold.

She wasn't that tall, but her arms were the size of many womyn's thighs, and her thighs were like the trunks of trees, rooting her into the earth. She was thick and strong, and as the weeks went on, her incredible skill as a carpenter became clear. She had worked on construction crews in Florida — high-rise work — and seemed to be confident in doing all of the relatively simple jobs we were doing on the Land. Like so many of us, she evolved over the long days in the sun and the sweet quiet nights around the campfire. That timid walk across the tall grass in that solid Amazon body evolved into a strut, her Carhartts slung low on her ass, butt crack showing whenever she bent down and plenty of times when she didn't. As her awkward self-consciousness loosened, she had a tough sexiness to her, and her wicked sense of humor started to poke out.

There were a lot of strong, confident, and skilled womyn on Long Crew, but even among the most-sturdy, she stood out.

Except when she stood next to Ira.

Ira was the largest womon I'd ever met. She was tall, thick, brawny, and muscular. She had a soft layer of subcutaneous fat covering all that muscle, designed to make sure she would survive a long trek across the tundra. She was blond, very blond, with broad Germanic features. This was in the '80s, when the Cold War was still dividing Europe, and Berlin tied with Austin one year for having the most workers from any single town.

She spoke with a strong, drawn-out accent, and though she spoke more English than many of the German womyn who came to work at Michigan at that time, she chose to speak very little. "Lieeesahh" is how she said my name, though she scarcely spoke to me back then.

Ira scared most womyn. She was surly and aloof, and often wore a sneer across her face, eyes squinted. That look and vibe in a womon over

6 feet tall made womyn simply walk around her. She valued strength above anything else and it took years of her being on crew for her to slowly learn that there were other things of value besides being able to lift 150 pounds by yourself. Physical strength was her goddess, and this sister was strong.

Ira photo by Moka Jane Suskind

"Are you going to give me one of those scrawny little ones to work with today?" she would ask incredulously. Yes, that scrawny little one is one of the few you don't scare, so try to be nice. Her smile was beautiful but reserved for rare occasions. I would watch her and imagine a dyke moving through the world in that body; I knew she depended on that strength and sneer to protect herself when the gaze of the world constantly took her apart. So large. So blond. So obviously female.

She worked on Lace Hardware, the crew that moved all the lumber and big furniture out of the storage barn, erected the stage scaffolding, and put up the big circus tents. She used a 12-pound sledgehammer, back when most still used an 8. The womyn on the crew were both intimidated and inspired by her, and she was, by them, for very different reasons. They relied on teamwork. She relied on herself.

At the end of Long Crew her first year, Baba asked if she could stay until the end of Strike, the dusty, gnarly time when we'd be down to about 30 tenacious womyn. That last week is hard. The days are longer, and everyone is bone-tired and emotionally spent from watching the town come down to milk crates and tarps. No chairs, no big tents to shade the sun or block the rain, just a lean-to here and there. The energy that carried us was the rich feeling of connection from what we had accomplished together. Deep teamwork. We said those days separated the womyn from the girls. Staying focused and sturdy as we put it all away for another season was our sacred and cathartic closure. Even though this was her first year, Baba had worked hard and we welcomed her to stay.

A group of us was sitting around the firepit after dinner, dirty from a long day of work, and Baba was teasing Ira that she could take her in a wrestling match. I imagined that with Baba's lower center of gravity she was betting she could topple Ira, but Ira was betting she could finally be rid of Baba's teasing. She sneered and said, "Come here you little gnat, I vill have to shut you up once and for all."

They circled each other in the field between the firepit and where there once had been the Worker Kitchen, now just a cooler waiting for pickup and a little pile of watermelons remaining under the tree. They both wore shorts and work boots and were naked from their belts up. Baba was having fun with Ira, beating her chest and shouting "Arghhhhhhhhhh! Come to Papa!" Ira sneered through her smile, her eyes dead on Baba's laughing belly. They circled, their naked shoulders and arms met once, and the anticipation around the circle of womyn watching was electric. Holy shit! They are really doing this!

We were all grown-ass womyn. Living on the Land for five weeks, we had undergone a cellular rearrangement through which we'd uncovered the wisest, kindest, most loving, and open parts of ourselves. But that was mixed with a childlike feral freedom that liberated us from a lifetime of shoulds: how a womon should look, what a womon should wear, how womyn are supposed to act. We wore priestess robes and tutus, leather chaps and ball gowns. We painted our faces, spit to clear our throats, danced in parades, and sat in circles to unlearn the ways of Patriarchy. We did whatever the fuck we wanted and reveled in the realization that what we wanted was OK here. We released the shackles of expectations that were wrapped tightly around our bodies, our minds, and our hearts. The freedom to be goofy through what would be considered inappropriate anywhere else washed us clean every day. Even so, this exhibition going down in front of us was unusual even on the Land, where bizarre lived a respectable life. It pulled our attention like performance art.

Once more, Baba beat her chest in an old-school Tarzan move and faded over to the tree where the watermelon cooked a little in the late evening sun. She picked up a watermelon, held it high, and with a burst of fierceness, broke it over the top of her own head.

The watermelon meat and juice and seeds flowed down her naked torso. She drilled her gaze firmly into Ira's eyes. There was silence in the circle of womyn who had gathered to watch tonight's operatic performance. Baba, trembling a little — as she did — juice running over her chest and down her belly. Ira, sneering a little — as she did — eyes piercing back at Baba as they both stood still. And then that rare, magic smile from Ira. She'd been out-butched by the crazy new girl. And she loved it.

Baba, 1997

CHAPTER 24

SHIGELLA

It had already been a hot summer, humid and sticky the way summers in Michigan can be. By the time we got to the Land in 1988, we were in an almost-continuous heat wave. Living in a tent and working in the forest, I always felt filled up by experiencing the immediateness of weather. Weather was part of life. No fans or air conditioning to roll back the heat. No furnace except the communal fire pit for those late nights and early mornings when you saw your breath, even in July. Weather just was weather, and you learned to work with it as it covered you.

Living in the forest for six weeks changed me, every year. To wake up, day after day, and put your feet on the earth instead of a floor or concrete, to live at the mercy and magnificence of wind, rain, sun, and every other mood the Great Mother served up was grounding, even if it was also exhausting. I don't think I'm disconnected from nature when I'm living in my house in the city, but I know I am part of the entire ecosphere when I'm walking through the woods at night, peeing under a tree, recognizing the sound of the first bird at dawn and hearing the coyotes as I fall to sleep. I would become feral, bit by bit. I liked what it did to my chemistry.

Usually, it was the big rainstorms with high winds that wrecked our confidence and slowed down the building of our town. Rarely had the heat been a factor, but this year's heat was real and relentless. Crews that were able to rearrange their schedules to start at dawn, take a break in the heat of the day, and then return in the evening. In July, the nighttime doesn't set in until 9:30 that far west in the Eastern time zone, but temperatures stayed in the 90s all night, a relief from the 105- to 108-degree days that sat on your solar plexus, soggy with humidity that hovered close to 100%. It was oppressively hot. Relentlessly humid.

Heat exhaustion was running through the camp of the 150 of us who were there to prepare for Short Crew arrival. Sunburn covered everyone. We drank Gatorade and encouraged each other to take breaks and jump in cold showers, wore ice packs behind our necks and took the bus to the Ake (Lake with the L blown off from some local's shooting practice) to go for swims in the now-warm water. It was daunting to carry on. We were sure it would break any day. But it didn't.

There were only so many days left before Festival and the long list of things that had to be done sat before us, so we struggled through. Sisters would be arriving, and everything was layered so that one thing folded in after the other, and there just wasn't that much wiggle room in the eternal punch list of things to be done before the gates opened. It went from being an interesting challenge to a fucking bummer as the heat and humidity persisted, with each woman pulling from her deep inner strength to show up and push through the cloud of white heat that met us day in and day out. Most of our tasks were physical — loading and unloading truck after truck, building the stages in open fields under the blazing sun, cooking under a tent where the heat now hit over 120 degrees, rolling pipe out to showers and faucets, sledging stakes into the ground, spreading wood chips for paths, laying rug for sisters in wheelchairs to move across. We had a job to do, and we would find a way to continue.

Short Crew arrived and with the addition of a couple hundred more womyn, the Worker Health Tent was wall-to-wall with sick workers. We only had one Amazon nurse for Long Crew, Nurse Betsy, and she was totally spent keeping up with the workers falling from heat exhaustion. Some got sick and then got better. Others were not getting better, but there was no real way to lower their body temperature besides ice packs. We were sure it was heat exhaustion, but what if it was also a flu? We put bleach hand-washing stations around so everyone could sterilize their hands. Evening meetings were filled with long announcements about hydrating. The Womb womyn had arrived with Short Crew and immediately started helping Worker Health while a skeleton crew set up the healthcare tents. As soon as they were even partly set up, their beds were full.

What the hell was happening?

We had docs, herbalists, naturopaths — and so many sick sisters. On Thursday before the Festival opened, two womyn who could not stay hydrated were sent to the hospital for IV fluids and blood tests. The next day, we got the test results.

Shigella, a highly contagious intestinal infection.

The womyn who went to the hospital were prescribed antibiotics and our docs immediately called in more. Could they be the only ones who had shigella? I phoned the health department to tell them our results, I shared what we were doing for prevention, and they communicated that we were doing everything that could be done. Everyone, whether they felt sick or not, was wearing gloves in the worker kitchen doing every task, as were all the healthcare womyn. I went to sleep that night knowing that the 30-by-50-foot healthcare tent was full of sick womyn, more throwing up outside their tents, and the night air was punctuated by womyn running to the porta-potties.

I had broken up with my lover of six years that June, and we were still working together, trying our best to be friendly and family, as good lesbians like to do. She invited me to sleep in her tent that night, and for the first night of the summer I said yes. It was such a scary time, and it would feel good not to be alone. I woke up around 3 a.m. and didn't see her next to me. Had she gotten sick? I rolled over and found that I had somehow landed on top of her in my fitful sleep, my sleeping bag on top of her sleeping bag. What woke me up this time was not another sister walking to the Porta-Janes but the fact that I had shit myself in the night, in my bag, on top of my ex-lover.

I cleaned myself up as best as I could and stumbled down to the Womb. I walked into a MASH unit that had exploded through the night. Womyn were stretched out on the grass outside the tent, moaning and alternating between throwing up and intestinal explosions. Sisters were tending sisters as more kept rolling in. All the time, each one of us knew that thousands of womyn were en route to the Festival.

It was 1988, and of the many things we taught ourselves on the Land, one was how to heal and care for one another without reliance on allopathic drugs. The Womb had row after row of herbal remedies made ahead for all the variations of illnesses that could walk into their tent. We used clay for skin infections, and massaged and prayed to heal pains. The healers made tinctures and salves. Yes, if you needed an aspirin or epinephrine for an allergic reaction, or some more traditional remedy, we had those, but one of the important principles of the community was that the Womb was always co-led by an alternative healer and a doc. We taught alternative healthcare remedies as a political ideal and lifestyle. It was a radical and new approach in the '70s when Festival began, and as the dozens and then hundreds of healers found their way to the Land and added their wisdom, the community learned self-care without drugs. We grew our self-reliance by learning healthcare skills from others. After a decade it was an ethos we held high and on which we depended.

That morning there was a meeting with the co-coordinators of the Womb. We agreed that anyone who was sick had to take the antibiotics, or they had to leave the Land to avoid infecting another round of womyn. It was an unprecedented time and we had to protect the herd. But still, it was a tough sell. We had to make this clear in a meeting with the entire working community, no exceptions. Billie Potts, one of our original herbalists/teachers/witches, would speak to the community first. She was highly respected, known to have never met an antibiotic that she loved, and a longtime Michigan community worker. Her book, *Witches Heal*, was on most of our bookshelves at home. She was our teacher. I never thought I would hear her tell us to take these drugs — it was like a speaker at an AA meeting suggesting everyone take a shot of whiskey together. That's how deeply we felt our communal belief of staying outside of the medical establishment. But we were up against the first challenge to our ability to heal ourselves, and we had to womon-up for the sisters who were arriving.

It was a matter of two days, and everyone who had been sick was feeling better. The sulfa drugs were nasty, but they worked. We bought out the entire county's supply of the drug prescribed by the hospital and were starting to clean out bigger towns farther away. By the time the Festival opened, there were no new cases of shigella, just the 5-gallon buckets with bleach water placed by all the Porta-Janes and food areas, along with flyers explaining what had happened and how to protect yourself. It was a quiet Festival, with no new outbreaks during the week.

That quiet was short-lived. On the Tuesday after Festival, I received a phone call from a health department in Wisconsin. Someone was in the hospital with shigella and she had been at the Festival. Then came calls from Ohio, Minnesota, Illinois, Kansas, Missouri, New York — the hammer kept falling and the phone kept ringing off the hook.

By Thursday I was in a meeting with representatives of the Centers for Disease Control in Atlanta, the Michigan state health department, as well as local and county officials. I was in an infectious disease shit show. Thousands of womyn had left the Festival totally fine, but then hundreds, we think over a thousand, had gotten sick while traveling or upon arriving home. The head of our county health department was an old-school John Birch Society member, and he had been lying in wait to get this lesbian Festival out of his county. He was the person I spoke to when we first got the results, and the person I made the follow-up call to when all the different states kept marching in with more results. He changed his tune so fast from, "You're doing a really good job in a tough situation" to some version of "Heads will roll." I could see what was coming. I called the phone company and asked them to fax me my phone logs from the past two weeks.

As the meeting unfolded, the head of the state health department hammered away at how this could have and should have been done differently, that they should have been notified at the first outbreak.

"Who was the appropriate person to notify you?" I asked.

His answer was Mr. John Birch Society dick, who immediately declared he'd known nothing until he started to get calls from other health departments. Since I'd smelled this rat two days earlier, I pulled out my phone bill and asked him if he remembered the 5-minute, 37-second call we'd had on the Friday afternoon before the Festival, directly after the hospital had called to convey that the tests confirmed shigella.

Mr. John Birch Society, down one; Lesbian Shit Show, up one.

It turned out that there had been a rash of periodic outbreaks throughout the Midwest that summer because of the heat wave. Outbreaks in hospitals, on airplanes, at other festivals, and in summer schools. We weren't the only ones who experienced it, but we were unique in that it traveled all over the country on that Sunday and Monday at the close of Festival. They embedded two CDC staff members in our post-Festival crew, a womon who moved among us conducting interviews wherever she could, and a male who was set up at the Front Gate. They gave us a lot of credit for how we contained the first outbreak — the female CDC worker even asked if we could send her a brochure for next year's Festival, as she hadn't enjoyed a field study this much in ages. Once the report came out, their assessment was that there had been two separate outbreaks, initiated by two separate carriers. The first was in the Worker Kitchen, although they couldn't identify through which food item. The second was the Main Kitchen's tofu salad on Sunday afternoon, obviously handled by someone who had arrived on the Land carrying shigella.

We got through it, and though I can't say we were better from having gone through it, I can say we were stronger and more prepared to meet the unexpected. But it was a rip in the cocoon of trust that we were safe together on the Land. We were forced to realize that with thousands of us in one space, the ease that many of us lived with relied on a few individual womyn working behind the scenes managing the health and safety factors so the rest of us didn't have to think about it. We were left with an even deeper understanding that among family, trust can be broken — and repaired, if all are present and willing.

Aerial view of Festival photo by Jennifer Campbell

CHAPTER 25

RIDING THE WAVES

I always say I am so grateful that I was still drinking and using drugs during the first year on the new Land, and nothing could be truer. I really don't know if I could have made it through the piling-on of one torturous problem after another unless I was walking through it three sheets to the wind. I didn't know I was at the end of my drinking and using career. Part of the steady mix of substances I was on at that point was a heavy rotation of things that kept me awake most of the night, which in some ways was good, because the list of things to do seemed to grow by itself during my few raggedy hours of sleep.

When I did sleep, it was in an RV, which had started as a modest, old-school, pull-behind trailer, but had grown into a swank, tricked-out, 38-foot mobile den of debauchery. I parked it right behind the Night Stage, just on the other side of the backstage tent we later called Central Heating.

I was in that RV late one night, trying to get some rest, when an enormous storm broke out. It was the first night a bunch of production crews arrived, and passed out around me were a miscellaneous group of tech folks who hadn't had a chance to put up their tents yet or had stalled partying on their way onto the Land. They would load all the production gear onto the stage the next morning at 8 a.m. After we finished visiting and drinking and carrying on, and they'd gone to sleep, I heard the rain start to pelt the RV and the pace of the wind shift.

As I had done for almost every August of my adult life, once the rain picked up I went down to the stage to check things out. The pouring rain had already filled the canvas, making an enormous bulge of water. Back then, two 20-foot-long two-by-fours nailed together is what we used to kick up the front of the tent, rather than expensive store-bought four-by-fours, or our eventual sturdy four-by-sixes. I could see the scabbed-together two-by-fours were beginning to bow. I ran back to the RV and woke everyone up, screaming, "Get to the stage!" Then I ran through the night up to Lace to find a sledgehammer.

This wasn't the beautiful 60-by-90-foot tent that we eventually had custom-made for our Night Stage. It was, I believe, a 40-by-60 that we had progressively modified over time. Generally, large tents have three 18-foot center poles; from there the canvas slopes down to 7-foot side poles. In order to use it for a stage, we used 20-foot center poles in the middle of the stage deck; and then used homemade 20-foot-long four-by-fours rising from the ground to kick up the tent along the front of the stage, facing the audience. This created a large, beautiful opening for the performance area, enough "trim" to have lighting on the stage deck, as well as a good opening for three follow spots that operated from the scaffolding in the audience.

But this redesign of the tent created a very unusual and very unstable tent structure, one that needed longer side poles along the perimeter of the tent to keep it tight to the ground. In some cases, we put stacks of woodblocks under the side poles so they didn't lift under a big wind; we even drove stakes next to the poles to tie them down. More than once, a big wind picked up during a concert and the side poles along the stage tent swayed like long loose teeth in the wind. The swaying teeth only happened if we got the safety (the little rope that connected the metal post at the top of the pole to the grommet on the tent) right. Otherwise, a side pole could get tossed in the air under a good wind. Now, in this deluge of rain, in the middle of the night, the section of the tent that we had kicked up high for performances was quickly pooling water. If we didn't get that side of the tent down it would rip, and the entire stage tent would collapse before we could load any equipment onto it in the morning.

Our sleepy-eyed crew of late-night deviants, none of whom but me had dealt with any of the big tents, tried to push one of the faux four-by-fours to the side, but it just dug deeper into the sand. We kept trying. The longer it took us, the heavier the water in the canvas pressing down on the four-by-four became, causing the wood to continue to bend. I took the sledgehammer and knocked it at the bottom, and it slid a little in the right direction, so I hit it some more while sisters pushed and pulled. The rain was pouring down on us, and lightning and thunder filled the sky, but we were too frightened to be scared.

Thud. Thud. Thud. The sledgehammer was moving the board maybe half an inch at a time. We were in a race to lower the tent against the canvas that was steadily filling with water. Thud. Thud. Thud. Pushing and pulling.

Craaaccckkkk!

Instead of the canvas ripping where this huge bulge of rain had formed, the scabbed-together two-by-fours cracked in half, 4 feet above our heads, and the top half, now a jagged spear of wood, plunged down with the weight of over 100 gallons of water above it. Somehow it came down between the five of us who were huddled right below. No one was hurt. Had it hit any of us, we would have been impaled by the force of the jagged spike, but instead, it came through the smallest opening that existed between us, barely space enough for it to fit.

Blessed. That is what we were. Blessed. Looked after. A blanket of protection all over that Land. And we truly needed an entire posse of guardian angels. We were pulling things out of nowhere to build this city for Amazons, making up what we didn't know, one trick at a time. But we learned from our mistakes. From that point on, there was always a Rain Crew at the ready, sisters who knew how to tie and untie tent ropes, ratchet the lines, and swing a sledge. We were in a continuous process of learning what to do the next time and were always grateful for surviving the lessons that were the bridge to each new system.

The Lure of Sisterhood

At this time, in 1982, my sister Kristie and I were business partners and there were a handful of coordinators. The crew consisted of whoever showed up to work whenever they showed up. They heard the siren call and made their way to the Land, somehow knowing inside their hearts how badly they were needed. Those Amazons who came in the early years were not afraid of the shipwreck that this seductive song foretold. They were made of the stuff that looked a storm in the eye and said I am ready to ride your waves. The lure of sisterhood was so much greater than the risks we all faced and the endless processing we undertook in our search for our lesbian nation-state.

It wasn't men that we were in opposition to, though this is what was said about us over and over. It was maleness we'd had our fill of, and Matriarchy that we wanted to remember. We needed time and space away from maleness to find our femaleness and love it back to life. We passed around Sally Gearhart's book, *The Wanderground*, reading it by candlelight in our tents, knowing we were creating our own place of wonder. We worked naked under the August sun and shared cuddle dates to keep us warm at night. Sometime before baster-babies were the lesbian procreation trick, we dreamt of parthenogenesis, and knew we were this close to feeling the Goddess in us in a way that could start our young eggs dividing.

We wanted to grow a female value system, a womyn's way of thinking. We deeply understood that we were born and raised in Patriarchy, that our everything was wired to be male-identified. This was all we knew, the ways of men. To learn something different, first we had to completely own our innermost truth, and own the maleness that lived inside all of us. Only from first claiming this truth could we begin to disentangle ourselves from Patriarchy and slowly unravel the hold it had on us and boldly start to create our brave new world.

How would our world look if we were womyn-identified instead? Our deepest and most continuous work was to ask ourselves this question. This meant we questioned everything. How we lived and worked together was our ground floor of learning.

How do we support one another?

How do we teach new skills when we are just learning them ourselves?

How do we take care of ourselves while working hard?

Do we know how to talk with each other through disagreements and not just try to talk one another into our point of view?

Do we overvalue verbal dexterity and verbal confidence?

How do we make space for quieter sisters?

Do we value physical strength at the expense of diminishing other contributions?

What do we do when someone is just fucking off all the time?

How do we handle difficult behaviors like theft and dishonesty?

How do we live in the woods respectfully with the forest and animals?

Class and race are a factor in every single thing — are we willing to remember this, always?

How Do We Relate to Leadership?

Leadership was always high on our list of questions, because the world of men was made of layers of hierarchy, some of it seen, but most moving under the murky cultural waters that flowed over everything. As our Festival world grew and our town became more complex, continuity of information and experience on the Land was critical to avoid reinventing the same rusty wheel each summer. The sisters who returned to work from one year to the next were the holders of past information because they were the ones who made up how to do it in the first place. Their guidance allowed tasks to be completed more safely and efficiently, leaving time to take on the ever-evolving new ideas that sisters brought to the Land. But this put us in the gnarly arena of leadership, something we often railed against in all the wrong ways for all the right reasons.

Ninety-five percent of the leadership on the Land came from womyn taking the initiative to handle something, whether it was to run plumbing to the showers or cook dinner for the workers or organize a safe sleep tent for the toddlers. It almost always started organically with someone taking on the responsibility and then the leadership, eventually the coordinating positions evolved from recognizing that. Many times over the years, I sat with someone who wanted to know how to become a coordinator, and my answer was always, "Take on responsibility as if you were a coordinator. You don't take on the responsibility because you were offered the job, you are offered the job because you already own the responsibility." When a new position was created or there was an opening from someone leaving, it usually felt obvious who would be next. It was the sister who already worked like she was the bottom-line responsible person in everything she touched. She owned it all.

Starting with Kristie and me, most of the initial leaders — the early sisters who just flung themselves on this open Land and put their shoulders to the tasks at hand — were working-class dykes. Working-class leadership wasn't always a comfortable thing when our numbers grew. As more middle- and upper-middle-class womyn joined the working group, it was clear these were sisters who had been raised knowing that someday they would be in leadership or ownership. That often-unexamined entitlement permeated their work. And now they were working in a team led by a sister who was raised knowing she would wash dishes, or work the line, clean houses, take orders, not give directions. We spoke different languages and had different styles.

The upending of the traditional caste system was amplified exponentially when more womyn of color became part of the crew and then became coordinators. There were always white womyn who interpreted the unfamiliarity of style and approach not as a cultural difference, but as a lack of appropriate leadership, a leadership style that felt intimidating, or that lacked what they considered proper communication.

Absolutely, most working-class womyn and womyn of color have different styles of leadership and communication than white, middle-class sisters. We had all been taught the ways middle-class folks communicated and operated were the right ways to behave. It could feel completely belittling to have a sister calmly, succinctly, put you in your place if you did a task differently than they wanted. When these are words honed in middle-class culture, they quietly but efficiently cut deeply, leaving no outward mark, no boisterous public outburst, only inside pain. This language style is thought of as acceptable. But having someone use a swear word or raise their voice during a disagreement, or any conversation — an integral part of most working-class communication — was often considered abusive in middle-class culture.

We were literally inverting the expectation of who would be in leadership, whenever possible. It was a messy process. We couldn't expect these things to happen overnight, but we could and did expect them to happen, and expected all of us to work toward change. We had to find language to discuss this, language that straddled different classes and cultures.

They say a hallmark of third and fourth-wave feminism is intersectionality, but we were knee deep in the second wave and completely committed to dismantling the hierarchy of privilege on the Land. We were committed to making this change, which is very different than an intellectual commitment to talking about it. We lived this.

The Festival community had one big advantage in our approach, however sloppy, to these massive issues: We loved each other. Even if we didn't always like each other, we loved each other. We brushed our teeth next to one another and held the porta-potty door and heard each other's farts and saw each other cry and danced topless covered in sweat and worked until our muscles shook and our bodies were covered in dirt. We wanted a growing unity that could only be reached by the whole community becoming willing to take risks. To own our privileges. To learn to listen to the experience and hear the feelings of others. To show the experience of being a womon of color, a poor womon, a disabled womon on the Land. To be witnessed. Together we were growing a community value system, not an intellectual system. We fostered something in our hearts that said we would learn about each other's lives and honor differences. We were willing to be a part of change.

CUNTS and LUNTS

Leadership, in all its forms, was always in question, as it always should be. Even in our early years, when we were mostly a ragtag group of low-to-the-ground dykes, things came up. There were some in the group who felt there was a need for an intermediary between Kristie and me, and the womyn who worked on the Land. They suggested a group that was called the CUNTS: Coordinators Union Negotiating Team. I believe the first year for the CUNTS was 1981. Everyone working was encouraged to write to the CUNTS if they had issues, concerns, or suggestions they wanted to discuss, and the CUNTS would discuss them with Kris and me.

We all met midwinter, and during this meeting in a cabin that was loaned to me by my roommate in New York, Kris and I reported on what we were working on, updated everyone on our programming with artists, and had some roundtable discussions about various issues. They brought up a couple of letters that womyn had written and asked some clarifying questions. I enjoyed having other womyn to bounce things off of, but when we left, I had a feeling in my stomach that I was now reporting to womyn who were mostly there in earnest, but I didn't know exactly why I was reporting to this particular group of womyn. I wondered if this had come into being because a sister or two who initiated the idea of the CUNTS more realistically wanted to be the boss of me, and then enlisted other sisters to agree to the importance of a union? Who doesn't want a union for Sappho's sake?

I am the same person who couldn't work in a collective because I couldn't handle doing so much of the day-to-day work of the Festival and then have collective members who did comparably very little have equal say in decisions, decisions about work that I would end up doing. Working with the CUNTS felt like another version of this dynamic spun into the form of a union team. In the real world I know there are members of management or boards who direct people's work but contribute zero hands-on effort. Festival was 1,000% about hands-on work. It was a community built on work and love. The work of directing and critiquing other womyn's work was not one of the jobs we brought over from patriarchal management, so what were we doing?

Both Kris and I had a natural flow in our work with coordinators, an ease collaborating on plans for their areas, reaching out often to ask for advice and wisdom on things that they were most knowledgeable about. We freely sought and received a ton of direct input from womyn who worked at all levels on the Festival; we worked alongside them, hands on, so we knew each other. I honestly didn't understand the need or function of the CUNTS, but I tried to go with the flow.

The following year on the new Land, the idea of another group — the LUNTS, or Land Use Negotiating Team — was put forward. The group would be composed of sisters who had a particular connection to the Land and were interested in preserving as much of it as possible as a wild forest, something we all were committed to. So now we had another layer of lesbian middle-management. Some of these womyn worked on the Land Crew or were Rovers. They worked directly preparing for the Festival, which included safeguarding the Land as well as the womyn living on the Land. That made some sense to me, but then, the sisters who comprised the LUNTS were already part of the immediate group making decisions about the Land.

The 1982 Festival came and went, with all its complexity. Very long story told short, I got sober in December 1982 and moved from New York City to Berkeley as my winter home. I didn't meet with the CUNTS over that time because I could barely brush my teeth or make a phone call. I arrived on the Land in 1983, hardly any skin covering my heart, and waded into the new territory of producing the Festival without chemicals. You imagine things will get better when you get sober, but truly, at first they often get a lot worse, and this was true for me. Whatever bullshit I had been hiding and shuffling and covering with monkey dances, when the cloud of smoke from my dancing feet lifted, there I was, with all my feelings, and my honest, unfiltered perceptions of everything in my life. I walked through that Festival with tears washing down my face, every day, in almost every inappropriate environment, but I walked through those tears. Once the most profound lie of my life had been faced — the denial of my alcoholism and drug addiction — I had nothing to do but walk forward.

Pretty much my whole world fell apart during that first year of sobriety. My business partnership with Kristie ended between the 1983 and 1984 Festivals. When I looked down the channel of what would make it possible for me to continue to do the Festival, I knew it wasn't possible for me to continue to work with a structure like the CUNTS. I had to be honest now or not move forward. And while I knew I would always seek the wisdom of sisters like Flowing, Jan Walsh, and Pamlin Pegg, who were part of the LUNTS, the committee was structured into two-year stints, and I was looking for a lifetime with those sisters.

Producing the Festival was hard. If I was going to continue to take on the overarching responsibility as producer, it was too much to agree to a structure that didn't work for me, one that provided nothing except a layer of separation between me and the womyn I had worked with for years.

Had I agreed to work with a layer of middle management to be politically correct? Was I afraid of claiming my own leadership? Some of these womyn were middle-class, and it was shocking how readily they occupied the place of looking at my work with opinion and critique, with little hands-on work to show for their own. I had so much class identity and reclaimed pride in my working-class culture, but I still didn't see myself as a leader in critical ways. I was the one who would start the earliest and work the latest. I would never say no to a task and never ask a sister to do something I wouldn't do. But I worked in ripped shorts and no shirt and as my mama would say, my sentences were peppered with dis, dat, and de udder ting. I made a great worker, I knew this, but other people were primed to be leaders, to be owners. Not me.

Shortly after Kristie and I communicated that we were ending our partnership and that I would continue to produce the Festival, I wrote to the workers and said I could no longer work with a structure like the CUNTS and LUNTS. I understood that leadership in our community was complex, and that Festival itself had gone from being a collective of different configurations, to a partnership of Kris and myself, and then the addition of the LUNT and CUNT committees, and now, it would be a sole proprietorship. But I had to be clear and honest about what I needed to move forward and do the work. I could not be more responsible to a group of five womyn than I would be to anyone and everyone who worked on or attended the Festival.

I would always keep my commitment to be a worker among workers, and be part of creating a hybrid of leadership in our Festival community, one where coordinators would define the content and intent of the work of their crews, where crew members were encouraged to be part of leadership in the clan as well as in the work we did in creating the Festival.

We would sit in circle every week in a community meeting, hammer out issues that affected our priorities in living and working together, building and rebuilding trust, understanding, consensus, and unity. I believed together we could create something different. We had all heard the call of the sirens, luring us to this place not yet known, and against all odds we stayed the course on this potential shipwreck, navigating the treacherous waters of Patriarchy, looking for solid land to place our matriarchal flag. Perhaps there we could create a celestial hierarchy, a collective body of angels, where everyone has an opportunity to make their offering, and an honorable place for all at the table of womyn.

No time for two baths, 1978   *Kristie and Lisa Vogel*   *Sister serious stance, 1984*

CHAPTER 26

WOMYN OF COLOR TENT

Past Gaia Girls, just around the bend, was the Womyn of Color Tent, a space for womyn of color and their guests. There were three neighborhoods within the Womyn of Color space: The Living Room, which at times welcomed all womyn to participate in certain workshops or celebrations; The Sanctuary and Firepit, located behind the brush wall, woven with ferns, which at all times was a haven for womyn of color only; and The Patio, the front porch that was open to all womyn, always.

It all seems so matter of fact now, so part of the fabric of the Festival, to describe it like this, just as it appeared in the Festival program, but coming to include and honor a womyn-of-color-only space on the Land was a journey.

Amoja Three Rivers and Blanche Jackson were the ones to propose it. I had known Amoja from when she had gone by Carol and worked in the Worker Kitchen, staying to the bitter end one year when we got to sit with each other in the evening, poke the fire with sticks, and tell stories. Blanche, from New York City, had been a womyn's record distributor and was part of the team of Festival womyn doing outreach to womyn of color in different urban areas. The next thing we knew, there were two passenger vans of womyn of color coming to Michigan from New York. It was clear that Blanche was on a mission, and I was glad to pitch in by offering Festival tickets to offset the cost of transportation. Blanche was one of the first to organize a bus to Festival — and possibly the only organizer who earnestly followed our sliding-scale guidelines.

We offered eight Festival tickets to every large bus that organized transportation on a true sliding scale to provide access to low-income womyn. But the Festival's eight tickets only eased part of the load. The home community had to actively participate in helping sisters get to the Land. Blanche got that.

Some years later, Blanche and Amoja would start Market Wimmin, selling Amoja's book, "Cultural Etiquette: A Guide for the Well-Intended," along with shekeres and other crafts, making space for other womyn of color just starting out to sell at the Festival. There were probably 15 years when a betting pool of sorts arose over how long it would take Blanche and Amoja to unload their packed-to-the-gills vehicle, one steady trip at a time up Old Inventory Road. Even with loads of volunteers, this unpacking could literally take days.

I knew each of them and they knew me. When Amoja and Blanche came forward to propose a Womyn of Color Tent, I first suggested that instead we add a co-coordinating position at the Community Center and use a section of the Community Center Tent for womyn of color.

This was my response, after years of committing to and prioritizing the diversification of the womyn who made up the Festival's staff, performers, and workshop presenters. A co-coordinating position was my offer, a decade after hiring sisters of color in the '70s from different cities to work as outreach coordinators, networking with WOC and promoting the Festival.

We often borrowed Virginia Woolf's title "A Room of One's Own" as our shorthand for what we desired when we created female space in a man's world. A corner of one's own. Did I really think that would be a good place to start?

"It's a hard time in finances, we're not starting new areas now, let's start this at the Community Center."

I had missed the point.

What womyn of color needed and were saying they wanted to create on the Land was a separate space — a space within the Michigan community, but separate. A place to support one another from the stresses of being at the Festival. The Festival, in theory, was a safe space for womyn, but one that was not always out of harm's way for womyn of color. A place to be together. A place to workshop. A place to party. A space to step away from the majority white sisters, whom they loved or didn't, but who could not hold the mirror of recognition that other womyn of color did.

Even with the best of intentions that together we were creating a multicultural community on the Land, we all arrived at the Festival as who we were in that moment. For most white womyn that meant living in a white-dominated culture as the only thing we knew, with little or no understanding that it was white culture, or that there was any other way of being that was OK other than the default of being stylistically white Anglo-Saxon middle class.

I think most white womyn came to the Land with the desire to be one big diverse community — to live, and work, and love together — but we had yet to do any deep work on understanding and truly respecting cultural differences, and most had not even heard of the concept of white privilege.

We desired diversity and inclusion but were not ready to take a deep look at what benefited white womyn on the Land disproportionately, even exclusively. We walked through the world never having to consider that ways we thought were "normal" or "correct" were in fact the ways white people behaved. We only saw ourselves. Most of us lived in a world that only saw white.

Our small initial group organically confronted middle-class norms from the beginning because many of us were working-class, yet we had no analysis of white cultural norms. As more womyn of color came to the Land and spoke up about the inherent whiteness of the culture, we were ignorant but not entirely unable to hear the feedback because of what many of us had gone through — being told our working-class behaviors were wrong, crude, intimidating, or overly aggressive. There was a certain level of translation working-class dykes could make because we had a partial understanding of what it was like to move in the world of the womyn's movement, a movement that was by and large defined by educated, middle-class, but alarmingly downwardly mobile womyn in the lesbian community.

We got it that working-class flavor was both fetishized and ostracized. Our clothing and demeanor were mimicked, while our language, etiquette, and volume were sharply criticized. We were often politely scoffed at for our lack of certain types of information, the kind of information that is silently transferred through class privilege. This experience gave us a window into understanding what was being said by womyn of color, though the sword that cut was one of race, not class. A cut that I understood was even more hidden. I wanted to see, but still stumbled every day in my own awareness that white was a culture, the dominating culture that expected everyone not white to act as if they were.

I understood that we were all so much more vulnerable on the Land because our hearts were more open and our souls closer to our skin. I knew whatever injury I experienced on the Land cut deeper and hit more fully than in the world, where I learned to carry all my armor. I could imagine that this was what sisters of color experienced on the Land, but I didn't truly yet get that they needed a space within the space to be with each other.

Amoja agreed to run WOC programming and utilize the space in the Community Center, and it was a great success, despite it being a corner of a bigger tent. Sisters were so happy to have a space that there were nights when womyn slept right there, so full of joy to be together. The feedback and input from womyn of color was profound. It was clear after this one year having space in the Community Center Tent that a self-defined Womyn of Color space was important and necessary. This was 1984. And in 1985, the Festival's 10th anniversary, the Womyn of Color Tent had its own space.

The homecoming for womyn of color at the Tent was immediate and powerful. The space provided a home base for a diverse, multicultural community of womyn, a space that was distinctly not focused on white womyn. At all.

It was revolutionary on the Land for womyn of color, for white womyn, and for the relationships we have with each other. Its presence and importance called more womyn of color to the Land, and with it, the call for racial awareness in our growing community spread.

It was not a smooth addition for many white womyn, who really struggled with the idea of a separate space for WOC on the Land.

"Isn't this just reverse racism?"

"The best drumming on the Land is happening at that firepit, but I can't be part of it."

"Aren't we all here together? Why does there have to be separate space?"

"Nowhere else on the Land is there space where we all can't go!"

The level of defensiveness from white womyn was intense, and as one of the primary people answering the letters that came in, I learned a great deal from these interactions with womyn who wrote about their confusion and upset. It was humbling to witness the painful, angry ignorance in the letters, and it helped me understand my own process as I struggled to have compassion for a sister screaming reverse racism when faced with this one place reserved for sisters of color.

It made my commitment to be in this process much stronger, as I attempted, with my own unskilled words, to encourage another sister to imagine walking the Land in another sister's shoes. In another sister's skin. These were the conversations white womyn had to have with each other, again and again, year after year, in workshops, in Community Meetings, at campsites, and outside the Womyn of Color Tent on The Patio.

The full fantasy of our utopia was not afforded to everyone. We could not go back and heal the original break in humanity, but we could start seeing with full eyes what we each had and didn't have in the world we were creating together on the Land.

White womyn could take what we understood about our need to be in all-female space for rejuvenation, just to get a fucking break from the beat-down of Patriarchy, to support and respect the WOC space on the Land. It was not an intellectual exercise, but a process of opening ourselves up to the experience of others, wanting a sister to have what she needs for her own healing.

Womyn of Color Tent Altar photo by Pat McCombs

The Womyn of Color Tent changed the very fabric of the Festival for everyone. By having a space of celebration and support for womyn of color at the Festival, it was tangible how aspects of different cultures became woven into the customs and traditions on the Land.

I remember when Mimi Gonzalez called the office seeking permission to drive her truck down with a pig for the Latina Potluck that summer. I had known Mimi from back in the Mt. Pleasant days, playing pool at the Bird Bar. She sold raffle tickets at early Festivals, and I believe was the first to offer a kiss for a sale. After those early years we went our own ways, and now decades later, Mimi was back at the Festival, bringing her big heart and energy to the community again.

"WHAT? I'm sorry Mimi, but you know we don't give car passes to deliver food items for group cookouts; if we did that we would never stop and there would be cars everywhere."

"But I got a whole pig I'm bringing to the Latina Potluck, and I don't know how I'm going to get it down there."

"How big is this pig? I mean, pigs are huge!"

"Maybe it will be a half a pig — but it's more than I can carry from Treeline."

I responded to Mimi with our policy, trying to be fair with everyone, and the best way to be fair was to have guidelines that applied to all. I did not get the significance of what the Latina Potluck was and the joy it brought to the Land, especially for Latina sisters and their friends. Eventually, we negotiated a drop off to the Womyn of Color Tent.

Every time a sister would come up with a little foil packet and offer me a taste of the delicious, shredded pork, seasoned, prepared, and blessed by Mama Rosa, I was excited to get in on some of it, and I never forgot that first conversation with Mimi about the pig.

I didn't get it. I was able to be supportive, willing to learn, but I really had no skill at actively centering the experience and the needs of womyn of color. Mine was in the center by default and I did not see that.

Barbecue, to me, was great food, cooked over a grill or fire, but it wasn't part of my cultural practice. It had become so integrated into U.S. cooking through backyard picnic parties that I didn't think of it as an ancient ritual, coming through the Caribbean islands, practiced at every family gathering throughout Central America.

The kind of white folks I came from didn't really have an important food culture. By the time I was a child, poor white folks just ate poor white folks' food like burgers, fish sticks, hot dogs, canned vegetables. But there are folks, poor or not, whose traditions sit at the interface of food and culture, where culinary practices are significant and sacred. Mimi and her sisters brought this powerfully to the Land to share.

I know now that you can intend to learn to be actively anti-racist, you can want to deal with your white privilege, you can be willing to confront that your way of seeing things isn't the universal way of seeing things, but until you are actually in community, build friendships, have loverships, make family, and shed real tears with diverse sisters, you will only know you and womyn who are like you. Stepping into the sometimes difficult, often messy, always challenging, and forever liberating process of living fully in a diverse community of womyn changes everything.

The WOC Tent was a space for the rejuvenation of womyn of color, and yet it gave everyone at the Festival more of what we came there for: community. In that process of creating a respected separate space, it sowed the seeds of a togetherness we could only imagine in our earlier years.

We had a heart advantage on the Land because we were living together, loving together, "going to church" at Acoustic — which is how we came to think of our Sunday mornings there with DrumSong Orchestra and One World Choir — playing basketball in the afternoon, and watching shooting stars at night in the grass. We lived in the same house, and we all loved that house so much that it made it so much more possible to commit to one another, to be willing, to be teachable.

Community photo by Desdemona Burgin

CHAPTER 27

HOLY, HOLY

In 1995, after the painful end of a nine-year work partnership, I was praying on a vision for an Opening Ceremony. For the past 11 years, the Opening Ceremony had been happening on the first night of Night Stage as a 15-minute offering that included a blessing, a prayer, and always, the song "Amazon," by Maxine Feldman. Originally it was sung by Maxine in her powerful uber-butch presentation with her acoustic guitar; then later, by Rhiannon, often accompanied by Edwina Lee Tyler on djembe and Kay Gardner on flute.

Before entering a business partnership with Boo in 1985, I had been booking and producing the Night Stage since the first Festival. I loved doing that work, but I also deeply loved the creation of the town, thinking through plumbing expansion with the plumbers, menu planning and ordering for the kitchens, estimating how much road gravel we could afford to add to the two miles of road that snaked through our Land. Our town kept growing more and more complex, and though we had coordinators who looked after all the details as they arrived on the Land, it was increasingly true that the details had to be held together as one whole piece. The free-flowing amoeba that was our beloved Festival was expanding and contracting with each year, and though every area had a growing definition, expertise, and autonomy, the connective tissue that kept it all working together — and carried the threads from one year to the next, one coordinator to the next generation — this had to be solid.

Boo, who was also my lover at the time, had worked in music production for a decade, and it was natural for her to move into stage production coordination when we became work partners. I followed my passion to focus on the coordination of the town. We still did the programming and bookings together, but the on-site coordination was divided for those years, and the Opening Ceremony was not in my purview.

As much as I loved the song "Amazon" and I loved the sisters who had shared their blessings, prayers, singing, and music during these Opening Ceremonies, it was true for me that the existing Opening was not something I could deeply relate to or feel. I knew it was very meaningful for some sisters, but I also knew others had a similar response to mine, staying far on the edge and watching, but not joining. I wanted to include more of us. All of us. I wanted to have a universal shared heartbeat.

The Shit Storm

The year before, 1994, had been the last summer of co-producing the Festival with Boo. The intense struggle about the dissolution of our partnership reverberated into huge underground conflict everywhere, much of it going back to which of us you felt connected to, and why. In our town of radical harmony, there was deep strife. The rumor had spread that I had been abusive to Boo, that I had literally choked her in an argument, and though I had behaved in ways I deeply regret, with constant arguing and rageful outbursts between us, the story being told did not happen. I walked through that year with so much pain. Numerous sisters who worked or performed at the Festival approached me to tell me they felt quite shitty about me due to the rumor they had heard and believed. This was often accompanied by their own painful story of personal abuse at the hands of a loved one. A lover. A father. So many fathers. In our community it is nearly impossible to say to another sister that the allegation coming from someone claiming abuse was not true.

We all have been not believed.

I understood that womyn who did not know me personally believed the allegation made against me and now questioned the essence of my integrity. Even some who knew me well were at least confused. The one thing that I had from my roots as a working-class dyke was the goodwill I had grown in the community, goodwill from earnest work, goodwill from a steady commitment to struggle through issues, goodwill from a deep belief in community process. This was the one thing I had of value in my life, and I knew if I did not have the goodwill of the womyn I worked with, I had nothing.

I was rough around the edges, and I swore a lot. I still do. I was loud and rambunctious and hung out with other loud and rambunctious womyn — poor and working-class womyn, Brown and Black womyn — and rarely were there privileged and refined sisters in our pack. We were not the ones who were thought of as owners, administrators, or leaders. As this dynamic of class conflict played out, I was Dad the plumber, with my butt crack showing. My former partner was put-together, polished, well-spoken, femme, aloof, and had a law degree.

And now we were trying to get through one last Festival after being business partners for nine years. We were not speaking. We were working in separate trailers, with separate crews of womyn.

In the meantime, Camp Trans appeared across the road for the first time, three years after Nancy Burkholder had been asked to leave the Land. That was a regrettable break in our intention to never question anyone's gender on the Land. The one and only time this had happened, with Nancy in 1991, became legend. Now, coinciding with this internally dramatic year, a group gathered across the road to protest that incident.

Inside, there was another protest boiling, focused on the punk band Tribe 8, who were booked to perform for the first time on the Night Stage. Some sisters working and attending the Festival that year planned to protest the performance, not because they had ever seen the band perform, but because they heard that they supported violence against womyn. I could get that some would be intimidated by a forceful and grungy, tattooed and soap-dodger-looking band that cut off a dildo right in the middle of their set. But how was this violence against womyn?

This was also the year that my beloved friend Sara Deerheart died before making it back to the Land, and when my lovership with Pyramid started, adding fuel to the flame of differences between me and Boo. She now wanted to somehow outlaw BDSM on the Land, and Pyramid was seen as part of that community.

Early in that Festival week, a call came into the office trailer from the Box Office, saying that they'd caught wind that the group across the road at Camp Trans was going to come over and buy tickets. "What should we do?"

"You sell them tickets. You can say you just want to check in that they understand that the intention of the Festival is to be a space for womyn-born womyn, and then you sell a ticket to anyone who wants to buy one."

The worker at the Box Office said she didn't feel good about that and didn't think she could do it. I told her that was totally OK. "Could I speak with the shift supervisor please?"

I repeated to the shift supervisor what I had said to the earlier woman and asked if she could do this. "I don't think I can," was her response.

"That's totally OK, but we are a house of cards if we question anyone's gender, and this is what has to be done. Ellen has the keys to my truck and is ready to go out the door; she is comfortable doing this. She can be there in seven minutes."

The shift supervisor decided she could do it herself. The group from across the road entered, a group made up of born female, trans-identified, and others from throughout the spectrum, young and old. They came in, had a circle-up and talked with folks, then paraded through the Festival grounds before leaving, claiming victory that they had liberated the Festival. (As we know, that was not the end of this long story.)

Sisters said I had let trans people into the Festival, that I did not value womyn's space. They said I was Boo's perpetrator. They said I protected perpetrators. Some womyn wanted a statement to be read disowning Tribe 8, and not only did I not feel that, but I would never set up an invited artist in that way. So clearly, I also supported violence against womyn. I was centered in multiple cultural conflicts happening in our beautiful town. The narratives swirling around the Land had their own life. It was the most complex and difficult Festival I had ever made my way through.

I came out of the shit storm that was 1994 and was soon in legal arbitration around the partnership dissolution that lasted until May 1995. I was now taking back all the administrative coordination, working with some new and some returning staff in the office and on the Land, booking the 20th anniversary Festival, and dealing with persistent rumors and yes, troubling truths. It was not a radical lesbian feminist breakup. But the breakup was finally complete, and the ruptures of trust that rippled through the working community were real.

Now, nine months later, I was planning the coming Opening Celebration, and with each step I took toward that 20th Festival, I was aware of how much healing was needed.

A New Tradition

I was contemplating what to do about the spiritual tradition of the Opening Ceremony, which I wanted to continue in some form. In my prayers, I began to imagine a completely different approach to the song "Amazon." I called Judith Casselberry and Toshi Reagon and asked them if they could envision a version of the song that would make womyn dance, something that could be felt to the far edges of the Night Stage Bowl and roll down your backbone. I imagined something that could have a funk verse, a reggae verse, a rock and roll verse. These sisters, both incredible musicians, and each channels of the Goddess, gave us something so much more than I imagined, something

to sustain us for decades, for a lifetime.

I asked the Dance Brigade, who were performing on the Acoustic Stage, if they could do a dance for the Opening. Along with a dance, would they be open to ending the dance by diving into a mosh pit filled with hidden Lace Crew members who would pop up and catch them? We would recreate what had been frightening for some

Krissy Keefer stage diving, 1995
photo by Janne Watson

sisters last year — our first mosh pit with Tribe 8 — and have it right there in our Opening Celebration. We added huge slides constructed by the Carps crew, 12 feet tall, lined with sheet metal, and powdered with dancing dust. The dancers would slide down, bounce on mini trampolines, run down the runway, and then be caught by the crew.

It was playful, and magical, and beautiful, and it started our path towards what Judith and I would refer to as "Holy, Holy, Holy — Let's Party!"

That new and wildly exhilarating approach to the Opening Celebration was only the first of the surprises we had planned for the 20th anniversary. The second night, a hot air balloon would float over the crowd at Night Stage.

That idea had arrived one day when we were doing electrical put-in prep on the Land, and overhead floated the most beautiful, gentle, ethereal hot air balloon. This doesn't happen in Michigan. OMG. This would be fantastic if it happened while we were all together! I called hot-air-balloon companies and described what I wanted to do and when. We discussed the winds and the time of evening, arranged for Pip to be on the ride, planned the launch location, sure the balloon would come over sometime mid-first set. It was so exciting. Sisters would love this!

The set started and a little while later the balloon was launched off-site, with a crackling FM radio between me and Pip — "Pip, how far away are you now? Pip?"

"We're up, but … ccckkkkrrrrrtttt … it looks like we are heading towards … sshhhewwwwwwwww … Howard's Barn" (the place we stored our lumber, 2 miles south of the Land). The sound of the fire filling the balloon with air was loud on the radio and Pip was barely coming across. "Pip, somehow, you have to get him to turn the balloon! What can we do to make it come towards us??" Nothing. The balloon went with the wind, parallel to Madison Road, and missed the Land completely. At least Pip had a good ride.

We tried the hot air balloon again that year. That time our best idea led us to launch in the back of worker camping, in a small field in the campground known by some as Cum-Again Acres. We were confident this time, starting so close to the stage, how could we miss? But we did. Why not just give up? Who knew hot air balloons were so hard to pilot where you wanted to go?!

When we finally had our hot-air-balloon success — in a different year — we had to give up on having the balloon appear like a mirage on the horizon. We started it right there in the Night Stage Bowl, the fire blowing air into the giant balloon as sisters gathered for Opening Night. Like the huge breath of the goddess, the enormous balloon slowly, then quickly, billowed first

Floating away, 1998 photos by Brynna Fish

within, then over the audience. The basket — still with Pip, and this time a female pilot — lifted as its huge lungs filled with air. As it rose above the crowd, roses attached to smaller balloons floated down into the crowd.

Dreaming up other surprises for the 20th anniversary year, I'd looked into parachute jumpers. I thought it would be so exciting if a group of female jumpers landed in the back of the Bowl in aerial formation, like you see on TV. Could they form a labrys? I found a club made up of female jumpers who had experience jumping in formation and they were in Michigan! I met with the leader on the Land. No way could they land at the back of the Night Stage Bowl. The closest they would come to the audience was the Day Stage.

"But we'll all be here at Night Stage, why would you land at the Day Stage?!" It would be something we observed from afar, like a live TV feed rather than something that made our hearts pound and produced a collective gasp of excitement. It needed to be part of us, and the Day Stage idea just didn't work. Maybe that idea just had to go.

But then a womon new on the Transportation crew, an Amazon named Cherie, said she was a parachute jumper. And a good one.

"Could you jump out of a plane and land in the Night Stage Bowl?"

"Yes."

"Could you hit a 40-by-40 tarp, right there, in the center of the Bowl?"

"I think so."

There would be no practice run. We hired a prop plane out of Ludington, and up she went. We had a crew sitting on the tarp who would clear out as she came down, and provide a safety ring, whatever that could really be.

We heard the plane, which looked and sounded like any of the prop planes that routinely circled over us to see the spectacle below. It circled, and suddenly, we could see the parachute pop out. As she started to float down, blue smoke came off her heels. When she came in for her perfect landing, right in the center of the tarp, we saw the full glory of her jumping outfit: a pair of leather chaps, a black bra, boots, and absolutely nothing else.

Out of the ashes came the phoenix of renewal — that was the 1995 Festival. For any who were willing, this could be a new beginning.

The 20th Festival was a celebration of our best. Our finest music, our most beautiful dance, our incredible innovative ideas, our passionate politics, our expanding hearts, our capacity to grow silence and join the peace of the forest. And now, we had introduced another level of communal expression, a celebration of ambitious Amazonian extravaganza, a spectacle of pageantry that would echo the magic we each felt in our hearts. A celebration of our wildness, our spirit, our innovation.

Holy. Holy. Holy. We so partied!

1st row: *Crafts entrance*; *I got this, 2006* photo by Angela Jimenez; 2nd row: *Quilting Bee, 2015* photo by Brynna Fish; *Womb self-service herbals*; 3rd row: *Loading in, 2014* photo by Desdemona Burgin; *Joy, 2008* photo by Chewy Kane

CHAPTER 28

OTHERWORLDLY

Every summer, for many years, I would be walking up the path toward the Night Stage parking lot, and just as I rounded the curve, ambling up the paved path toward me would be Karen Dodson, arriving after her drive in from northern Illinois. I thought nothing of it the first few times it happened — I was just delighted to see this old friend, and we would greet each other with deep family familiarity. The third or fourth time I had a huge wave of déjà vu. "Wow, we've done this before." And then we would meet, year after year in the same spot, always on Karen's arrival, which was on different days and at various times of the day, but we would meet. Right there. We started to greet each other just laughing as we saw one another. "Here we are again." Everything was right. And everything was also just a little weird.

Time warp. Had we ever even left that little bend in the path? Or were we simply living in Land Time?

Did that happen just today?!" you'd hear one sister say to another. Or, "Wow — that was this morning? It feels like it was last week!"

It wasn't just a little step out of time we experienced, but a large-scale bending of time and space. When a womon would say, "She was here just a few minutes ago," and another would lovingly correct her, "Actually, that was early this morning," others would shrug and laugh a little and say, "Oof — Land Time." Or, "I've been on the Land for a week, but it feels like an hour, and it also feels like five years."

We knew what we meant even if we didn't know what IT meant. We lived in a porous relationship to time and space. When meeting someone on the path, like I would meet Karen every year upon her arrival, it was common for one of us to remark, "No time has passed." And mean it. The veil that held time blew wild in those woods, completely flexible. It sped up or slowed to a crawl, not uncommonly at the same moment.

A day felt like a month. A week went by in a flicker. It was like we had never left for those 51 weeks between Festivals, which led us to all agree with Elvira's joke and refer to that other time and place as Area 51.

"Where do you live in Area 51?"

"I'm not at all ready to return to Area 51."

I remember the first time I walked on the Land, my car parked at Treeline because snow covered the road. There was no one there and the woods were quiet in their white blanket. When I was midway to Triangle, I heard womyn talking and laughing in the distance, just over the hill. It was very vivid.

Were we always here? Or were we simply returning?

The metaphysical force generated by thousands of womyn intentionally gathering to form community, rediscover our ancient culture, and create something completely new — this was potent energy. A continuous vibrational power that washed over us, it gave us the strength to be more open, more real, to challenge ourselves to change, to grow. We were there for a community gathering and we were hungry for so much more. Among us were teachers, seers, healers, and priestesses, and yet the very real motivating force was the community energy itself. Each one of us strove to bring our best to the tribe. Our growth — individually and as a group — blossomed from that one primary commitment. Our best. Our kindest. Our most helpful. Our most willing. Our courage to change.

In the spring of 1995, after two painful years of counseling, mediation, and finally legal arbitration with my business partner of nine years, I was preparing for the summer, deeply concerned about the rupture in the family that the dissolution process with Boo had generated. Not the business dissolution itself, but the harmful side-taking that had been generated by stories told by Boo and her closest friends that often included asking womyn to take a side. I kept my confidences close, my truth in the arms of just a handful of womyn, even though I knew that sharing my side of the narrative could vindicate me in the eyes of those who believed the stories as they were told. What good would it do to the larger community to tell my side of a deeply conflicted business breakup? An immediate reprieve of my reputation, but one that would be followed by an even larger rupture in the heart of our community. I couldn't do this.

I reached out to a psychic, an elder who was in her 90s at the time, who came highly recommended as the super real deal. I called her on the phone, and simply told her I was looking for guidance on how to be of service in healing the wounds of divisiveness that were festering in a community I was part of. I didn't talk about specifics, didn't tell her it was a music festival or a womyn's thing, but just that I was part of a group that came together every year, and there had been a rupture of trust. She listened, didn't ask anything else, and then began that breathing, snorting, and silent thing that psychics do. After a long silence, she began to speak.

"I see womyn. Many, many womyn. It's like they are coming from everywhere, in caravans. And I mean everywhere. All over the world they are coming. And actually, they are coming from outside this world. Is this gathering all womyn? Only womyn? Do you know that womyn come here from everywhere — literally out of this time and space — out of this actual world that we know?"

"Maybe. Maybe I know that."

"My dear child, you have nothing to worry about. What I am seeing is that the energy you all generate brings the angels to you. It's like you are singing for the angels and they are so happy when you are together. They come to you every year. They are part of this, always. And all you must do is stay out of the way. That energy will heal everything."

Her words ran chills up and down my arms and warm water down my spine. I recognized what she was saying. She so easily put into words the feeling I would have when I first walked into the Acoustic Stage bowl in the spring, the absolute abundance of spirit, the shimmering of energy, the sweetness of life. She so simply named the source of at least some of the grace that looked after our group of ragtag Amazons through all our journeys, every one of the potential dangers, all our political trials. Yes, I can believe they will stay with us through this as well.

I wasn't always comfortable with taking the spiritual side of our community completely seriously or embracing it as I do now. At first, I saw more differences than similarities between me and the sisters who gathered in moon huts and spread their blood on the Land for renewal, who gathered to raise the Goddess energy or make rituals at the new moon. I had too much work to do to dive into a moon hut and lose my mind, and besides, I wondered how crowded those tent huts were, with everyone's periods aligning after a few days of being in the force field of so many womyn. I was always happy when womyn were together with intention. But really, I was busy.

It's not that I didn't feel spirit, it was more the way that spiritual practice was presented that I couldn't connect or relate to. I would get swept up in the magnificent channel that was the drum of Edwina Lee Tyler — this was the kind of spiritual call I could hear and feel through every cell of my body. When Edwina would drum, it stripped away our armor and anything else that held us separate from one another. She led us back to the ancient ways of all the cultures, when womyn would drum around the fire, channel the spirit of all that lives, crack us open to the point where you didn't know if you were animal, plant, or spirit. You knew you were all things.

Edwina Lee Tyler, 1987
photo by Jill Guttman

In the early years on the old Land, Z Budapest would come and sell books and do palm readings in the Crafts Area, and would always send messages that she wanted to do ritual on the stage. I had been around Z at the Midwest Festival. I had even joined in the Full Moon Ritual and the Breast Dance she led there, where sisters would spiral dance topless, and as they passed one another, face to face, they greeted each other by brushing breasts back and forth. My 20-year-old self could totally get behind that and I was already over the moon with the nakedness of my very first womyn's festival. I thought it was weird that at the end of the dance we were to dance by Z and kiss her, so instead I spiraled myself back to my Mt. Pleasant posse. They were standing on the table to see, laughing their asses off at me, that my breasts and I had joined the dance.

So when Z would send word down that she would like to bless the Festival, I honestly didn't take it seriously, or regrettably, very respectfully. I just didn't relate to it. I remember once there was a long and rambling late-night message on the phone machine at the office (also my house) from Z, saying that she was now tired of us not making room for the Goddess, and if we did not offer a blessing, she would hex the Festival and make it rain. She stopped coming to the Festival shortly after that, and years later, I regretted not making proper space for this sister who brought the Dianic Wiccan tradition to so many.

Looking back, I realize that despite our initial cynicism toward the spiritual realm, so many of our organic actions were actually communal rituals that reconnected us to our innermost sacred selves. We cooked over open fires, meticulously stacking 20-foot-long pits with dry oak that we lit at the beginning of the week and cared for day and night, all week long. At a time when processed foods were sacrosanct, we ate vegetables, beans, grains, and fruits. Before anyone imagined Whole Foods or Pharmacia, we healed with herbs and touch, used clay on our skin, aloe vera to treat burns, tinctures to calm our spirits.

We didn't want a piece of what men created; we chose to recreate the Amazon ways of living in the world, and our dignity grew as we embraced the ancient traditions. We did our work with reverence, whether we were cooking food, digging a ditch, caring for another sister's child, or building a stage. Every piece of what we did was spirit-driven and fueled our connection with our labor, our love for each other, and for the Land that held us. This is what had been taken away from the human spirit, the inner connection to making with one's own hands, feeding with natural food sources, healing with plants, and caring with touch. This is what we rediscovered and grew again in those woods. We created rituals out of everyday life, and all our efforts became sacred.

The Land itself was our touchstone, and for many of us who came from urban centers around the world, it was our first experience of living in a wild woodland. It was our priority to be gentle with the forest, to leave as much as possible completely untouched by our hands rather than sculpting it into a park or campground. We marked big areas throughout the Land as animal sanctuary, limited vehicle uses to what was absolutely necessary, gently bent aside ferns to put up a tent so they could revive more quickly. The Land itself became our spiritual site because of the devotion of the womyn who came there, the deep love and connection we all grew with those woods and meadows.

Getting to know Kay Gardner, feeling how totally cool and deeply spiritual she was in her life, was my personal turning point. She was so NOT a goody-two-shoes witch, and she didn't take herself too seriously, even though she was a monster talent and a force in any circle. She was just Kay. Being Kay. Making music and ritual just like others would pound a nail or bake a pie. It's what she brought into the world — art and ritual, without much fuss.

Kay used to camp right behind my tent on the Land, the only performer I could handle camping so close to me, right between me and the path that led to Central Heating, the backstage tent. I would climb out of my tent in the morning and slide around the back to pee, and that started our little morning ritual where she would say my pee was her wake up call. It wasn't weird, or boundary-less like it would be with someone else, but just a sweet good morning between neighbors.

It was Kay's vision that created the Acoustic Stage, and her energy that found the exact right place. It was also her witchy ways that birthed the Candlelight Concert, our closing ritual of music, dance, and spoken word illuminated only with candles and torchlight. She asked us not to clap, but instead to hum. At first many of us would titter at the idea, but we slowly came to appreciate and feel the vibration that our shared "mmmmmm" offered

Kay Gardener, 1985
photo by Lucinda Smith

to the circle of energy. She started the Singing in Sacred Circle tradition that carries on today, sisters raising their voices in ritual and healing. She changed me, I know this. She changed many of us with her magnificent and accessible ways of approaching ritual and her belief in something bigger than ourselves.

Because ritual is really what you make it, perhaps it's an act of being conscious and intentional that makes the shift into spirit. Showering with 20 womyn became a cleansing ritual instead of just a shower. It was spiritual and shifted everything in me energetically as well as got me clean. Singing to a Ferron song with 4,000 of my sisters under open August skies broke me right open. It burst my heart chakra free and cleansed me from a year of slogging my way through the Patriarchy. And dancing — sweaty, joyful, no-one-needs-to-look-cool dancing with my sisters — healed everything.

Along that path by Acoustic Stage and near the swamp road, there was a particular energy field some of us felt. Probably many of us, but some of us eventually talked to each other about it. I felt comfortable walking everywhere around that Land, in the day, in the pitch of night, alone, with or without light. Yet more than a few times when I walked along that path, I felt a dank veil fall over me. Once walking there with Pyramid, we both unconsciously reached out for each other's hands, and admitted we were scared. What was this that occupied the space so close to our sacred circle of the Acoustic Stage? The temperature was different, the smell was slightly of rot, eerily different than the mix of compost and new life one smells in a natural forest. I remember when Jeanette and Cyn came to me one night and said, "This sounds a little crazy, but we felt someone or something on the Land — we didn't really see them, but we were both frightened." When they told me where they were, I could only say I understood. Perhaps this area of darkness that carries fright and seeps the shadow side through the forest is the balance to the light that shines everywhere else for us on that Land. Fire and ice. Equilibrium of the spirit. The balance that our stability rested upon.

One night during the Long Crew dance, I went for a walk with a new womon on crew who had caught my eye and that I was having a bit of a flirt with. It wasn't common for me to butch flirt, but it wasn't unheard of, and this strong and quiet one caught my energy, and I could tell I caught hers. She asked to take a break from dancing and go for a walk, and we did. When we sat on the grass over by the Main Kitchen, she suddenly flew on top of me, making out madly at me, not with me.

Whoa!!!! This really wasn't working for me, and I quickly shut it down. But the dance was closed by now with the 1 a.m. quiet time agreement, and I walked myself slowly home past the Cuntree Store and up to the hill that led down to the Night Stage bowl, wishing I had stayed and danced.

But instead of the large Night Stage bowl, there was a lake, vivid and clear in my view. I could hear womyn laughing and splashing and then my eyes focused and I could see them swimming, the moonlight spilling down on them and across the water. It was like everyone who closed the dance had jumped in for a swim, but that couldn't be. I stood on that hill and watched, dangling on the edge of being very frightened and overwhelmed, but the beautiful scene happening in front of me could not elicit fear.

It was the angels swimming in the moonlight, and I was so very happy they were here.

CHAPTER 29

SARA DEERHEART WAS THE FIRST OF US TO DIE

It came without much warning, the cruel and rapid extinction of one of our brightest beacons of tribal love. A life, lived just 39 years, crumbled before our eyes as her bones turned to dust inside her skin. It seemed so quick, even as we knew (though could never truly understand) how this seed had been planted many years earlier. Her ridiculously beautiful, charismatic light was snuffed out an earth-shattering 15 weeks after we'd heard the word that would become more and more part of our collective experience. Cancer.

Cancer of the breast.

Cancer of the bones.

Cancer of the brain.

Cancer of the vulva.

Cancer of the appendix.

Of the uterus. The colon, pancreas, skin, liver, kidney, blood.

I guess we were lucky that out of the thousands of us tied together in this exquisite family, our spiral-like tendrils stretching over the entire planet, it took until we were in our 30s, 40s, and 50s for these chips to start to break off from our sparkly patina of immortality.

We had been so gloriously invincible.

Ours was the generation that reclaimed Amazon culture as our birthright, that tore away at the tentacles of Patriarchy buried deep in our psyches, jumped naked into raging rivers and fearlessly into unknown seas. We were a cultural and political revolution, and we knew it — it was cobbled together one hand-published book, one self-defense class, and one herbal remedy at a time.

When a handful or more of us were together, we were greater than the sum of our parts. We traveled in packs, gravitating to each other at bookstores, coffeehouses, living rooms, rallies, and Festivals, all of which we created to have something that was in our likeness. In a world that repeatedly exalted the extreme masculine, we revered the divine female. It was all new, yet somehow we knew exactly what to do, making it up as we stomped along, living our lives by the sacred creed we had just created.

It was that time of life in lesbian feminism when even though we were living in the belly of the patriarchal monster, we believed everything was possible. We wanted to be a part of the unfolding solution. We were young of body, or young of heart, and everything we imagined fed our radical and loving mission to create something better, truer, safer for the world of womyn.

And then Sara died.

Before she ever had an email address or saw a cell phone.

I was on the Land; it was during Long Crew. Though we had painfully accepted that Sara could not be on Long Crew, we still had hopes that she would make it to the Festival. But as the days of Long Crew piled on top of each other, it looked less and less possible. I was her medical significant other, but I was on the Land. Her girlfriend Ann was on the Land. Pat, her other bestie, was also on the Land. None of us really believed she was going to die.

Dying was not something we did.

How could this possibly be happening to someone so full of life and love? Someone who would make time for everyone and anyone, who had the gift of welcoming everyone in, who would lean in as you told her your tale of woe, and gently say, "Tell me more."

When she had asked me to go with her to meet with the cancer doctor for the biopsy report in the early spring, we both knew it wasn't going to be good. Good news, they let you know over the phone. We loved the cancer doc, Lisa Baily. If you had to hear shit news, let it be from her. But Sara didn't have insurance, so together we maneuvered through the appointments, the sitting on the linoleum floors in crowded hallways, the smell of desperation that filled Highland Public Hospital in Oakland, California. As her medical significant other, I attended every meeting, every test, every wait-in-line, up to and through her surgery that spring. We were hopeful, optimistic even. When Sara stopped by the office on the Saturday before I left for Michigan, she looked good — her spark was back. That was the last time I would see her alive.

I left for Michigan in late May, and in just a couple of weeks, we found out that the pain in her back that we thought was from surgery and her recuperation was from the cancer that was everywhere, deteriorating all of her bones. All of her everything.

She would call me in Michigan late at night, addled from morphine, meandering through her memories, hopes, her cold fears. Then the calls stopped. The call that did come was to say if we wanted to see her, we had to come now. I coordinated a vehicle and a driver and found Pat and Ann so they could start driving toward the Grand Rapids airport, two hours away. By the time they arrived I had found flights that would get them to Oakland as soon as possible. They would have to stand in for the dozens of us left reeling back on the Land, the hundreds who had worked alongside Sara, the thousands of hearts she'd touched.

They arrived minutes before she passed.

Joan Ellis

In reality, Sara wasn't the first of us to die. I don't know how I could forget Joan Ellis. It was probably because Joan had slipped away from contact with any of us a few years before she was killed in a drug deal in San Juan. Drug addiction has that sluggish, slow-death way about it. Even if it ends in a bullet or a car accident, the life force has already dripped out slowly, eaten away from the inside.

I knew more than most about the monkey that crawled on and off Joan's back because I knew her from the city as well as the Land. We lived on the same block in New York, on East 4th between A & B, back when it was chop-shops and shooting galleries bookended by a Wing Ding and a Hasidic butcher shop. It was rough in the late '70s, foretelling nothing of the gentrification of the East Village that would trick out those grungy streets not many years later. I was still drinking and doing coke as often as possible, feeling so hollow and scared those nights I circled the block looking for the right-side-of-street parking so I could sleep past 8 a.m. without moving the van. I would see Joanie leaning against the building at the Wing Ding, a cigarette constantly burning. I knew her way was to shoot her drugs alone in her fourth-floor apartment, but she was attractive and salty and often got her first bump on the dealer if she would just hang out for a bit. Addiction makes us particularly flexible.

She looked pavement gray in the city, deep rings under her dark brown eyes, stiff shoulders on her 100-pound frame. But each summer as she left her block for those weeks in the woods of Michigan, the sparkle in her eyes would come back, the sun turning her olive skin such a beautiful reddish brown.

Joan was a poet, a performance artist, a hairdresser, a hustler. I watched as she cut hair one summer at the Midwest Womyn's Festival and I thought she was too cool for me to talk to. One day, a couple of years later after I'd moved to Manhattan, Joan tapped on one of the street-level bedroom windows in the manufacturing loft that 100,000 cockroaches and I called home.

Iris and Joan, 1985 photo by C. Elliot

Even the very cool among us get lonely, and at times, desperate enough to reach out and tap on a window.

I never saw as many locks on a door as I saw in Joan's apartment. Deadbolts showing a variety of colors from decades of paint jobs — dirty pink, smudged tan, grimy powder blue, muddled mint green. A floor-to-door angle security post combined with a 4-inch-wide horizontal barricade bar reinforced against a power break-in, with two different door chains to peer through when looking into the hall. One chain just wasn't enough on East 4th in 1979. Joan wasn't the least bit skittish walking the streets, but she knew where she lived, and the life she led, and understood that some of the rough of the city lived right inside her building. She taught me the best defense against cockroaches was hand-to-hand combat. "You cannot let those motherfuckers think you're afraid of them — you take them out with your bare hand."

More than once, I saw her cross the street, calling out to some guy pissing against a building, "That's right muthafucka, the whole damn world is your toilet, the whole fucking world is for you to piss in!" as he collapsed against the urine-splashed building in a shyness he hadn't felt since he was 12.

We heard about Joan's murder sometime after it happened. That's a particularly stunning grief, when you realize someone is long in the ground or already turned to ash by the time the news of her death hits your heart.

It was different with Sara. We spoke late into the night every day, even as morphine clouded her mind and weakened her voice. I could hear her slipping away more with each call and yet her death was a shock I could barely survive. When Pat and I spread her ashes on her campsite the following summer, I couldn't imagine then how many more sisters' bone shards would find lasting peace on those acres.

We spent our first couple of decades on the Land in the longest series of delicious hellos, assembling a chosen family out of the most disparate group of feminist idealists. No matter where we came from — and we came from everywhere — we made each other believe in the daring ferocity of our shared undertaking, and somehow that inspired us to believe in ourselves and each other in the process. We might not have been friends or even noticed one another on the street, but here, here our hearts softened to our differences *Deerheart* photo by Ann Smith and understood that each sister placed a unique block in the towering pyramid of our collective endeavor. Even if some could not recognize the importance of each person's particular addition

(What DOES she do around here??), we didn't doubt the power of our cooperative creation.

Nothing in our prior lives could compare to the experience of walking through life accumulating this enormous chosen family: sisters and lovers, adopted mothers and daughters, intimate friendships, soulmates, homegirls, workmates, and comrades. And nothing in life's balance could have prepared us for the reality that with every new family member we were blessed with in our lives — sisters that we camped next to, confidantes we emailed over the winter, and soulmates we called when our heart was crumbling — there would be, at another time, a reckoning, a season of goodbyes.

Lorraine

Lorraine and I first met the year the Inventory Crew dropped off the Community Center basketball hoop at the Belly Bowl for a few days before it landed at its proper home. She and I were fierce competitors in the dust bowl games of street basketball played in the dirt. Both of us had grown up playing basketball with rough brothers, and I recognized the grit with which she stole the ball from me, bobbing and weaving through the clouds of sand created by our furious feet. I liked that she didn't give me leeway on the basketball court, or anywhere really. She also didn't give me undue shit because of my job. She was just herself: smart, rough, mouthy, and an amazing dyke-of-all-trades.

She became the coordinator of the Inventory Crew, overseeing the movement, stacking, and storage of all the Festival stuff in a 10,000-square-foot building filled with all the raggedy inventory that made the Festival run. She transported buckets of 10-inch nails for carpet paths with as much dignity as the glass jars for herbs at the Womb. She taught womon after womon how to use and care for the loaner tools, oiling, sharpening, and tightening as she went. Lorraine never refused a 12-year-old intern who wanted to tag along with her, but she would suffer no adult fools who overpacked their boxes or returned broken gear. Her wrath was epic and feared — and her kindness emerged in the stories of hundreds of sisters.

When she came to work at our summer office in Walhalla, she and I had more than a few good fights that cleared the room. The very thing that made

Lorraine in Walhalla photo by LV

us so genuinely comfortable with one another felt awkward or even agonizing for others. She didn't care about being polite. She wanted someone to know exactly what she thought, with all the salt and pepper that covered it. We could yell and swear at each other until it morphed into a belly laugh. Like family. Like blood.

Over the last dozen years, she was always the first in Walhalla, and I was always the second. She would come get me and Billie dog at the Grand Rapids airport, waiting for us inside, leaning against the wall outside of security, even though I always told her a curbside pickup was cool. It was always great to see her, that handsome smirk on her face, the tenderness with which she held Billie while I collected my luggage.

One year when a huge storm cancelled all connecting flights out of Chicago, I called her to say I would drive up, and we agreed she would meet me in Muskegon so I could drop the rental car. Back at the house at 3 a.m., I was toast after a frazzled, fucked-up day of travel. I drew a hot bath. Relaxed after a good long soak, I pulled the plug on the tub. The gurgling sounds of a crazy monster started rumbling through the entire house. The toilet was backing up. Black water was filling the tub where I'd just knocked the road off me. Naked and wet I ran for the plunger. As I plunged one toilet, I heard the monster in the quarter bath and arrived as it spilled over. Blood-curdling sounds from the bowels of hell filled the house. I plunged my little heart out and heard the guttural groans again in the first room with the tub.

Lorraine yelled down from upstairs, "What the hell is going on down there?!"

I started up the stairs at the same time she started down — me, butt-naked and dripping wet, wielding a plunger; her, equally bare, stumbling down the stairs with a T-shirt in her hand. When our eyes met, we both collapsed laughing on the stairs, the howls of the doomed septic tank bellowing throughout the house.

After the end of the Festival years, Lorraine drove up from her home in the Ozarks to join us for the summer in Walhalla, planning to help us care for Julia, my 89-year-old mother-in-law living with dementia, who had been staying with Lia and me in California. Lorraine arrived not well; Lia, Marge, and I just thought she needed to recharge after the stress of dealing with the isolation nightmare of the COVID pandemic. Ten days later, we were calling an ambulance. Her blood pressure had tanked, she couldn't walk, and the paramedics had to carry her down the stairs on a gurney and take her to the ER in Ludington.

She was with us for two months in Walhalla, in and out of doctor's visits, in and out of the ER. We were up and down the stairs to bring her food, change her sheets, tell her stories, and ease her discomfort when we could. We watched her dwindle. We recognized the scent of her body was changing. No amount of cajoling or begging could make her appointments come faster. Her time was near, and there was nothing that could be done. We were perplexed at how this could happen so fast — why did she come here this damn sick?

But we understood. She had come to Walhalla to find the help she needed to face this truth, to be among chosen family, to know she was wanted in her dwindling, as much as she'd been wanted and needed in her days of exploding strength. She was one of our giant oaks, slowly falling.

Nan, Rose, Paij, and Pat, 2009 photo by Diane Butler

The Land is now dusted with the burnt bones of hundreds of sisters — scattered under trees, encircling tent sites, mixed into fire pits. We say their names at rituals, feel them in the wind as we walk through the woods and tell stories of their goofy humor, their tireless work, their pain-in-the-ass processing, that super-sexy suit she wore. We are slowly learning not to collapse in the face of our own sorrow, or another's, to find strength in the gentle letting-down of the fortress around the softest part of our tender hearts.

It is time to learn new skills of letting go of the body and connecting more deeply to our universal soul. We have been here before together — this we always knew.

This is the Wheel of Life.

It is a privilege to live this full cycle with such a fierce Amazon family, eyes wide open. To look into the shadows and face the loss of so many, to feel the hollow echo of mortality as we release yet another to go on ahead.

Your furiously incandescent souls are everywhere now, part of everything, like dying stars. And I know with my full spirit that I will see you on the other side, on that path we call home.

CHAPTER 30

GONNA TAKE A MIRACLE

I remember first hearing Laura Nyro when I was in my first month of college. It was the record she did with Patti LaBelle and the Bluebelles, featuring covers of older soul, R&B, and doo-wop tunes that were part of the soundscape of the streets of New York when she was a child. Labelle (as the group later was known) had put out Nightbirds a few months after I'd come out as a dyke, and it became the theme to my political/sexual/female awakening. So many sweaty dance parties where the rhythm, the sexual friskiness of "Voulez-Vous Coucher Avec Moi (Ce Soir)?" pulsed as the soundtrack to my liberation, my coming of age. The entire record was so deeply female, so personal, and really fucking hot.

I backtracked, finding out everything I could about the womyn in Labelle — Patti LaBelle, Nona Hendryx, and Sarah Dash — and started buying their earlier recordings. That's how I discovered Laura Nyro and *Gonna Take a Miracle*, the record she made with Labelle as her supporting vocalists and collaborators. Soon the dance parties were filled with all the contemporary dance tunes — Gloria Gaynor, Gladys Knight, Rufus — but always, somehow, we knew that Laura and Labelle — they were ours.

Diving into Laura's earlier recordings, I almost instantly became a devout student of her musicality, her lyrics, her changing rhythms, and her crazy-ass, inspired singing that could go from a touching melody to an insane wail in one second, seamlessly. I studied her records like they were my graduate class in music appreciation. I realized that the sound and emotion in her voice that burrowed their way into my deepest feelings were minor melodies. Had I ever let myself hear this before? I learned all the players and producers on her albums, every lyric. I waited and waited, sometimes years, for each new release. I found her music when I had just turned 18, in 1974. She had already retired for the first time in 1971, when at the age of 24 she was already weary of this business of music.

So, when I was producing my first record in 1978, *Tattoos*, by Sirani Avedis, it was a long shot to call (212) 555-1212 (the old-school information line for long-distance numbers) and ask for a phone number for Nydia Mata. Her number was listed. Nydia played congas on Laura's record when she came back from that first retirement in 1976, as well as on her live album in 1977. I got the number and made the call.

"Is this Nydia Liberty Mata?"

"Who is this?"

"My name is Lisa, and I'm producing a record for an artist in Chicago. We love your playing on Laura Nyro's records so much,

and I'm calling to see if I can talk you into coming out and playing on this record we're doing. We don't have much money, but we will feed you really well, and we're exceptionally good cooks."

Long pause.

"What kind of food do you cook?"

The whole record project was a bit of a lesbian drama shit storm, but it was the fertile food that fed my friendship with Nydia. Because we could not afford the rates of a quality recording studio in Chicago, we found a studio just opening 90 minutes north of the city, a fabulous, state-of-the-art, 24-track studio at a price we could afford. Ironically the studio was inside the Playboy Resort, so every morning as we drove into the parking lot, eight dykes in a big cargo van, we would pass the huge rotating bunny sign. On break, Nydia would head out to cruise bunnies, leaving half the crew offended while the other half thought it was funny. It wasn't super-feminist in a super-lesbian-separatist time, but it was super-fun. She was an equal opportunity flirt, and I liked it.

Nydia came to perform at the Festival that year with the band that played on the record, and later with her own Latin jazz band in '79 and '80. Laura had come out of retirement, released three records, and was now back in retirement. On a road trip across the country in her RV in the summer of 1979, she decided to stop at the Festival. She was low-key and lovely, and even though everyone kept asking me — and her — if she was going to play, I knew enough about her vibe from listening all those years to hold back. She was there to be a part of it, and she didn't need her music on stage to do that. We partied into the night after the shows in my little backstage trailer, and she told me one night that when people asked her if she was going to play, she said, "I'll play if Lisa asks me, and she hasn't asked me." It wasn't a lead-in question. It was an acknowledgement that I hadn't asked her, and she liked it.

I had just broken up with Sirani, who was there with her new girlfriend. The energy between us was not good and was about to get worse. They were handling T-shirt sales and distributing the comp shirts all artists were to receive after they played. Someone had gotten hassled when they went up to get a comp shirt, so I'd gone over to get a medium black for her. Sirani's girlfriend started to hassle me, screaming in my face, asking me who did I think I was! The T-shirt sales tent was maybe only 100 feet stage right.

Everyone was watching this go down. She grabbed me by the collar of my T-shirt, face red and eyes intense.

"Let go of me" I said, as I tried to talk myself down.

She hit me on the arm.

"Let go of me or I swear, I will break you in half."

She shook my collar. Hit me again.

"Let go of me."

We were surrounded by stacks of big T-shirt boxes. I picked her up and stuffed her inside a T-shirt box, her arms and legs flailing out of the top.

Sirani ran up screaming, "You are SO ABUSIVE!" as she hit me, ripping the necklaces I wore (two saxophones and a labrys) off my neck and throwing them onto the ground. All eyes were on us. I did not return any blows to either of them, or even protect myself much, except for having stuffed the girlfriend into the carton.

I got out of there as quickly as possible. I went backstage, incredibly shaken. Nydia and Carol Fenster, who worked with me backstage, came up to me and said, "Come on, we're getting you out of here." They had a borrowed big Ford LTD-type car. They threw me in the back, tossed a blanket over me, and whisked me away to the cabin where Nydia was staying. They drew me a bubble bath and lit candles. I never went off-site during the Festival, only lived on the Land, where the showers were so cold it made your head hurt and we ate very simple vegetarian food. At the cabin they served me meat and smoked fish, cheeses, and crackers. By the time I got out of the bath, Laura, who had her RV parked by the cabin, had gotten out her electric piano. "I heard it's been a rough day. I'd like to play some music for you."

I moved to New York City in the fall of 1979, still reeling from my breakup with Sirani and needing a place to hide — what better place than the biggest city in the U.S.? I lived on the Lower East Side and worked for Nydia's Harp Band and a couple other Latin jazz, Afro-Cuban, and jazz funk bands. This incredibly green and incredibly white girl from Michigan had a van, and I wasn't afraid to use it. That made me popular with all the musicians because hauling congas and drum kits, bass amps, and a concert harp took a van, and those were scarce in the city. I put up flyers advertising the gigs I was working on every street pole in the Village and spent my days and nights loading equipment in and out of clubs. I also worked the door for the bands and talked to the money person, hawked tickets on the sidewalk, and learned to dance salsa in the back of the room with Nina, Nydia's mama.

I went to parties where I was one of the few white womyn in the apartment. I learned how to be in a room where only Spanish was spoken. I learned to be OK not knowing. I learned to be a part of something even if I wasn't always completely included. I learned not to ask people to change so that I could be more comfortable.

Two years later I moved into Nydia's building, on the 7th floor, taking a long-term sublet from a guy who was touring with a Broadway play. Two bedrooms with a concert grand in the dining room and super cheap rent for early 1981. Laura would come to town and Nydia would throw her congas in the elevator, and up they would come to jam in my dining room, a bottle of sake always simmering on the stove. Looking back, I feel like I should say I was amazed that Laura Nyro, whom I had listened to so fervently for so long, was now playing in my living room — but it felt so perfectly normal in my new, very not-normal world of living in Manhattan in the winter, Michigan in the spring through fall.

I moved from New York to the Bay Area in December of 1982, and I continued to work with Nydia pretty much every year at the Festival, as she appeared with one band or another. In 1988, I was ending a six-year relationship, my father was dying of lung cancer, and the Festival had exploded in an outbreak of shigella. At the end of that year's Festival, Nydia called and said, "Laura wants you to come to New York, she's doing a series of shows at the Bottom Line. She wants you to be her guest."

"I can't. I have to move when I get home, my dad is dying, my life is in upheaval. Please thank her so much, I would love to come, but I can't see it."

Laura had been in retirement at this time for 12 years, and though I'd had the joy of her singing to me in a cabin and in my living room, I had never seen her in concert.

Nydia called me when I was back at the house.

"Ru (the nickname she and a small handful called me), come on! If your life sucks, you need to do this!"

I did. I packed up that year's Festival and went to NYC. There were a handful of us at Laura's table for three nights, totally lost in the groove of the set lists that took us through 25 years of her music. The line formed around the block for tickets that would not materialize, the small house filled with a who's who of the music world, coming to pay their respects to this Amazon whose songs they all covered, whose ability to live her values they all coveted.

The last night, as the house cleared and the line of industry folks waited to pay their respects in Laura's dressing room, Nydia came to me and said Laura wanted to talk with me in the dressing room.

"It's OK, Nydia, I'm not a backstage person, and I see she has a lot of folks waiting to talk with her."

Paul Shaffer, Phoebe Snow, and Sandra Bernhard were three I could recognize in the line.

"Ru, come on, she wants to talk with you."

I followed Nydia into the flower-filled dressing room, Laura chilling in an easy chair.

"Lisa — tell me, how was the Festival this year? I think about it so often. It's a beautiful thing you have going there. How come you never ask me to play?"

"Argh, ahh, I would love for you to play, but you know, you've been in retirement for a long time. I never wanted to try and reach into that. Let's see if we could make it work this year. The sisters would so love to have you play on the Land."

With my father dying and my relationship in the grave, I was unhinged. I decided to rent a place in NYC. The city had healed me during my last breakup, and maybe it would heal me again. I rented a room from a filmmaker who taught upstate, so she wasn't around much. It was cheap and in the West Village, a neighborhood I couldn't afford when I had lived there a decade before, and still couldn't afford unless it was a weird share like this. I stayed for a week here and there, doing my work from the little apartment and stopping in Michigan to see my dad on my way to and from California. I was pretty much isolated, covered in grief from morning to night, but it was somehow comforting to be there among millions of isolated people. One night the phone rang, and it was Laura.

"We heard you were in town, and I know your dad's very ill. I thought you might like to come to the Anna Magnani film festival with us. Take your mind off some things."

The next call was an invitation to come to Connecticut to help pick out a puppy from the pound. And then an invite for sushi. No process, no coddling, just company and community which I could barely receive, except for the absolute gentleness of it all.

That summer Laura came and played Festival, solo with just her piano, no band. Many in the concert field that night had loved her for years, and many others had never heard of her because of all the years she had stepped away from the music business. My personal anticipation was huge, because it was a certain kind of dream coming true and I knew how rare this moment was.

Brewing that day was a Festival-wide conflict, part of what came to be known as the "sex wars" on the Land. Some BDSM womyn had announced a "slave auction" to be held Saturday night, a version of a heavy-duty play party drenched in painful racist imagery and language that cut deep through our community. This was during the time when BDSM exhibitionism was at its high point, and the philosophy of safe, sane, and consensual hadn't fully taken root. The Festival's position was that consent had to include those viewing or experiencing the sex scene, understood to mean, "Go on and do your thing where sisters who don't want to experience it won't have to hear or see a whipping, won't witness a cutting in the shower, won't have to see someone fucking in the food line." In addition, nothing titled "slave auction" could happen on this Land.

Our position was thought of as being old-school '70s sex-timid — like the new sex liberators had any idea of the sexual temperature of the '70s! When we found out when and where the event would take place, we organized a group to go there and break it up. They'd planned to hold it in the workshop tent at Triangle, directly across from Quiet Camping, scheduled to start just before the Laura Nyro set. The sisters who went in to ask them to break it up were shouted down and physically threatened before they retreated to the Triangle. I was on the radio with the Security Coordinator, and through it I could hear the screaming from the beatings happening in the tent. It was the first time Festival Security womyn had been physically threatened by womyn attending Festival, and the first time they were unable to talk their way through an issue.

A slave auction — how could this be? A loud play party directly across from Quiet Camping was totally rude. But something called a slave auction? This became my experience of Laura's show at Michigan. Radio in hand, blood-curdling screams coming over the radio, talking it through with the Security Coordinator, who was both angry and frightened by the very real threat they were experiencing.

There was a follow-up slave auction scheduled for the next night. I went to the coordinator of Lace, the crew that put up the big tents. "I would like you to take that tent down. I don't want to give them a space to take over, and certainly not tent poles to tie womyn up to in common space." It was 1989, and the pressure on the Festival for being sexually conservative was wrongly placed, but it was real. That the Festival was a place where hundreds and thousands of womyn found their sexual liberation, in all its forms, was lost in the debate. BDSM liberation was hot news, and so lesbian feminists raining on that parade was even hotter news, and a weird rap was out about the Festival, painting us as sexual conservatives. The Lace Coordinator said she didn't feel good about taking the tent down and didn't want to take a side on the issue. OK. I went to another coordinator, and she too turned me down. Fine. The next day I went in my truck, with three other womyn, and we took the tent down, moving the party back out to the Twilight Zone.

Laura at Festival, 1989
photo by Toni Armstrong Jr.

I know for the sisters in the audience, Laura's performance, just her at the piano, was stunning. After that one and only time that Laura played Michigan, we really were not in touch much, just an occasional call from Maria, her partner of many years. I only kept the New York apartment that one winter, and Laura didn't travel or really talk on the phone. I was in Hawaii on vacation in the spring of 1997, listening to the radio, when I heard it announced that Laura Nyro had died. I was sure I had heard it wrong. I learned she had been sick for a couple of years and had kept it private, just as she had lived her life. Her death would not be consumed, just as she had not allowed her life and her art to be consumed.

After that year's Festival, I was in Walhalla, exhausted. Maria called. She'd been working on a memorial concert for Laura with traditional producers in New York. It was scheduled for October. It was falling apart. The producers were disrespecting Maria, and she couldn't go on. Would I consider producing this show?

Laura Nyro, circa 1970s

CHAPTER 31

GONNA TAKE A MIRACLE: THE CONCERT

When Maria called to ask if I would produce the memorial concert honoring Laura Nyro, I had been off the Land for about a week, so exhausted I was talking in tongues, missing my mouth with my fork, and falling asleep on the toilet. My fatigue was so bone-deep I thought I would throw up if one more person spoke my name. At the same time, my body was sparking from the electric energy that had kept me going for the last three months, 18 hours a day. I was a racehorse with my leg in a sling, that mother picking up a Volkswagen off her baby girl, all eight pistons firing hot with the garage door closed.

I needed to rest and find my equilibrium, but how could I say no to this invitation to honor a sister, a cultural warrior who had brought so much into the world, a friend who had reached out to me during some of my darkest moments.

Maria rattled off the names of artists who were committed, and they read like my record collection. Patti LaBelle, Chaka Khan, Phoebe Snow, Carole King, Rickie Lee Jones, Bette Midler — and the list went on. The original production company had started the artist booking and secured the Beacon Theater for October 27, 1997 (less than two months away), then things had gone from rough to totally shitty. Maria could not work with them. After living with and loving Laura for 17 years, she wanted this to be the loving feminist show that Laura would would have wanted.

Even before the Land dirt was fully out from between my toes, I started to piece together what this could look like. Maria had two ideas for music directors, and she would handle that piece. I would start following up with musicians, get contracts set, plan rehearsals, accommodations, and schedules. Instead of going home to California I would travel to New York to meet with Maria and visit the hall. I had been to the Beacon, the mainstay pop/rock house in NYC, but only once while working with a band that was part of a big multi-act presentation. All I could remember from that night is that I met Colleen Dewhurst backstage, and the bliss I felt from hearing that phenomenal rusty voice with my own ears.

One of the most important acts to Maria was Chaka Khan, one of Laura's all-time favorite artists. Chaka's people had laid out that she only stayed at Le Parker Méridien hotel; that drove home the standard we would have to meet for a lot of these people. It seemed likely that with all these acts, this show had to sell out. But still, how much can you charge for one night? The hall held 2,800 people. I knew I would have to hustle.

Before leaving Michigan, I got on the phone with the manager at the Méridien and explained I was booking a multi-artist show and we would like to feature their hotel. To do this, I was looking for a considerable discount, and in exchange, I would bring to their hotel artists like Chaka Khan, Carole King, blah blah blah, people who traveled into NYC all the time. And, of course, we would acknowledge them as a sponsor of the performance. To my amazement, they continued to talk. "I'd like to visit the hotel on my next trip to New York, sometime in the next 10 days." They offered to put me in a junior suite during my stay as their guest.

Why is this so easy?

I decided to play a little harder to get. I said that since I would need to stay at the hotel with all our artists during production, could they please book a block of rooms for me to assign later. They gave me half-off on the rooms and they upgraded both Maria and me to suites for the entire time of our stay (which would likely be a week to 10 days), charging us only half the price of a standard room.

This must be meant to be! I hadn't done this before but already I felt like dropping these names was magic.

I had lived in NYC from 1979-1982, but other than returning for a few months in 1988, I had not been back. I would have to hit the ground running and dive into some phone books. Although email had taken root by 1997, I hadn't yet used a search engine, but since modem access was still dial-up, Ask Jeeves wouldn't have helped much. I met with Maria, whom I hadn't seen since Laura had died in the spring. She was as beautiful and charming as ever, and together we formed a pact to do justice to the music and legacy of Laura.

After seeing Maria, I was 100% committed. I took all her notes and returned to California, stopping in Michigan to visit my mother. At night while she slept, I made schedules, looked at song lists, and roughed out budgets. I went to Kmart and Wal-Mart and shopped for 99-cents-per-yard black fabric. I couldn't believe how dirty and funky the backstage areas and dressing rooms were at the Beacon; somehow, I had to create a green room with food, a place where all these artists and tech folk could gather in a feeling of community. One hundred dollars' worth of black fabric would hide a lot and create a clean and beautiful backstage.

Things Fall Apart

Once I started to dig into things back in California, I realized we had a major problem. None of the artists I'd been told about were booked or committed. We had already set a very high ticket price, I had booked a block of rooms, we had a hall, but the only band committed was the Harp Band, a local band made up of Laura's good friends. I worked my way through a little stack of phone numbers, and one by one, I heard how folks loved Laura, loved her music, and they just weren't sure about the date. I freaked out.

Desmond Child, a famous songwriter who had written for everyone from Bon Jovi to Aerosmith ("Dude Looks Like a Lady!") really wanted to be on the show. I'd first heard of him when I'd booked an artist in the '70s who had been in a duet with him — somewhere I had a cassette with his song, "I'm Gonna Eat Hard Bagels Till I'm Sore." Unfortunately, though he'd written hundreds of pop and rock hits, he wasn't a great singer. But Laura had inspired him to be a songwriter and he would do anything to be on the gig. I quickly realized that since he'd written songs for Cher and Joan Jett, Ricky Martin ("She-bang!") and Kiss, he had a Rolodex that didn't stop. Soon I had personal phone numbers for Carole King, the inside line for Bette Midler, and lots of little stories about how to approach them and what to tell them when they asked how I got the number that rang in their kitchen.

Patti LaBelle, a longtime personal and musical friend of Laura's, finally confirmed once I agreed to a white stretch limo from Philadelphia to NYC, her musical director playing piano for her, and to keeping the car and driver running in the alley beside the venue all day and night. Phoebe Snow said "yes" next, then Kenny Rankin — I was getting a little traction. Chaka Khan, whom I had booked Le Parker Méridien for, ended up a "no." Carole King and Bette Midler sent their best wishes. I was fucked.

I don't know if Maria had been bullshitted by the earlier production company or if she was blowing smoke at me. Either way, it was all sand running through my hands. Laura's music had meant so much to me personally, but I also felt that for who she was, for what she gave to popular music, there should be a tribute to her by her peers. Was it not coming together because I was now the person in the driver's seat? Or was I now the person in the driver's seat because it wasn't coming together, and the pass off to me was the only thing that could give it some life?

Laura's star had long since crested, and after two prolonged periods of retiring from the music business, her audience was now comprised of artists who derived part of their music from the building blocks of Laura's unique sound, music lovers who held her recordings from the '60s and '70s as collector's items to cherish, and younger music buffs who bothered to dig deeper than lowest-common-denominator contemporary music. The whole thing was a harder sell than I had imagined in the beginning. My personal admiration for Laura and her central place in my worldview of music had influenced my expectations of how this would be received by artists asked to participate and an audience being asked to buy tickets.

Meanwhile, I was also in a co-dependent mess with Maria, who was slogging through her grief while dealing with complicated estate issues. I was fronting production expenses, which I was starting to worry could really plow into the red zone. I trusted that Maria would catch up with the finances soon and felt so confident in the solvency of the estate that I wasn't overly worried. Of course, they weren't married in 1997, though they had been together 17 years. I just couldn't handle anything but a forward-thinking process.

I decided that the show was happening. I would book artists — not necessarily famous artists, but great artists — to fill out the program. One day when I was driving across the Bay Bridge listening to a mixtape, a Tuck & Patti song came on. I knew someone who could get to them. I started thinking of artists I had worked with who would do the songs justice. I was doing this for Laura. What the fuck was I doing feeling like success had to do with famous names, the very thing that drove Laura out of the music business? The very thing I abhorred about popular music. I called Rhiannon — she would so kill the song "Emmie." I called Toshi and Big Lovely — their rendition of "Eli's Coming" that opened the show remains one of my deepest memories of that night. I called Jane Siberry; she had played the Festival the year before and she would bring that same enigmatic energy that Laura personified. I needed an emcee, and I called Reno, a New York performance artist and comedian who had played the Festival. It was coming together — in a very different shape — but it was coming together.

The Beacon was a union hall and had a lighting crew, stage crew, and a shitty sound system. It would cost more money, but I decided if I was going to keep this ship afloat, I wanted to have the team I knew and knew I could count on. I called Myrna Johnston to bring her sound system from Boston and brought in Linda O'Brien to design the lighting. They were the head sound and lighting womyn from the Festival, top-notch and hardworking. I flew in Cristi Delgado, Elizabeth Brassil, and Lisa Zawacki from the Festival's Oakland office crew and rallied Festival crew womyn who lived in New York to do artist support, food, and production tasks. We were a circle of Festival womyn and we were going to rock this thing.

We rolled into New York, me and a few artists camped out at the swank Méridien, where the rooms were not filled with the superstar list I had initially given them. Instead, I kept trimming the room number down, assuring them I would give them the names before people arrived. I had the out-of-town crew and most of the artists staying at the Floatele, where I had worked out the same deal, using the same names, even though this was a more modest accommodation.

By now I felt like an ass for booking Le Parker Méridien based on it being the hotel Chaka Khan "normally" stayed in, the same Chaka Khan who was not now and probably never had been playing this gig. But by then I had offered the hotel to a few other artists and paid a deposit, so I was committed. These types of gigs pay very little money to the artists stepping in to do one or two songs. In the late '90s it was an honorarium of $500 to tie up a night for someone who might command $15,000 to $20,000, so it came down to the perks. The right hotel room. The first class or business class seat on the plane. The town car or limo. The right food. Comp tickets (how many did they want for the show?)

Finally, I was in New York. The Beacon's marquee featured our show, with "Cyndi Lauper" (who had only recently confirmed) in big letters. She called the day after I arrived and canceled. Doctor's orders — pregnancy bed rest. Having learned the address (years ago when I lived in NYC) of the building where both she and Madonna owned apartments, I said with confidence, "But Cyndi, we can have you in and out of there in an hour. It's right down the street from where you live!"

I'd kept up my feverish calling to Rickie Lee Jones' people — everyone knew how influenced she was by Laura's music. Finally, the day after Cyndi bailed, Ricki said she would come. Last-minute business class seat from LA — I had to suck this one up.

I remembered that back in 1988, when Laura did her run at The Bottom Line, Sandra Bernhard would make tracks after her show "Without You I'm Nothing" — which was having a sold-out run at the Orpheum Theater across town — to stand in line for a ticket to Laura's sold-out shows. She was a devotee, and even though she was a scary mofo, she was now on the show.

Rehearsals were happening at the space we rented downtown. I was figuring out seating charts for guests and banging away at my laptop with the budget that was out of control. We had gone from Paul Shaffer being the musical director to Jimmy Vivino to now a nice young guy who did not

work leading a late-night talk show band. We were able to book most of the supporting musicians who had played with Laura over the years, people who knew her sound, her style, and the feel of her music. The night Rickie Lee Jones came in for her rehearsal the band started to play her first tune. She sat still. They continued to play. She put up her hand.

Rickie Lee Jones at Laura Nyro Memorial Concert

"I thought you understood Laura's music... listen. You're too far ahead of the energy. I'll sing the lyric — stay slightly behind the lyric, not ahead."

That rehearsal changed the whole show. Rickie's insight and

feeling for what made Laura's music so emotional was so simple, and yet deeply difficult to capture.

Tickets were not selling well and expenses were mushrooming. Everything was last-minute and barely in my hands. I was smoking my head off and the womyn working with me in my hotel room kept all the windows open, even though the cold and rain of October blew through the room. I didn't have the time to take the elevator down to the street to smoke, and I didn't have what it took to not live on cigarettes and coffee. My fibroids were kicking my ass, and I was hemorrhaging so much I wore two maxi pads. My skin was a most-sickening color of gray, the combination of blood loss and cigarettes making me look more like dirty cement than anything human.

The day of the show, everyone had their schedule of when to arrive for soundcheck, a schedule we had built around Patti LaBelle, who was starting her day by taking our limo to do a morning TV appearance and would arrive after that. We were informed that she would not wait around. Our schedule was already running late, so I slipped someone's soundcheck into Patti's time when she hadn't arrived. And of course, right after we started that soundcheck, in swooshed Patti and her entourage, 40 minutes late. I went up to introduce myself and explain that we'd had to go ahead with someone else.

"Well, Patti needs a cell phone, who has a cell phone? Can anyone give Patti a cell phone??"

OMFG, she speaks of herself in the third person! I had purchased a cell phone for the first time right before I left for New York, and I wasn't about to give a third-person-talking diva my phone, no matter how much I loved her music.

"So what song am I singing?" She had been the only artist who hadn't come to rehearsals because her conductor was going to play on her song; they would rehearse separately. But none of that happened. I told her the song we'd sent a month ago to her then-husband/manager, along with the finale that we'd asked her to lead.

"Do I know that song?"

She looked at her conductor, and I took him in for the first time. Oh shit, this guy's eyes are totally pinned. He kinda laughed and said he didn't know. She looked at her husband, who acted like he knew nothing. I ran to get the lyrics and the sheet music and handed them to her and him.

"Patti can't read that, I need those lyrics BIG."

I turned to Joey, the only runner in our group. "Joey, run, fast as you can, stop at nothing, go to the nearest copy place and blow this sucker up four times as big as you think it should be and then run and give these to no one but me, no matter what I'm doing."

Amazon Country in the City

We made it through the soundcheck, running into two hours of union overtime for the guys we had to pay to be there even though they weren't working the show. One by one, the artists would look around, and say some version of, "Is this entire crew womyn?" or "Wow, look at all the womyn on crew!" It either hit them right away or seeped in as they went through soundcheck: They were in Amazon Country.

All these womyn in music, touring and playing for years, and they had rarely seen a single female on a crew, let alone the entire sound crew, the lighting designer, all the production support, everyone in the green room. Laura was an anomaly in so many ways — among all the womyn in pop music, she was matriarchal. She loved the goddess, she loved other womyn, and her music came from a womon's perspective that was written for who could hear it and unconcerned about how acceptable it was to men. She left the music business twice because she could not play it that way. I knew she was smiling at us for bringing the goddess into the Beacon.

That night when Phoebe Snow arrived with her guest, Gloria Steinem, who was carrying a bouquet of flowers for Phoebe's dressing room, she barked, "Gloria — look at this place! You know how many times I've played the Beacon? This place is a dump! I've never seen it look so good. Look at that food!"

Staring at the walls, noting the over-the-door hangers for stage clothes, little flower bouquets in each room, she continued, "There's a place to hang my jacket, those dirty walls are covered with all that fabric. There's a pitcher of water in my room. Look. At. That. Food. There are womyn everywhere. Did you see that womyn are running sound and lights? You know why it's all so good? These are the womyn of Michigan doing this. Ever heard of that place? Goddammit. We never had it this good."

The show was beautiful musically and spiritually, so full of heart. The Michigan artists were hits, a surprise to everyone but all of us working. We all knew they would honor Laura's music and make us proud. Rickie Lee Jones, who simply channeled Laura in every inch of her bones, stayed into the night at the after-party, hanging with the crew.

See, everywhere we go we take our Michigan clan, in spirit, or in flesh, sometimes in large numbers, sometimes small. And sisters will join this circle, knowing what they are entering, or just knowing what they need, and then come in close.

Alice Coltraine at Laura Nyro Memorial Concert

CHAPTER 32

THE SEX WARS

A young womon with fiery red hair approached the rickety rental table under the 20-by-30 tent floored with upside-down carpeting. It was our Staff Services Office, and I didn't normally work in there, but at that moment I was the only one there. I hadn't met her yet, though she had been on the Land for a few days. You couldn't miss the hair.

> *"I'm just checking to see if my mom has showed up yet."*

> *"Excuse me?"*

> *"I thought she would be here by now and I'm worried she's lost."*

> *"Is — your mom on crew?"*

> *"On crew? No, my mom is dead. I had her shipped here because she was cremated after I had to leave for crew, so I had them ship her urn here."*

Definitely a first.

She floated in almost every day to see if her mom had arrived, and my opinion shifted from thinking she was a bit of a wingnut to realizing she was a complex and sweet womon, exorcising her grief in all the ways, as we do. She was working in the Belly Bowl, the area that kept the coffee, lemon water, and toasters happening for the workers, and where we lined up for our daily meals cooked by Galz Diner. After a week she started to relax — her mom had arrived — and she was in the groove of her crew and settled on the Land. Land life is an excellent distraction for much of the day when dealing with a recently dead mother. I learned this firsthand some years later.

Turns out that V, the redhead reunited with her mother's remains, would become a prominent force in the leather community on the Land. She and her partner, Whitewolf, eventually a coordinator at the Recovery Support Area, did workshops about BDSM that kept feminism wrapped in the concept, not a prevailing combination at the

V Kingsley, in her glory!

time. Through their workshops and presence on the Land, V and Whitewolf were a voice encouraging the leather community to be a part of the whole Festival, not simply push against the community. V's energy was so deeply accessible to a myriad of people. She was naturally nonjudgmental and lovely with everyone she met. The love she engendered in many in the community, in and of itself, took some of the sting out of the tension that many felt about the disrespect to Festival mores exhibited by some in the S/M community.

There was an infamous event that happened most years in the Twilight Zone, the Stations of the Cross, led by Drucilla, a regular camper who was the Town Top out there. It was not at all in Drucilla's interest to work toward harmony within the community because her position was stronger if there was a rift. The vast majority of womyn at Festival were not up for participating in these events, but the Stations had become so well known in the gossip circles that many would plan a trip out to the Zone after Night Stage to see what they could see and raise their pulse a little by the badness of it all. Often womyn either got lost or came upon a whole lot of nothing happening, but occasionally they would hit the timing right and there would be a dramatic scene in progress.

Most people were intimidated by Drucilla. V and Whitewolf were about the only ones who would call her out when she was out of line, and they for sure did not pander to her topiness. They too were quite well known around town; their workshops were popular and for many were an introduction to the SM community. Their modeling of how to do your thing and be respectful of other womyn at Festival started to carry more and more weight. Pyramid, another worker, also started doing workshops on flogging, strap-ons, and various kinky additions. With beloved and respected members of the crew facilitating these workshops during Festival, workshops that were scheduled and printed in the program, BDSM was no longer solely a renegade opposition force. It became increasingly clear over a few years that although the Festival community had a huge range of politics, feelings, reactions, and analysis about dykes and BDSM, the Festival itself wasn't taking a position on it.

The conflict around BDSM at Festival was tangible; the division in our community was real and quite complex. Our goal was not to homogenize the debate by removing the conflict, but rather to build a town where we could coexist with the tension of difference without demanding that anyone change or leave to make that work. We had to learn how to respect and even embrace differences, even though some of these differences felt completely fundamental to our individual cultural and political identities.

Some womyn felt passionately that participating in BDSM and enacting the power dynamics and role plays — or the beating and bondage that were incorporated in that play — were directly embracing the oppression of womyn. It was caving into patriarchal fantasies that we had spent years clearing out of our psyches: Healthy dykes should have no part of this mindset, and Festival should declare it didn't belong on the Land.

Leather dykes felt liberated to claim their own relationship to power, to explore issues of trust, to work with dominance and submission as a path to personal freedom — and to connect with a community where sexual freedom was available on a group level. It was a new sexual revolution, and they were not going to allow old-school dykes from the '70s to harsh their freedom.

Most womyn were somewhere in the middle, not part of the leather community, somewhat to very interested in exploring more radical sexual options, but far away from wanting to be anywhere near the inside of the Stations of the Cross.

We were roommates living together in a big, open-air house, sitting around the kitchen table of an oak forest three times a day, lying next to each other's heads, sometimes a mere yard away, with only the very thin layer of nylon that composed our tents between us.

Finding a way to coexist in our differences was not going to be a fast process. Saying everyone belongs, and we agree to not diminish anyone whether in the minority or majority — whether we agree with you or not — is not a simple practice. We ask you to respect community guidelines, and if you don't, we will talk with you. And then talk with you again. Maybe someone else will talk with you. Slowly, community ethics take shape.

Through this process, public flogging slowly moved out to the Twilight Zone, the scenes in the shower lessened and stopped, the sisters who wanted to expel the leather dykes lost their focus on what was happening at the Zone. And even more slowly, our shared love for the community, the actual reason we were here on the Land to begin with, grew to be a more significant bond than all the differences that seemed insurmountable.

Photo by Brynna Fish

CHAPTER 33

A DIRECT HIT FROM THE RIGHT

At the 2000 Festival, Tristan Taormino, a well-known author on radical sex, came to the Festival as an Intensive Presenter. She had a full lineup of topics: Anal Sex 101, Hosting Play Parties, How to Ejaculate. It was our desire to have something for everyone, and Tristin covered the edgy sex crowd as well as those who wanted to explore. Her workshops were a big hit. In particular, the one on Female Ejaculation captured the imagination of both those completely unfamiliar and those who found home ground.

Many sisters recognized their own unspoken experience during the Female Ejaculation workshop. Having only attended one workshop in 40 years, I was not there, but the stories ran through the camp like wildfire. My own therapist, who had come to me in the spring and asked if it would be a boundary issue if she came to the Festival (OMG no — I will never even lay eyes on you) said it was one of the most liberating experiences in her life. It showed womyn who never knew that womyn ejaculated that it could and did happen. During the session a parade of womyn took turns showing how far they could ejaculate. I imagined it lost most of the sexual reference at a certain point and became more about body liberation and celebration. This is what my therapist took away, and what I imagined when I thought about the workshop. So cool. So open.

The Festival came and went, and womyn piled onto the online Festival bulletin board chatting about all their experiences of the Festival. The ejaculation workshop was discussed right along with the Redhead Parade and the nut-loaf recipe served on Tuesday night. Just another integral part of that year's Festival.

This year, however, there was a lurker on the bulletin board, a right-wing journalist from the Americans for Truth About Homosexuality. She pulled from conversations about the Twilight Zone and the ejaculation workshop and juxtaposed them with conversations on the boards by mothers navigating how to have children at Festival, in all its complexity. After she published her article in her right-wing hate rag, it was picked up by the American Family Association, who had sent an operative to the state to rally support for anti-gay legislation. They sent the article around to local and state newspapers, and it started to get some play.

So titillating. So scandalous.

This was a decade before the AFA was listed as a hate group by the Southern Poverty Law Center, for the "propagation of known falsehoods" and the use of "demonizing propaganda" against LGBT people.

I was less than a week off the Land when my phone started ringing off the hook with calls from the local sheriff, the state police, the local newspapers, and finally, the state attorney's office in Lansing. I was exhausted from the Festival and hadn't been reading the online discussion boards, but as soon as those calls started flooding in, I pulled the boards down. My imagination was horrified by the image of everyone with a local paper and an internet connection jumping onto the bulletin board we thought of as private and going through, thread after thread, to look for lurid details while religious right voyeurs from all over the county peeped into our cloistered community of no man's land.

I had spent 25 years building bridges in the local community — bridges built with sticks and duct tape and carefully shared pieces of information about lesbians that provided a fuller picture of us as human beings, not the salacious tricks that men fantasize about or the wife-stealing bull-dykes they feared.

Now I was having conversations with some of these same men about what constituted lewd public behavior, the difference between a lap dance and a public fuck, whether children were around public sex, how nudity in an all-female environment in my mind wasn't lewd, though yes, I agree, public sex is against the law. It was like a bad B movie playing out through the phone in my bedroom office in Walhalla. Every time I walked into a business where I knew I was recognized as the Festival producer, I found myself wondering if they now imagined me ejaculating with a hundred of my closest friends, teen girls watching from the bushes.

I understood that things happened at the Festival that were against the law in the public sex arena, but if our community agreements were kept, that was contained to the consenting-adult area of the Twilight Zone. I felt morally OK with that, and I could say with conviction that of course public sex was in no way sanctioned. Festival could be an edgy space to navigate with children, no doubt, but I felt confident that children were not in the Twilight Zone or in sexual exploration workshops. As for the blustery talk on the internet about workshops, I couldn't and wouldn't speak to that. All of this in my mind was really fucking uncomfortable to have to discuss with law enforcement and the press, but still, it was not illegal.

At times I was moved by how much support the Festival had in the local community. I could tell that the sheriff wanted to deal with this about as much as I did. "If it hadn't made it into the newspaper, Lisa, you and I would be having a private conversation about this, and that would be that. But it did make it into the newspaper, and I have to follow up. And it did make it down to the state attorney's office, and you know, that's my boss's boss."

Come spring 2001, I had to meet with the sheriff and the chief of the state police, and they said they needed to see the Festival layout when it was all up and running.

"I'm sorry, that won't be possible."

You see in all of the years and all of the Festivals, the police had never been inside the grounds while it was happening. The head of the state police was really pushing for this. I compromised and said we could do this the week before Festival, when all the areas were set up and the crew was there, but before Festival attendees arrived. They wanted to see for themselves where the workshops were, where the Twilight Zone was, where the childcare areas were, and how much potential overlap there was between these areas.

I had clothing I always traveled with for just this kind of thing. Nice slacks, a womyn's blouse, clogs. If I had to drive around with three law enforcement officers talking about an ejaculation workshop and where it happened, I would have to go in drag.

I had a borrowed purse slung over my shoulder.

I would show them how far the Gaia Girls camp was from the workshops. Nearly a quarter mile.

I wore lip gloss.

The Twilight Zone was nearly three-quarters of a mile from the childcare areas, and deep into the woods.

I pushed sensible earrings through the closed-up holes in my ears.

I would bring them a list of childcare activities and schedules, day, and night, to show them the girls had so much fun on their hands, who could be bothered to spy on adults?

Was the touch of eyeshadow overdoing it?

I was shameless in my attempt to remove anything in my normal presentation that would make this harder. As I walked to my truck in the Night Stage parking lot to head out to meet them by the Front Gate — with my purse, earrings, slacks, and lip gloss — I felt confident in my drag presentation. I was on a mission. Catcalls pealed across the field from the Carps crew building the Night Stage.

The girls were getting a kick out of this, and I did not blame them.

I drove out to the front gate, sweat already starting to soak through my tailored Banana Republic blouse. It was not that hot, but I was that nervous. The confidence I felt leaving the parking lot had slipped away on my ride to the gate. I was sick to my stomach with that doomsday kinda feeling, like when I arrived to pick out the casket for my mother, or that time I found a box of letters my girlfriend had stashed, letters from her other girlfriend. It's a nausea that feels like your whole being is one big upside-down stomach, stuck hanging inside the cage of The Zipper at the county fair. But there would be no relief from throwing up. This ride would have to be lived.

Sheriff and state police squad cars had already pulled just inside the gate when I arrived. It was before the Festival opened, but there were already nearly 450 womyn on the Land, and of course everyone knew this was happening. News like this travels fast, plus I needed everyone to be scarce during the tour I was about to lead. I depended on everyone remembering so that I wouldn't have to manage naked womyn popping out of the woods here and there as I took these guys for a tour.

I got out of my truck, said hello to Sheriff Bob, whom I'd known for 25 years. As a young under-sheriff he'd done so many of the Festival paid shifts on the road — and he was so well liked — that we called every subsequent sheriff on duty "Road Bob." I introduced myself to the state attorney rep and the head of the state police for our district, shaking hands in a show of confidence, my borrowed purse slung on my arm. Bob wasn't his regular warm, easy-going self and I got it. This was his watch, and if there was something wrong here, his being hands-off with us all these years was not going to bode well for him.

The other two were stiff and awkward, more like Baptist preachers coming to bust a whorehouse than to review a Festival layout. I didn't know what was magnifying their energy, that they were on this locally famous piece of lesbian land for the first time ever, or that they believed that we were in fact inappropriate with underage girls and they were totally skeeved. I knew that the blunter and more comfortable I could be, the more disarming it would be to them. They were counting on something sheepish, because really, we were in trouble. The more I could be affable and matter-of-fact, the more it would telegraph normalcy and that would be my most precious commodity.

"Since there are four of us, I think it's too tight for us to take my truck. Who would like to drive on our tour?"

I wanted to get right down to business, and I also wanted to show I wasn't avoiding anything. As I expected, we piled into the dark blue state bull squad car, Bob and I in the back seat, the top of the pecking order in the front. The state bull led off with a directive: "Let's start by going straight to the workshop area and see how far that is from where the children's areas are." I was going to have to be the Town Top if I was going to survive this, and I knew that meant setting the pace from the start.

I countered, "Since this is the first time you've been here, I'd like to give you an overview of the whole grounds, and part of that of course will be reviewing the areas where it was alleged that children were endangered. Drive down the road to your right, and please note that our internal speed limit is 5 miles per hour."

I was willing to wear the lip gloss, carry the purse, and punch in the earrings to try and normalize anything I could. We all knew they were here to put eyes on how far the female ejaculation workshop was from the childcare areas, and how far the Twilight Zone was from any kids. I was the living, breathing representative of that ejaculation workshop, and though I had never been to the Twilight Zone, I was its representative. I wanted to look like their daughter, or sister, or cousin, and not like anything that would signal a big old ejaculating dyke to these guys who probably never experienced a female truly having an unfaked orgasm, let alone ejaculating across the field.

We set off, driving by fields that had mushroomed with dozens of large circus tents in the past few days. Benches were distributed alongside the road and outside tents; flag poles were set up to hail the shuttles that would soon be circling by. Tables and chairs were in place, webs and passageways of carpet paths stretched between everything, and scores of hay bales were placed in circles here and there, ready for the conversations that would continue from last August. Trash and recycling containers were strategically placed, colorful light strings strung between areas, large banks of porta-potties stood at the ready, water faucets and drinking fountains just where a person would need them.

And not a single person.

"That's our Night Stage over there," I said, signaling to the south.

I trusted that this would be the anticipated grand finale of sensory overload for their already glassy eyes. No one expected the stage that these girls built to be such a looming figure, or that those lighting towers stretching into the sky were something we constructed. They were impressed, there was no doubt.

"Now let's circle back and revisit exactly how far apart the Workshop Area and the Twilight Zone are from Gaia Girls Camp and Sprouts."

The Land is only a square mile, half of which is deep forest where humans rarely go, but when you take it in the way we did, it feels like an immense sprawling city. By the time we got back to Gaia Girls Camp, putt-putt-putting down the road at 5 mph, they were duly confused, and I could sense, very ready to get their feet solidly back onto patriarchal terra firma. I showed how Gaia and Sprouts were both up on large hills, each in expansive areas, and One World, where workshops were held, was a world apart.

"Where exactly was the, the, uh, um, demonstration workshop?"

"Oh, the ejaculation workshop happened over here, in the workshop area where we schedule things that need privacy. As you can see, it is far away from either childcare area, and besides, all workshops with a demo component have monitors to make sure even adults don't randomly walk in." That was the truth, if just a wee bit of a stretch, but being the only one who could say the word "ejaculation" out loud, I needed to say it to keep my edge.

Since spring we had known that the American Family Association was planning to infiltrate the Festival with a mole, someone tasked with gathering proof of our indecent behaviors. I cannot lie, it unnerved me, because if someone was looking for inappropriate behavior, they would likely find it. It was just a matter of whether they could manipulate the information to make it appear that sexual behavior was taking place in proximity to children, warping the liberty of the Land that everyone enjoyed into a false narrative of exposing children to inappropriate behaviors.

On the ride back to the gate, these law enforcement officials informed me that they would be sending a pair of female state police officers undercover to the Festival, so that they would have eyes on the ground. They knew the groups Americans for Truth and American Family Association were both sending moles and they had to have their own people there to document what was — or was not — happening.

For fuck's sake. After a quarter-century of peaceful private seclusion, the upcoming Festival was being used to empower a religious right-wing organization's attempt to define state policy in Michigan. Even in many straight circles, the concept of "lesbian" just can't whomp up enough sexual imagery to form a lewd fantasy — they just can't see it without a male in the mix. But the press about the ejaculation workshop took the image of us to a new level, and what was once the granola lesbian man-hating camp was now being studied as the local den of debauchery.

It was hard not to panic.

That year more than 300 children were due to be at the Festival. Though some in our community wanted Festival to be adult-only, in my heart I felt the growing inclusion of children of all ages was our lifeblood. The freedom that the kids felt for that week was contagious. They radiated a brave openness, moving unharmed within the net of extended family that included just about everyone they passed. Running feral through the ferns, bodies free, hearts on fire, never needing to track the signal of adult caution that constantly monitored their safety on the streets of Patriarchy. Instead, they learned a new wild freedom as they explored the world, feet in the dirt, unfettered and alive.

I had decided months before that we would not bend to the microscope; we would not stop booking and scheduling workshops about sex. We would send someone to make an announcement at the beginning of each workshop that no sexual contact should happen during the workshop and ask that everyone please participate in honoring this agreement.

Likewise, we would not bow to the same pressure by eliminating the wanderer option for girls in Gaia. If given approval by their guardian, this meant that a child could sign herself in and out of Gaia and become her own independent wanderer throughout Festival at her own will.

When it came down to it, we really weren't willing to change a lot. It was more important to us to be in the center of who we were and live our moral truth than it was to avoid dealing with any judgment or legal mess from law enforcement or right-wing groups. We knew that the Festival community was a far safer place for kids than Area 51. We lived in a complex world at

Festival, full of diversity of all kinds, and that meant we rubbed up against each other in complicated ways. But that was ours to work out, and not something someone from outside our community was going to start defining in year 26.

The energy around all of this shifted from anxiety to comedy by the time the Festival opened. Someone new who was watching a group from a distance — was she the right-wing mole? An artist rep that was being a pain in the ass — ah never mind, she's probably the mole that tagged on to the band. Elvira's Top Ten List that year was a countdown of the ways to find the religious-right mole in the crowd, the subtext of that week brought into the bright comedic light of Night Stage to be met with gut-laughing recognition. It was the punchline to so many nonsense conversations that when a plane flew circles over the Day Stage with a GOD'S LOVE SAVES banner floating behind it, it inspired cheers and waves.

No hiding.

No shame.

No fear of being found out for who we are, in all our complexity.

This Is Us.

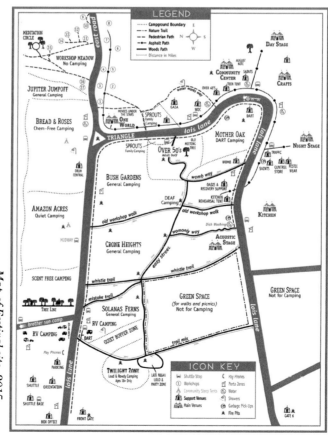

Map of Festival site, 2015

CHAPTER 34

THE ACCIDENT

In 32 years of Festivals, with tens of thousands of womyn and kids coming and going from the Land and cohabitating in the city we built together in the woods, we had seen some serious accidents and many near misses. But the worst had never happened. We had never suffered a fatal accident. In 2008, tragedy struck, and we were forever changed.

Caity was working the midnight shift in the Ops Trailer on Opening Day. This was usually a slow shift. The campgrounds were buzzing with the first day's arrivals, but in the office trailers it was a chance to get odds and ends done. For me, Monday night was usually my last shot at undisturbed desk time at night. That night, however, it was far from quiet. The phone rang off the hook with artists stuck in Chicago — a massive storm rolling through the Midwest had completely shut down O'Hare airport. Members of our Driver crew were also calling in, stuck in Grand Rapids waiting for artists' flights that would not arrive. Caity and I were each talking to at least two people at a time on different lines while simultaneously searching online for hotels. The hotels closest to O'Hare were solidly booked and we were desperate to find our artists someplace to rest for the night. We took turns dissuading the sisters who wanted to rent a van and drive the five hours from Chicago. It was not a great idea, given the late hour and the weather. By the time we both went to bed, everyone was set for the night. We had left copious notes for Erin Driver, the Transportation Coordinator, who no doubt would be in by 7 a.m. the next morning to begin overseeing the day's arrivals.

She would have a mess to untangle, and not just those late-night changes. The entire day before had been rough. Thousands of arriving sisters had been forced to unpack and set up their campsites in that storm. The hundreds of flights canceled or rerouted scrambled the arrival of both campers and artists, with drivers stuck overnight in Grand Rapids waiting to shuttle womyn who just did not arrive.

I had the coffee on for Erin when she arrived. My eyes usually popped open around 4:30 a.m. just before and during the Festival, adrenaline pulsing through my body, my mind immediately on the tasks at hand. I loved being up and focused while the city still slept; I could think my own thoughts uninterrupted, focusing on my tasks without any friendly intruders. Erin and I worked silently in opposite ends of the trailer as she pieced together how to fetch the artists and campers who were stuck overnight, along with the hundreds of travelers who were scheduled to arrive that day. Her Tuesday numbers had almost doubled because of yesterday's canceled flights. She knew she would have to recruit additional drivers at breakfast. She was good at this, and I knew she would figure it out.

Erin produced updated rosters of passengers and drivers for the 10 a.m., noon, and 4 p.m. shuttles, posting copies in the Ops trailer and sending clipboards down with Tasha Driver for the drivers already in GR. When she arrived at the airport to load the 10 a.m. shuttle — two 15-passenger vans with 14 womyn each and two cargo vans for their luggage — she found well over 50 womyn hoping for a ride.

The day would clearly be a mess, but continuing contact between Erin and her drivers confirmed that womyn were headed our way. Then a call came in from a driver saying their van would be late; there was a major backup on the highway with traffic rerouted around an accident. My ears perked up. This involved an artist who had been kept overnight in Chicago and would now need to go directly to a rehearsal when she arrived on the Land. Next I received a call from Holly Near, who was visiting with family in Muskegon. She called to let us know the local news was reporting that one of our vans had been in a major accident.

Everyone in Ops spun into motion, pulling up news reports on the internet, scrutinizing photos and video of the scene. We could not see who was involved, or even which van. Panicking, we tried calling the drivers who carried cell phones. No one was answering. Was that simply because they were driving, or because they'd been in the accident? As we scrambled for information, vans began arriving on the Land: Two vans with artists, one of the vans with campers, and one cargo van. It had to be the second van with campers that had been involved in the accident.

The rosters that Erin had made early that morning had gone completely to shit during the mayhem at the airport. Some of the womyn scheduled for the noon shuttle had rented their own cars and left, some of the womyn scheduled for the 4 p.m. were trying to get on the noon, and some of the womyn scheduled for the noon shuttle were on planes that hadn't yet made it to Grand Rapids. One of the volunteer drivers that Erin had recruited at breakfast had left the airport without crossing the names of her loaded passengers off the master list. We knew who had made it to the Land on the camper shuttle that had arrived, but we had no idea who was in the van that had not yet returned.

We knew by that point that the accident had been catastrophic. The back left tire had blown out, sending the van into a spin and then a roll-over, landing on the side of the road. The state police and the county sheriff were loath to give us any information about the condition of the passengers because we ourselves could not tell them names. Calls started to come in from womyn who were at hospitals near the accident. Holly, Kim, and Barrie were on the phone constantly, talking with womyn who had been in the accident, piecing together who was at each medical facility, and tracking injuries and information. They organized drivers to pick up the sisters as they were released from the hospital. In all our years of transporting hundreds of womyn, we had never had a road accident with injuries. Our minds were racing with overwhelming thoughts. Our hearts were pounding in our chests.

Slowly, the list of people and their current whereabouts was becoming clearer. We were told by womyn at the accident scene that someone had been taken away by helicopter. It had to be one of the last womyn we had yet to identify. A longtime worker and first-year coordinator of our on-land Shuttle, Susan Martin, was still awaiting her sister's arrival. She had never been to the Festival and was coming to share in this gathering that had meant so much to Susan for decades. To witness her community. We knew she was one of the Tuesday travelers, but we hadn't located her yet and prayed she'd found another way to the Land.

After 8 p.m., I decided to take another pass at the state police. I explained who I was, that the van belonged to our Festival. We had pieced together a list of names. A few of these womyn were now on the Land, others we knew were still receiving medical treatment, but there were still two womyn we could not locate. We knew one of our travelers had been medevacked from the scene of the accident. Could he please help me identify who that was?

He put me on hold and someone else came on the phone.

"I regret to tell you that the person who was medevacked died in transport. Her vitals crashed while in the helicopter and she could not be revived. We have not been able to reach her family yet, and I hesitate to tell you her identity until we have reached next of kin."

A shot of ice ran through my veins. I felt nauseous, on the verge of vomiting. My co-workers told me later that they had heard me scream. I had to pull it together.

"I understand your guidelines, and I respect them. I ask that you consider that everyone involved in the accident was part of our community, and we may be able to help you reach the family."

He told me the person who did not make it was Lynn Marshall, and at that point, we didn't know who this was, but feared it was Susan's sister. Chris Cozad, the longtime Mechanics coordinator, was in Ops, and I asked if she could go find Susan at the Front Gate.

I had just hung up the phone from another phone call when I heard Susan in the middle room of the trailer.

Susan's face encapsulated everything the day had held: shock, grief, trauma, fear, disbelief, confusion. We held each other and wept. I tried to hold Susan's devastation, shoulder her grief as best I could. I asked if she was up to talking to the state police and told her they had yet to speak to any family members. She wanted to go to her sister. She wanted Chris to drive her, and after speaking with the police, they left.

Eventually those of us working in the trailer that day made our way to our tents, weighed down by the heaviest hearts imaginable. The grief I felt was indescribable. It clung to every part of my body and spirit. My mind was consumed with chaotic thoughts and emotions, with fear, sadness, despair. I slept only for little bits here and there. By the time I got back up, sometime before dawn, I was utterly exhausted, both physically and emotionally.

As I drank my first strong coffee, I made a list of priorities for the day. First on the list was an update on all the sisters involved, and what they needed. We would do everything we could for them. Some would want to stay on the Land and some would want or need to make other arrangements. There would be Susan and her crew to care for, and the need to communicate to the rest of the Festival community, with care and skill, what had happened. Later that week, a healing circle, led by Ruth Barrett, was held with all the womyn involved who wanted to gather in this way, under Grandmother Oak in the Night Stage Bowl.

But in those pre-dawn moments of that terrible morning after, I knew we also needed to figure out where the van was and what we needed to do with it. And then the realization hit — we were not just in the midst of a community tragedy, we were also in a serious legal situation. I emailed Alan, the attorney I had worked with during the drawn-out legal struggles with Boo. The legal ramifications were something Alan would lay out to me. He called at 7:30 a.m.

"Lisa, when I saw there was an email from you in the first week of August, I thought to myself, this cannot be good. I am so sorry to hear this has happened. But you didn't call me for sympathy, you called me for advice. My first piece of advice is to get our own investigator on the ground, reviewing the accident site, talking to witnesses, memorializing what happened while everyone's memory is fresh. Do I have your permission to get my guy on the road?"

He had already called his investigator. His guy went to the accident site, took measurements of the accident scene, picked up the shredded tire, talked to police, and would head to our Front Gate to interview any of the womyn who were willing to speak with him. But first, he arranged to put the van in a storage facility so that the van itself would stay in our custody.

With the investigator in motion, Alan made clear, without any doubt, that we could not, from that moment forward, transport a single person off the Land in a Festival vehicle. No artists, no crew, no campers. It did not occur to me that we wouldn't be able to drive anyone back to the airport in any of our vehicles or any of the rental vehicles that were part of our fleet. We had to figure out how to get everyone back to the airport with only commercial drivers or privately arranged shared rides. This was only Wednesday, but we had to begin the hustle of booking buses and commercial vans, and communicating to people that all their departure times would be conflated to the most common denominators. Crew would have to figure out rides to the airport from other crew members. Somehow, it all happened.

Alan hooked me up with another attorney from his firm, Greg, who had served as assistant attorney general for the State of Michigan. Shortly after returning to the Walhalla house post-Festival, I met with him, and then later that afternoon, with a representative from the state police and Department of Transportation.

I thought one of the biggest legal issues would be that there had ended up being 16 people in a 15-passenger van. This happened because a family had laid a child across their laps in the back of the van and the driver didn't see the child. I knew this was an error on our part, a function of the chaos of that particular day. I also knew that we'd heard from many of the womyn about how expertly our driver had handled the blowout — many considered her responsible for saving multiple lives that day.

It turned out this was not what was on the mind of the state authorities. The biggest issue, as far as they were concerned, was that we were running a livery service without registered commercial vehicles and without commercial drivers.

"We rent 15-passenger vans from commercial companies. We insure 15-passenger vans as a company with a commercial insurance company. Do you mean that we are not allowed to drive those vehicles?"

I quickly learned what I'd never known: As a business, we were not allowed to drive anything larger than a seven-passenger van without a commercial driver's license and a DOT registration. Ignorance of the law was no excuse. Even our DART buses would have to be trailered in from our storage barns by commercial drivers. As we were closing the Walhalla house for the summer, we sold our other 15-passenger vans and bought a used seven-seat van to get us started the next summer.

Bankruptcy

Back in California, the insurance company booked a local law firm to represent me (and themselves). I met with them numerous times, always running everything past Alan, whom I trusted implicitly. In mid-October, he called me to say:

"I must tell you the real deal. There is no way that you are going to get to the other side of this. My advice to you is to declare

bankruptcy now. You were insolvent from the moment this accident happened. You might have a window to buy your assets back from the bankruptcy court, assuming they act on it soon, that there are no other buyers, and they approve you as the purchaser. You would have to go completely dark from the time you declare bankruptcy until the time — if there is such a time — you are able to buy it back. But it gets you out from under the impending doom of these lawsuits. The very fastest that could happen is three or four months."

My mind exploded with the complexity of what he had just laid out. I told him I would need to seriously think about this. I let the hard cold reality of what he had just said settle in. I understood that it would be a year or two until a lawsuit was even filed, though there was no doubt one was coming. I could understand, somewhat, his suggested pathway to continue the Festival under a different entity, one not involved in a lawsuit. It felt super corporate crazy.

I set about planning for both the 2009 Festival and bankruptcy, with the hope of purchasing the company's stuff from bankruptcy court and continuing the Festival under a different banner. Planning for the bankruptcy meant everything had to go into fast-forward — booking as many artists as possible, inviting and confirming coordinators, sending out crew materials and confirming crew, setting up rental contracts. I was in a heat to see what we could accomplish before the first week of December, when I would have to pull the trigger on the bankruptcy. We could put out an initial flier, even update our website, but at the point we declared bankruptcy, we would have no further access to our office. We had never gone dark for more than a week between the winter holidays. How could we do this and go dark for three or four months? I had to act as if this could actually happen.

There were so many ways this could go wrong. If we pulled a right-wing bankruptcy judge, we would be screwed. We were already a bit infamous in the state, especially among those on the right-wing side of things, and they would not want us to continue with our heathen ways. Closer to home, Alan asked me delicately if I thought Barbara (Boo) Price would get wind of it and make a move to buy the company.

December 1 came, and I decided that if we were going to risk it all, having one final Festival for the community was too significant to pass up. It would provide a chance for conscious closure after 33 years. Despite the looming legal consequences, I was willing to take that risk to allow the community to gather one last time.

Lawsuits

A year went by, and then another. I was served by the plaintiffs in September 2010. WWTMC, Cooper Tire & Rubber Co., Ford Motor Co., and Lisa Vogel were all named as defendants. The fact that they had named Ford and Cooper was not a surprise. I had spent endless hours on the internet looking at Ford 15-passenger vans that had gone into a roll-over after a tire blew out. I had discovered that this particular Cooper tire had problems with delaminating and blowing out. These big companies are known to keep popular profit-making equipment on the road, despite facing lawsuit after lawsuit, because it still makes them more money than taking them off the road. Alan told me to be prepared now for Ford or Cooper to file a cross-complaint lawsuit against me.

"Their job is to make you at fault; it puts them in the clear. And I do not need to tell you the resources they have to fight this thing. The chance of you surviving in the eye of the hurricane is incredibly small. But the emotional toll is something that will continue to build now that the multinationals are directly involved. I have seen this absolutely ruin people emotionally. The stress is too great. I don't know if you want to face that. Live your life. Walk away."

I had long meetings with the attorney appointed by the insurance company in his office high above Grand Lake in Oakland. I bought lady drag clothes for my long-ass day of interrogatories sitting across from a panel of Ford and Cooper attorneys. We all understood that I was the tail on the donkey. The plaintiffs were primarily focused on Cooper and Ford, while Cooper and Ford were primarily interested in directing everyone's attention toward me and WWTMC.

WWTMC and I had two things that everyone wanted: The van itself and the tire that was left by the side of the road by the state police and recovered the day after the accident by Alan's investigator. We also had the fact that I resided in California, which gave the plaintiffs the right to sue in California, more favorable for their case. We had joined with Cooper and Ford to ask the court to move the case back to Michigan, where the courts were known to be loyal to the economic engine of the auto industry. Meanwhile, I had hired a local attorney who was a specialist in insurance and accident liability. Alan reminded me daily: The attorney representing you via the insurance company works for the insurance company. Your team has to keep them on track, watching out for you and WWTMC.

Our strategy was to negotiate with the plaintiffs' attorneys to extract WWTMC and Lisa Vogel from the lawsuit in exchange for the policy limits of my insurance, along with our transfer of the van and the tire, the physical evidence they needed to hold the corporations accountable. They would never get more from us. Could we possibly make this work? But my insurance company was balking. Then the big legal guns hit my insurance lawyers with the reality that if they did not settle, they would be legally responsible under California law to cover whatever we were exposed to in the lawsuit.

Checkmate

This was all so complicated legally. I had to read each email exchange two or three times before I could fully grasp the details. Then I'd have to translate the dynamics into my own language so I could play their game and be part of the decisions that defined my life. The constant stream of emails was the equivalent of brandished swords menacing my every move. In the end, it boiled down to something rather simple: We will give you, the plaintiffs, everything we have to extract ourselves from this lawsuit, and you can then focus on the folks who have the deep pockets. Once my lawyers agreed that we would support keeping the venue in California, my insurance company understood they had been checkmated. They either had to agree to play ball and settle, or they would be exposed to a potentially much larger settlement down the road, and countless dollars in legal proceedings.

I do not know the conclusion of the remaining part of the lawsuit. I've done internet searches to see how it was resolved but didn't find anything. I hope all the sisters received strong settlements. While we'd done everything we could for the womyn involved in the accident when they were on the Land, the investigation and litigation meant I could not communicate with them outside of their lawyers. I expect Cooper and Ford settled their suit eventually. Both companies will no doubt go on making their products and huge profits, with these lawsuits just a small part of their cost of doing business.

For myself, it was three years of walking through storm surges, living in the eyewall of a legal hurricane with huge multinational corporations. But there was an eye in this hurricane. Somehow, we slipped through and got to the other side. Forever changed, but still moving forward, and still able to continue doing what I felt I was put on this earth to do. Susan Martin returned on crew every one of the remaining years of the Festival, and through her beautiful heart, brought her sister, always, into the community on the Land.

CHAPTER 35

MY LOVE LIFE ON THE LAND

I was unlucky in love at Festival for my first 20 years, though not for lack of trying. In the early years of the Festival, the mid '70s, I dove deeply into the free lesbian love on the Land, partaking in many affairs, at times having more than one sexual partner in a day. We were young, liberated from the constraints of heterosexism, in love with everyone and excited to share that love in all the ways. So many womyn found their partner, or lover, or love affairs on the Land. The same was true for me, although I would come to learn that mixing the business of producing the Festival with the pleasures of love on the Land could be excruciatingly complex.

The Festival was an incubator for so many things, not the least of which was lesbian matchmaking. Thousands of womyn came from all over the world, bound together by the desire to be in a womon-identified world, to live within the ecosphere that nurtured a realm of feminism in every aspect of our living community. We fell in love. We fell out of love. We had lovers; sometimes more than one. We saw monogamy as a construct of patriarchal heterosexism, a compulsive societal norm that we needed to confront within ourselves, like all the other tendrils of limiting beliefs we sought to uproot in our psyches. Nonmonogamy and polyamory were challenging and at times sloppy life practices, but they were also a practice that were enabling us to break free from the ownership model of patriarchal relationships. On the Land we made friends with sisters from all over the world. We saw our exes. We saw our exes with their new lovers. We did all this in a town that was only a square mile large. It impacted all our lives in glorious, challenging, and growthful ways.

My First Big Love

My first big love on the Land that turned disastrous was with an artist whose music I loved, whose message spoke to my sense of social justice in a radical way. We booked Sirani Avedis, then Sally Piano, from a cassette submission sent to us for the first Festival. She quickly became an office favorite. She was young and hip and a separatist — we liked that. A bit of a pathbreaker in womyn's music, she sang about being a Rainbow Womon, had a song about womyn living with disabilities and signed one of the verses, before we ever had interpreters at the Festival. Her soundscape matched what we were trying to learn together on the Land.

The second Festival was recorded on a reel-to-reel tape recorder by Martha Oelman, and I had plans to travel down to her place in Yellow Springs, Ohio, after the Festival to listen to the tapes. But first, I was to stop in Chicago to meet with the band Alive!, who had asked me to consider moving to Oakland to work with them. I called Sirani and her manager, Copa

MountainMoon, who lived in Chicago, to see if we could catch a meal while I was in town. Sirani had now performed at both the first and second Festivals, and I wanted to know more about both womyn.

At that meal together I ate the first crêpe I ever had. I was trying to be cool with the all-new-to-me French bistro vibe while managing the surprising but crystal-clear sexual energy flowing between Sirani and me over dinner. She asked if she could come with me to Yellow Springs. Absolutely.

The tapes of that second Festival were no good — some muffled or faint recordings of great music mixed with technically decent recordings of music that didn't warrant repeat listening. My fantasy of having a live record of the Festival was dashed. But the sex was great that weekend, and Sirani and I were off and running on what I thought would be a brief but awesome affair.

Sirani returned to Chicago, and I proceeded to move to Berkeley to pursue the exciting idea of working with the womyn of Alive!. I had maybe a couple hundred dollars when I arrived, enough to rent a trashy in-law unit that was more chicken coop than a house, without a refrigerator or furniture. I was eating out of a cooler, sleeping on a borrowed foam mat, with just a folding chair in the kitchen, and barely enough money to pay the toll to get across the bridge for our occasional gigs. I looked for work everywhere and relied on pass-alongs from friends. Martha — from Yellow Springs, who also lived in Berkeley — received a box of Harry & David's pears from her wealthy father at one point but wouldn't touch them because they weren't organic. For a week I ate pears, morning, noon, and night. Otherwise, I collected bottles on the street to buy cigarettes and quarts of cheap beer.

I was doing work here and there with Alive! but I also needed to earn money, something women's music didn't really provide. I found a job painting a house. The owner made me a low-ball offer of $400 to scrape, prime, and paint a two-and-a-half story house with two porches — with oil paint. I was so desperate, I agreed. I constantly reeked of turpentine. I had meticulously scraped off the old paint, sanding down the edges, and was nearly done with the prime coat when the legendary rains of 1977 started. And never stopped. I would wake up on that little mat on the floor, hearing the rain again, and my heart would sink. Some mornings I just sobbed into my pillow, as I lay tortured on my little foam mat. No work again today.

I was still spending time with Leni, the lighting designer from the past Festival. We had started an affair after being up all night together during a rainstorm, climbing the scaffolding to cover the lights while sparking mad energy between us high up in the air. As captivating as Leni was, we both knew this wasn't an ongoing thing. And my heart was with Sirani.

When it turned out that I wasn't a good match for managing Alive!, I started to plan to return to Michigan, closer to Chicago and Sirani. In the fall of 1978, after that summer's Festival, I got an apartment in Chicago and proceeded to book gigs and plan an album for Sirani. I didn't have a clue that I was joining the well-worn stream of sisters who would put their lives on hold to become their lover's free manager and booking agent. Sirani also started to work on the Festival, primarily handling graphics and promotion. It was she who came up with the beloved "treeano," the PianoTree logo.

Once we finished the album, we went out on the road on a little tour. By then we were having horrendous fights, always on the same topic — monogamy and nonmonogamy. I was 100% dedicated to free love, and she was 1,000% insistent on one-on-one relationships. We fought so much about this that we had neither — no outside lovers and no real love between us because of the strife. On tour in her van, I finally gave in and agreed to try monogamy. Soon after my concession, we had a gig in Bloomington, Indiana, where I watched Sirani get energetically pulled into a womon at the pre-gig dinner, charming her with her humor and laughing at all of her jokes. This same womon arrived in Chicago to visit her shortly after we returned. She spent the night, and they were off and running. My free-love self was wracked with jealousy. Sirani's one-on-one love now wanted to be one-on-one with someone else.

We tried to keep it friendly, and even continued to work together after the breakup. She did the graphics for the 1980 Festival, one of my favorite designs. When it came to her job on the Land, coordinating T-shirt sales, things took a nasty turn. At the end of that Festival, she left the Land with all the T-shirt money, what I estimated to be more than $20,000 in cash. I naively thought it was just a matter of timing. I didn't think for a moment she was actually taking the money. Maybe she was holding it for some kind of leverage? I went to Chicago to discuss the T-shirt money, still raw after the breakup even though it had now been over a year. I was shocked when it became clear that she had no intention of giving the money back to the collective. She had already been paid for the design work that year, as well as for her performance. The funds she'd taken were most of what we had to pay the six members of the collective something for our work, and all of the necessary seed money for another Festival.

I returned to New York and continued to try to communicate with her by phone and letter, still not believing this person whom I'd loved could have just taken that money. I was a sad sack, still feeling like I was in love, or still being obsessed — I don't really know if I knew the difference then. I was talking with Boo Price one day on the phone, she said, "Really, you'll need to sue her to get that money back." But I couldn't sue another sister.

I could see my way to having Boo, who was an attorney, write Sirani a stiff letter; maybe then she would take this seriously. No response. Time passed, there was some useless back and forth, then come that summer, I was served a lawsuit from her, with an appearance date of July 6, my birthday.

She was suing me for the logo, which we had paid her to design, and she was suing us for misappropriation of name (she falsely claimed we had listed her on the 1981 promotion). And she wanted money to leave the Festival.

Boo said, "It is now time to countersue. This is what amounts to a palimony suit."

I still couldn't do it. "Why would you sue someone for palimony who doesn't have any money?"

"She wants the Festival."

Of course, by now Sirani had an attorney. I had a strong suspicion that this was someone she was sleeping with, as weird as that would be for the big bad lesbian separatist to be sleeping with her male attorney. I wasn't wrong. The $20,000 she had taken was a lot of money, but I already knew enough to understand that even that amount could go away very fast when you have to prepare for and then go to court. I asked Boo to make a deal that Sirani could keep the money, and in return, sign off on any claim on the logo, the Festival, and me. I couldn't bear engaging with the legal arena any further. That was the tool of the Patriarchy, and if I had to let go of this huge sum of money, I would rather deal with that than use the master's tools.

My First Sober Relationship

Meanwhile, after nursing my bleeding heart while hiding out in New York City, I had started to date again. The annual gathering on the Land was a glorious time to meet hundreds of womyn, and though I worked from morning till midnight, I was young and completely open to hookups that didn't take a lot of time out of my schedule. In the fall of 1982, on a trip to California, I started what I expected to be a no-strings affair with Boo. She had represented Margie Adam at the first Festival and come to work on the stage for the second, so we were friends. A light affair seemed like it would be fun. I lived in New York, she lived in Berkeley, we both had nonmonogamy agreements with girlfriends who were extremely unhappy with our affair, but regardless, it persisted. Within the year I had moved to California. This dovetailed with the start of my sobriety; it was Boo who had said to me, "I cannot be with you when you do cocaine."

I didn't think I was moving to California, but I was going there to go through treatment. I needed to remove myself from New York City, where my whole life involved drugs and alcohol. I stayed with Boo and her son, Andres, in their fine house in Kensington, in the hills above Berkeley. She was there as I started to learn how to make phone calls sober, how to reimagine my world without drugs and alcohol. She came to the Festival a little longer that next summer in 1983, and even longer the following summer, the first after my sister Kristie had left the Festival. In 1985, Boo and I became business partners. I hadn't imagined this step, but it was her strong feeling that if she were to continue working on the Festival in any ongoing capacity, she needed to be a partner. I was still very vulnerable in my first few years of sobriety. Even though it had come time for me and Kris to stop working together, I missed her, and I missed having someone else who would share overall responsibility.

I didn't think of myself as owning the Festival, though that was legally and literally what was true. I thought of myself more as the steward, so when I made her 50% partner, I naively didn't realize that each of us actually owned half. Now we were both co-stewards, right?

We spent the first few years figuring out how to mesh our strengths. She was smart and had a world of experience I didn't have. She came from a wealthy family, had gone to private college and law school, and worked in music production on the side. She was completely adept at the kind of information access and worldly savvy only deep privilege from birth can bring you. I had dropped out of college in my second year, had accumulated a ton of hard-earned street smarts in my life. I knew how to work with people and had been producing the Festival since 1976; I knew the details of producing our stages and putting up a town inside and out. I was rough-and-tumble, and she was quite refined. She carried an entitlement that I will never have, that I will never want. Our differences, which at first were not separating us, grew into a flying wedge once the gloss of new love wore off and my sobriety took root. There was a growing number of things about which we had strong differences of opinion and divergent approaches. Not surprisingly, these often fell along class lines.

The work and political differences were the clearest to see. The interpersonal dynamics in our home were much more elusive. I had come to the relationship with a strong identity as a working-class womon and had thought my self-esteem issues around growing up unskilled blue collar had mostly been resolved. I certainly had a lot of working-class bravado, but that doesn't really carry you that far, it turns out. The hidden injuries of class rear their painful heads when you start swimming in privileged waters. During those years I slowly became less and less confident with who I was and grew increasingly vulnerable in the world in which Boo moved, the world of many forks on a dinner party place setting, the conversations among her friends who had gone to similar private bespoke colleges, the trips to destination restaurants with menus that broke a sweat on my forehead.

Where was the young Amazon who had no interest in assimilating into middle class culture? She disappeared during these years. Instead, I allowed myself to become smaller, feel less than — and I felt Boo agreed with that assessment. But more than anything, she was intensely interested in the Festival, and that was the one thing that I had pulsing through my veins.

In 1986, we booked Dance Brigade for the first time. I still remember my initial experience watching them perform at a theater in Oakland. The entire troupe was remarkable; I loved their strong choreography and their fierce theatrical political message. One dancer — a short, fiery, dark-haired powerhouse — stood out to me. Krissy Keefer had muscles in her calves that pounded across the floor, seamlessly transitioning between emotive, delicate gestures into furiously powerful movements. After their scheduled performance on the Acoustic Stage, we invited them to perform on the Night Stage the next night because we wanted everyone on the Land to see what they had brought to the Acoustic Stage the day before. They returned the next year, and that's when I had my first real conversation with Krissy. Our connection was electric, and I found myself keeping an eye out for her, if only just to say hello. When I complimented her jacket, she surprised me by leaving it outside of the tent I shared with Boo the morning she left.

"That womon!" Boo yelled. "You're not going to keep this, are you? And you certainly won't wear it around me."

After I returned to California at the end of the summer, Krissy and I made plans to go for a walk in Oakland. Afterward, she invited me to join her the next week for a performance by another dance company. I told Boo about it, and she flipped a biscuit. After one affair Boo had early in our relationship, we had been monogamous in recent years.

"She's after you, I just know it."

"I just want to be friends with her," I replied. "I like her a lot, and it's okay if we have different friends."

We argued for a while, but eventually Boo agreed to see how this went, and decided to take care of herself by inviting someone over for dinner the same night. Later that week she told me that if I wanted to see Krissy without her being present, I would have to move out. I was furious at the ultimatum, unable to admit to myself that she knew better than me where my energy was focused. The girlfriend always knows.

Despite this, I started seeing Krissy secretly and kept it from Boo. We made out in the car like teenagers. I was completely captivated by her. She was smart, sexy, deeply political, and so funny. I convinced myself that I wasn't being honest with Boo because Boo was being a controlling asshole. True, she was being controlling, but I was cheating and lying.

I had to get my shit together. I was in recovery. Honesty with myself and others was critical to my sobriety. I had fought too hard to live a life of true recovery. I was torn up from having deviated so far from my true path.

Krissy and I stopped seeing one another. We were both trying to repair our primary relationships, something we could not do if we were still deeply in each other's space. But it didn't make things better between me and Boo. We went the standard lesbian trial-separation route and I moved into a little sublet. I was better with myself because I wasn't lying every day.

I left for Michigan in the spring and Boo was to come later, after her son, Andres, had gone to his Costa Rican family for the summer. While I was in Michigan, she dug through some of my boxes, found a months-old letter from Krissy, and FedExed me a breakup note.

Who breaks up by FedEx?

When she arrived in Michigan, all the bedrooms in the Walhalla house were already allotted to other womyn; we would have to share a room, unless one of us slept in the living room. After a couple of weeks, she asked if I would be willing to commit to a monogamous relationship. If I could, she wanted us to get back together.

I couldn't agree to it. It wasn't because I didn't care about her or because I was seeing someone else. I wasn't in touch with Krissy at that time or running energy with anyone else. I just couldn't agree to something that didn't feel true for me at that time. I had lied enough.

The transition from life and work partners to only work partners tumbled before me and filled me with a sense of dread. One night, I searched for our partnership papers in the office at 10 p.m. when no one could see me. Did I have what I needed inside myself to end this now?

I didn't. I was too afraid.

What I was afraid of, I wasn't even sure. But I know now — after having crawled through the ensuing years of counseling, mediation, and finally, legal arbitration with Boo — the person I was that summer in 1988 couldn't have handled it. It was only the 1994 version of me, the me who had found myself again, that was able to fully, finally, free myself.

Boo was the first and only woman I had lived with up to that time. After our breakup, I dated womyn, sometimes for a year or two, but the reality that my primary relationship was with my Festival work always became an issue. I always had to wonder if a romantic interest came my way because of the attractiveness of my position in the community. Those same romantic interests flamed out under the distraction of the actual hard work and focus involved in my job. I worked extremely long hours all year, often unable to put it down even on weekends and evenings. I moved to Michigan for three and a half months every year, and while there, I worked 12 to 16 hours a day, seven days a week. I didn't want to talk on the phone at the end of the night — that's where I had spent my entire day. I could be totally present and attentive, and a lot of fun in the winter, but my passion for my work and my love and commitment to our community made it my primary relationship.

While I found it hard to resist, I knew it would be better if I didn't date anyone on the Land, this place where so many came to find a date. If I dated an artist, it could be fraught with the kind of narcissism that often comes with the artistic temperament, and the ever-present question of whether I would book them or not book them based on a romantic interlude.

If I dated a coordinator, it made it more complicated if we had to have a difficult conversation about work expectations. If I dated crew members, the triangulated power dynamics would be super-uncomfortable once the coordinator of her crew knew we were sharing a tent at night. I laughed with friends that if I wanted to date, the only group that felt remotely safe was the Interpreters.

My friend Pat Simon put an end to this idea and helped shift my focus. Pat was my dearest friend from home. Part of the success of our relationship was our pledge that I would never see her as a chiropractor, and she would never come to the Festival. We would know each other not by what we did in the world, but by how we danced. And we danced like mad fools together, three to four nights a week. But after the explosion at the end of my relationship with Boo, I needed her on the Land and she knew it. She came and set up alongside the Massage Crew, doing chiropractic treatments for workers. I put up her tent right by mine so we could see each other coming and going. That was fine until her second year working, when I started an affair with an Interpreter. Pat was kept up by the loud sounds of sex through the night.

"Why do you have to be dating a screamer?! Why don't you date someone sweet and gentle, like Lia, over in the Workers' Kitchen?"

My Life Partner

I had no idea who Pat was talking about. I hadn't even noticed Lia until then. And then I saw this person, sitting on the ground around the firepit, leaning her back in between Belinda's legs, and realized this was who Pat meant. She was attractive, absolutely, but Belinda was a coordinator I worked closely with every day. Was she having an affair with Belinda? That was a tangle I couldn't afford.

The next summer Lia arrived to work early and from the moment she walked onto the Land, I felt a buzz of connection in my stomach. I was already dating two womyn who were yet to arrive, and I really didn't need more complication, but the pull was nonstop. She was beautiful in a soft, unassuming way. I tried to keep my mind off her, but was totally unsuccessful, instead finding myself joining the circle down at Galz just to be around her. She didn't seem to notice me much, and certainly didn't give me undue attention. Her energy was gentle, her eyes soft, though they rarely met mine regardless of how often I placed them in relation to her. I felt a swirl of emotional desire whenever I was around her and it was pulling me off my focus. She seemed to move through the Land like a gentle goddess.

I finally asked Lia for a walk, and we toured the Land on the interior road one evening. She seemed shy. Or maybe she just wasn't that into me and didn't know how to tell the producer person "no." That was always a concern of mine, so I tended not to be the one to initiate things.

I continued to be spellbound. I was so confused because I felt like I was falling in love, but falling in love with someone who barely knew I was there. She didn't seek me out, but if I asked her to do something, she was receptive. We had a meal. We danced at the dance. Another walk. I asked her if she wanted to join me in my tent, and she said yes, but only if we wore our pajamas. And she meant it.

Slowly we became lovers on the Land that summer, and each morning when I woke up before dawn, I would lie in my tent and watch her sleep before getting up to go to my trailer to work. I wanted to remember exactly how she looked, there in my tent. The one time I went to her tent that summer, as we walked up the path I realized she had put her tent up exactly in Deerheart's old campsite, on top of her ashes and still-visible bone shards. No one on long crew had taken that spot since Deerheart had passed, but Deerheart was before Lia's time.

I wondered if we would see each other back in the Bay Area, where we each had a girlfriend at home. It turned out that our first time seeing each other off the Land wasn't in California after all, but in New York City, where Lia was from originally. That was the year I got the call asking me to produce the memorial concert honoring Laura Nyro. Lia would be back in the city at the same time and I was thrilled I would see her there. She got a crash course in what it would be like to date me that fall. I worked nonstop on that show, ordering room service at 2 a.m. after a grueling day, barreling toward that unwieldy concert. But she hung in there.

On our return to the Bay Area, neither of our girlfriends was agreeable to our continuing to see each other. Even though we were all nonmonogamous, it was clear that Lia and I were in love, and that was too painful for anyone else to be up next to. Neither of us knew where this relationship was heading, but we were compelled to find out. Those relationships ended and Lia and I dove deep into one another.

As hot and loving as our lovership was, we were both committed to nonmonogamy. This was the priority of so many of us in the '80s and '90s. It was our ideal — a life of freer love and passion shared with more than your partner — but had I ever really been able to pull this off, cleanly, once I was in a committed relationship? We are all still products of our context. Our context held this belief, while at the same time, our interpersonal skills were sadly lacking.

I saw couples who were able to navigate this on the Land, or at least it looked as if they were, but even in our first year, Lia and I suffered explosions when either one of us had another sexual partner. We blustered through those first few years, breaking trust, repairing faith, but always finding the ease of harmony that flowed so naturally between us. As strong as the bond was between us, I still doubted whether I could find long-term love.

My two most significant relationships had ended in long, painful, and complex breakups. Each of those womyn had become enmeshed with the Festival's inner workings because of our involvement, and those entanglements with the Festival added greatly to the complexity of our endings. After the incredibly painful parting with Boo, I tried to accept that a long-term relationship wasn't for me. I certainly wouldn't interweave my lovership with co-working on the Festival again. I had a thread of fear, always, that the Festival was what a lover truly wanted, not me. That they wanted me because of their desire for proximity to the Festival or the perceived value and influence associated with it. They were fucking my job.

Lia and I tried to find another way, warily at times, but steadily. She continued to work in the Workers' Kitchen, first as a crew member, then a few years later — at the request of her coordinators — as an assistant coordinator. Then a couple years later, she became a co-coordinator. During this time, she worked summers in the Walhalla office, doing office work and cooking. We each had our own bedroom and did our best not to triangulate between ourselves and the other womyn we worked with there. I watched for signs that she would end up as Sirani or Boo had, focused increasingly on their position in the Festival as our loverships withered. But with Lia, it never happened.

Lia cherished her independence and pursued her own path. She went to acupuncture school, immersing herself in learning Chinese characters and the use of herbs, and practicing her needling on me at night. Engrossed in her studies and the new life she was making, she stopped working in Walhalla for the summer, then stopped coordinating in Galz, and soon came only for the 10 days around the Festival. We still struggled with my long working hours, and my inability to fully land with her when she arrived. But now when she came she worked in the Office, or put her creative magic to work on the Opening Celebration, bringing me food for lunch and straightening up my exploding office when I was out in meetings.

I know she struggled a great deal during those years, no longer really having a crew at Festival, being seen as married to the producer. She too experienced the weirdness I did, the conversations stopping when you entered a circle, no longer being invited to a party at someone's campsite. Who she knew as her partner back in Berkeley — there was very little of that available to her for months at a stretch, and her frustration and sadness about this would come out the side of her neck from time to time, always at the worst of times. But she never left. And I always stayed.

Lia asked me to marry her when we'd been together for five years. On so many levels marriage wasn't my thing, but it was never about not choosing Lia. I chose her on every level from the beginning. Marriage went against my hippiness, my feminism, my need to live in the present and not plan the future. Each day was a gift. And still I understood what marriage meant to her, and so I said, "If we're still together at 10 years, yes." But at 10 years I still couldn't marry, though we'd moved in together after year seven and my love for her was deep and true. It wasn't just my enduring squeamishness about state-sanctioned marriage, which, like monogamy, was one of the pillars of Patriarchy we'd resisted for so long. I had also come to realize that I was so damaged by my past relationships that I still couldn't see a future with anyone. That damage lived in me and colored the corners of my heart. I would not allow myself to trust — or want — a forever relationship with anything other than the Festival.

But even through the layers of my self-protection, I recognized that year after year it was Lia's eyes I looked for across the circle in a heated meeting. It was her body I wanted to be up next to at the end of my long days. It was her feedback I sought and her input I heard most willingly. Rather than attempting to blend our relationship with the Festival, Lia blossomed in her own world, becoming a talented acupuncturist and an amazing triathlete in her 40s, off swimming under the Golden Gate like the badass that she is. We made an incredible home together, one where we live in harmony, a home that welcomes our community. We do political work together, make massive dinners for friends, hike in the hills, and love each other through all our changes.

My unlucky-in-love story at the Festival turned into a relationship that stayed steady for the final 14 years on the Land. Lia saw me through the most difficult days and nights during those years and held steady as I let go of the Festival, as I learned to build a different life. And after being together for 25 years, we married legally, after having been married in all of the ways for so many years.

I am blessed to have more than a few intimate friendships, sisters who have stood by me through so many trials by fire, who know my intentions even when I fall short, stumble, or flat-out fail. But without believing this would ever be in the cards for me, I found Lia, someone who has stood with me, helped to hold the stress I brought into our home, never suffering in silence. It was always her eyes I could find at the end of the night.

Photos by Chewy Kane, Desdemona Burgin and Sara St. Martin Lynne

CHAPTER 36

I COULDN'T SEE THE FUTURE

The day I first realized that I couldn't see the 41st Festival, I felt like the air got sucked out of my lungs. No intake to be found. I had been moving through the fall of 2014, the autumn after the 39th Festival, managing all the normal things for the 40th Festival — updating information pieces, organizing rental contracts and food orders, inviting coordinators, envisioning the performance program. I hadn't recognized I was doing all my very familiar fall work with an almost imperceptible but all-telling distinction: I wasn't simultaneously preparing for the following year, the 41st.

I did not include "Notes for 2016" when revising the crew numbers list for 2015, as I always did. At the time I thought I was too busy, and I would get back to it when I could. Experience told me doing it now would be quicker, easier, and more informed, but I just wasn't feeling it.

When working on the Main Kitchen food orders, I left no comments in the spreadsheet cells reminding me that the number of 5-gallon tamari tubs was a little lower because we had 16 gallons in storage from 2014. I asked Sandy to work on other things rather than do the mockup of information forms with 2016 dates. And I just didn't have my usual programming worry that often accompanied a big anniversary year — if we invited all the most beloved artists for the big year, who would be the tent poles for the next year's artist roster?

It was as if the reality that the 40th would be the final Festival was seeping into my work before I could handle facing the question. Of course, the continuation of the Festival had been a question for a while. How long could this go on with the shifting cultural sands, the continuous political stress, and the resulting financial strain of all of it? The Festival had outlived so many of the lesbian feminist institutions that had erupted from the '70s, but cultural changes combined with the relentless public political bombardment was weighing heavily on everyone.

Even so, the idea that any Festival would be the last Festival was still unimaginable to me.

Forty years of community. Womyn who had been babies on the Land were now community leaders. Young dykes from the '70s were now stomping around as wiser elders; I was one of them. A hundred thousand souls of the Forgotten Sex had healed each other, year after year, through the precious gift of remembering, together, a time when we were truly free. Wherever we lived in Area 51, these woods were home, whether we made it back every August or every six, even for some womyn who had only come once. It meant everything that there was a place where womyn lived together deeply connected to the mother planet, in celebration of all things female, moving boldly without fear, alone in the dark of the forest. We remembered. The matrilineal web of recovery from Patriarchy carried us from year to year to year.

And as much as I needed Festival community, I knew thousands of womyn needed Festival, too. I thought first of our beloved rainbow unicorns, sisters like Lisa Lisa and Baba, who lived an exalted life on the Land, full of love and meaning and appreciation, but who were continually harassed, demeaned, or overlooked in Area 51. In my heart I wanted the Festival to continue always for womyn who needed it more than they wanted it, this Land where square pegs fit beautifully into round holes.

A Political Shit Storm

I had come out of the 39th Festival in a shit storm of unbelievable political complexity. The task of preparing for the upcoming epic 40th anniversary needed all my love and attention. Instead, I was being pulled in dozens of directions as the leaders of LGBTQ organizations were attempting to manage the mess they'd made by signing on to a boycott against the Festival that had been launched by Equality Michigan less than two weeks before the 39th Fest.

EQMI had called for a boycott against not only the Festival, but targeting all Festival artists and vendors, and shaming every womon who attended the event. They'd reached out to all the big organizations and asked them to sign on. Without so much as a phone call to find out what the Festival's position actually was, most of them went with what EQMI had alleged and just signed. Many of them went further, supplying inflammatory sound bites or position letters. None of the statement writers had been to the Festival. The loud exception to this groupthink was the National Center for Transgender Equality, which took a pass on signing the petition.

The Festival and Festival community had been under constant reductive criticism for holding an intention that our gathering was for womyn who were born female and who currently identified as womyn. The onus was left up to each person to decide what that meant to them and to choose how they respected that intention, but we remained clear about where our focus was for the Festival. For all that the Festival was labeled "anti-trans," I urge you to reread the last two sentences. It was our intention, not even a "policy."

Contrary to the thick forest of incorrect information out there, once, and only once, had the Festival asked a trans womon to leave the Land, and that regrettable break in our intention was in 1991. From then on, we were faced with a tsunami of wrong information and literal lies about what we were about and who we were as a community. False stories about panty checks and tales about trans folks being expelled were repeated and even printed. The assumption that this diverse community had a single political view about sex and gender became ingrained in those who had never been to Festival. Bold misinformation about our community went unquestioned and traveled all over the LGBTQ community and beyond. Those who went knew differently.

The irony is that we existed as the most gender-radical space for womyn on the planet. You could walk down the hippest streets in San Francisco, Portland, or Brooklyn and not witness a more radical expression of female gender presentation than you could walking a mere 100 feet on the Land. The Land had been home ground to gender outlaws for decades. We elevated and celebrated all gender expressions. For so many womyn, their life made sense once they found the Land. In a world that said they didn't fit — that you had to do X to pass as a womon, or Z to pass as a man — on the Land, you could just fucking be. As the center of the LGBTQ world increasingly abandoned lesbian-identified womyn, Michigan would remain one place that was centered on womyn, in the broadest range of that lived expression.

The boycotting of this lesbian space by the National Center for Lesbian Rights, the Human Rights Campaign, the Task Force, and others was for many of us the final nail in the coffin of hope that womon-identified lesbians were represented under their rainbow flag. No questions, no conversation — just a boycott. Their actions said they were confident they could attack our community, boldly attach their names to a boycott against a lesbian institution, threaten the artists and vendors, and there would be no political consequences, only political gain. They acted as though the womyn of Michigan no longer had a voice.

But they quickly heard our voices. They heard from us in eloquent letters, posts on Facebook pages, hundreds of phone calls and donation envelopes returned with a piece of a sister's mind, instead of her credit card numbers. Photos appeared on Facebook showing womyn scraping HRC stickers off their cars, and long-ago Festivalgoers, who were now sitting on boards of directors and had become handsome donors, picked up their phones. The shit storm started to blow back on them.

One by one I heard from these organizations, who were now attempting to placate the Michigan community while not endangering the supporters who had applauded their participation in the boycott. I had meetings, I had phone calls, I was in email threads. Each leader communicated that they had acted rashly, that they wished they hadn't signed the petition to boycott, and they were sure we could work something out. Their apparent shared goal became to get Equality Michigan to pull the petition rather than to have to publicly remove their names. Essentially, in my view, they didn't have the guts to do what they were saying was right, but instead wanted to get EQMI to solve their problem by pulling the petition.

"They want me to fall on my sword," is what Emily of EQMI said when I finally spoke to her. Somehow in this mess I could appreciate her position, because, as ill-informed about the Festival as she was, she believed in what she was doing. The rest of the organization heads were likely doing what they thought was popular and therefore politically expedient, assuming they would win points, and lose nothing.

Allies in Understanding

The head of the National Center for Lesbian Rights, communicating to me on behalf of multiple petition signatories, invited me to go to Washington, D.C., to sit and discuss the whole situation with several heads of the organizations. I took a pass. They were shocked when they found out that our intention was, in fact, an intention, there was no policy we enacted, and we didn't stop anyone from coming to the Festival. Trans men and trans women had always attended the Festival, and either did so honoring that the focus was female or didn't. It was on each person. Petition organizers and signers had no idea that for some years we had been sponsoring Festival workshops designed to deepen the dialogue around the complex discussions around sex and gender, that we sought to learn to speak with each other with respect, and listen with our hearts, especially over this most divisive issue of our time. These Allies in Understanding workshops ran most of the Festival days and included all who wanted to attend, and always included trans women and trans men who were at the Festival.

When I explained the deeper feminist point of view of holding an intention, rather than laying down a policy, and monitoring and controlling who attended, they countered with how close they were to being able to 100% support the Festival. But they continued to insist, "Just come to D.C. and we'll all talk about it." As if their approval was the holy grail for the Festival or for me.

I suggested instead that they come to the Festival the following summer. After they'd been part of the gathering, they could have a realistic point of view about our community. I had no doubt that our conversations would be substantially different after they experienced for themselves what the Festival was about. I also proposed that we hold a communitywide Allies in Understanding workshop series in San Francisco — a weekend-long event that their organizations could sponsor — to provide an opportunity for all who wanted to attend to sit with each other and have the very difficult conversations we were learning to have on the Land. The purpose would be to learn together how to have this complicated discussion across differing opinions and life experiences, without the metaphorical tearing of flesh.

I gave my best pitch to involve them in organizing real dialogue within our community. I shared with them that in my experience, there's so much fear about this conversation — and so much political correctness on all sides of the issue — that we have no idea how to actually have this dialogue without fear of attack, anxiety over being deplatformed, and real concern for loss of funding if we take anything but the dominant line. This is why people signed onto a protest against the Festival without knowing anything about it.

We can do better. We must learn how to have this conversation and not have it be a zero-sum game, where someone must lose in order for someone else to gain. We can all be whole. It has to be possible to feel the pain in one community without denying it in another. This could be an opening for a revolutionary healing in our LGBT world.

There was no interest.

As the fall progressed, months of daily slogging through all this complicated dialogue was taking its toll on me. I had lived the past few years under a great deal of personal strain. Michigan had been the flashpoint for cancel culture before it became the rampant tool to punish anyone who exercised a different point of view. I had attempted to stay in the shifting sands of dialogue online in recent years, but everything blew up faster than I could even read it. I was called George Wallace in *The Advocate*. I was compared to Adolf Hitler. I hadn't even heard the word TERF (trans-exclusionary radical feminist) until I heard it used to describe me.

Cancel culture became focused on Festival artists. It only took one person to threaten a boycott for a gig to be canceled, a speaking engagement to be axed, or a DJ to be shut down. An entire generation of younger sisters was learning about the Michigan community through Gender Studies classes, where they weren't hearing about a group of radical womyn who were reclaiming the matriarchal Amazon strength of sisterhood across divisions of race, class, age, abilities, and gender expression. Instead, the story being told about our community was one of a group of TERFs exercising the biological privilege we had from being born into female bodies. The avalanche of misinformation had found its way from the gossip mills to the press and now into contemporary textbooks. By the fall of 2014, my heart was breaking into shards of glass and my mind was exploding with each bit of incoming turmoil and chaos.

Meanwhile, as I was planning the 40th anniversary, and in steady communication with the LGBTQ organizations, I did attempt to map out how a 41st Festival budget could look. Was it possible to get the budget down to the income a post-anniversary year would bring and keep the Festival that we love? I had moved the business through many changes over the past 20 years and attempted to make those changes in a way that didn't structurally change the experience of the Festival. There was now nothing I could do that did not involve deep structural change like eliminating one of our three stages or other core areas of programming or community life.

Right about that time I went to my favorite mud bath place. I'd been going there for 30 years, from when it was a super simple, rough-in-the-mud place to when it became cool and swank. Now it was a trendy, fancy, wine-country resort. Over all those years of changes, they always had a large container of water with lemon and cucumber slices, and that simple thing was pretty much my favorite part. Spa water.

On that day trip to soak in mud and steam, I noticed more changes, not the least of which was the increased price of the mud bath. I could handle that, but really? No more spa water? I was incensed. I was totally focused on this detail and complained to Lia too many times about how little it would cost to keep that small perk happening.

Was I just being petty, or was this a gnarly truth of human nature, that we are offended to be charged more and receive less, especially less of something we really enjoy, however simple? This was the reality I was facing. To make the Festival sustainable at the number of womyn that were consistently attending, I would have to charge more and cut back on many services and programs. In my mockup budgets I couldn't see another way, and each way I shook the numbers, they didn't work. I could not imagine being the person to produce a much smaller event, the only Festival that I could see possible. I simply couldn't do it.

In April 2015, I received a letter from Autumn Sandeen, the publisher of the *Trans Advocate,* who had dogged the Festival and me personally for the past couple of years, always with explosive statements and veiled threats. She wrote that she had bought a ticket to the 2015 Festival and was awaiting my statement that she was welcome. In the same week, I also heard from the heads of NCLR and the Task Force. They had been silent for some time after their attempt to get me and Emily from EQMI to make a joint statement, something neither of us wanted to do, even though our direct conversations were candid and reasonable despite our points of view being very different. They asked to come to my office for a meeting and wanted to know if I would consider including a representative from the trans community at the meeting. Autumn had tipped me off in her letter that this would be her, something the organizations had not disclosed. Autumn said in the same communication that she would come to my office and stay outside until I addressed whether her ticket to the Festival was good. Since Autumn Sandeen was the same person who had chained herself to the White House fence a couple of years before, I knew she had it in her. She was a loose cannon in everything I had ever seen of her, and I wasn't really interested in having this sit-down.

I was on my fourth draft of an email communicating that I wouldn't be interested in this meeting at this time, but that I would welcome such a meeting if both womyn who headed these organizations attended the Festival, something I had said to them before.

"Come and see what it is you are seeking to change. Walk on the Land with this community. Until you have been there, you really have no right to be part of this process or right to attempt to influence a community that you are not part of, that you have invested nothing in."

I thought it was reasonable, and I knew they wouldn't do it. But my point of view was clear. This community has a sovereign process. If you want to be part of our process, you are welcome.

I called Holly in Portland to read my current draft and get feedback, something I did often, because Holly is such an awesome wordsmith. As I described to her everything that had been happening, that my email was responding to, I started to sob.

I was pacing in the backyard of the office, away from where anyone else could hear. "I don't want this to be my life. I can only do this work from a place of love, and I have been covered in so much anger and conflict, I have a growing fear that it is actually going to kill me. My nervous system is shot, and my adrenals are chronically blown off the chart. I don't see a way through this."

I was never one to have a five-year business plan, but I was continuously working on the next year's Festival and always able to see several years ahead. But now, when I looked, there was nothing.

Holly gently said to me, "Sit down and write the letter you would write to tell the community this truth. See if it feels right."

She didn't try and talk me down. She didn't try to talk me out of it. She asked me to find my truth. I got off the phone, sat down with my chest heaving, cold sweat running down the sides of my neck, my hands clammy on the keyboard. It was like I was surfacing through cloudy, brackish water and suddenly the light broke through. The letter I wrote on that Thursday ended up being the letter I mailed out the following Monday with some changes, but not many. I sent it to a few friends to read and give feedback. I prayed over the weekend. I made an altar in my backyard with a copy of the letter.

I lit candles.

I burned palo santo.

Dear Sisters, Amazons, Festival family,

It has been my honor and privilege to produce the Michigan Womyn's Music Festival for 40 years. It has been my life's work, my deepest commitment, my constant challenge and my most profound joy. Every single thing of value I have learned in the world I have learned in the process of being part of building this beloved community. Almost every friend and family member who I cherish I have met on that hallowed ground, and every single way I have learned to put my mind/heart/shoulder into the purpose of creating something beautiful that honors womyn has come from the sweat I earned on that Land.

I am writing to tell you that the 40th Festival will be the last Michigan Womyn's Music Festival. The spirit of this community will live on forever, the friends and family we have found on the Land are eternal. Everything we have created together will feed the inspiration for what comes next. It's possible that I will come back with something else, or that other sisters will take the inspiration of the Michigan community and create the next expression of our Amazon culture. What is true for me is that now is the time to bring this 40-year cycle to a close, stepping out on joy at our most incredible anniversary celebration.

We have known in our hearts for some years that the life cycle of the Festival was coming to a time of closure. Too often in our culture, change is met only with fear, the true cycle of life is denied in order to avoid the grief of loss. But change is the ultimate truth of life. Sisters — I ask you to remember that our 40-year Festival has outlived nearly all of her kin. She has served us well. I want us all to have the opportunity to experience the incredible full life cycle of our beloved Festival, consciously, with time to celebrate and yes, time to grieve.

There have been struggles; there is no doubt about that. This is part of our truth, but it is not — and never has been — our defining story. The Festival has been the crucible for nearly every critical cultural and political issue the lesbian feminist community has grappled with for four decades. Those struggles have been a beautiful part of our collective strength; they have never been a weakness.

For many of us this one week in the woods is the all too rare place and time where we experience validation for our female bodies, and where the female experience presides at the center of our community focus. A place to lay our burden down from the misogyny that pervades our lives from cradle to grave ... a place to live in intergenerational community, and to live in harmony with Mother Earth. I know this is true for me. And I have a deep trust that each and every one of us can take what we have experienced on that Land and continue to create space that feeds our spirit, creates diverse community, honors our experience and supports our struggle as womyn making our way through the patriarchal world. Please take what you love about Michigan and use it to create something new and beautiful.

It is important that each and every one of us knows she is empowered to build on what we have experienced together on the Land. Everything you feel on the Land, everything you see — is something of spirit, and love, and passion for female empowerment ... for womyn's community. The Festival's 40 years of culture and community are a powerful seed and our communal experiences have created fertile ground to plant in. I know that we will find inspiration and vision to create our next time and space.

For those of us who will be gathering for our 40th anniversary this August — let's joyously hold up our incredible community and allow ourselves to be strong enough to consciously let go of this incarnation of her, with all the love we each hold in our beautiful hearts. Let us gather this August knowing that what we truly cherish about the Festival lives on in each of us, and more will come from this fertile ground. Let's do this up together — Amazon proud!

I will meet you there in August — my eyes meeting yours, heart wide open.

With all of my love and respect,

Lisa

1st row: *Night Stage, 2009* photo by Diane Butler; 2nd row: *Fireworks over Night Stage, 2015* photo by Desdemona Burgin; *Myrna at the mix, 2007* photo by Chewy Kane; 3rd row: *Acoustic Stage, 2013* photo by Desdemona Burgin

1st row: *Closing Ceremony processional, 2014*; *Videomania, 2015*, photos by Desdemona Burgin; 2nd row: *Eggs for breakfast!, 2007* photo by Angela Jiminez; *Meditation Circle, 2015* photo by Brynna Fish; 3rd row: *Marshmallow tree* photo by Katie Yealland; 4th row: *Odd late '80s game* photo by Jennifer Campbell; *DART campground, 2009* photo by Diane Butler

CHAPTER 37

SHE WHO WILL NOT BE NAMED

Lisa Lisa invited me to lunch to celebrate the pulling of her teeth. I had never gone to lunch with her, and I wondered how she had worked out the cost of a complete set of dentures, though I had witnessed some incredible resourcefulness from her over the years. Her teeth reminded me of so many mouths in my family — tobacco-stained, crooked, separated by gaps where there once was a tooth, pulling away from receding, diseased gums, to be replaced in middle-age by ill-fitting dentures. No matter how busy I was this month before I left for Michigan, you bet I would meet her for lunch and celebrate this moment of releasing pain from her mouth and emerging with a full set of new, sorely needed dentures. I wouldn't miss it for the world.

The story with Lisa Lisa went like this. She had African roots and a Canadian background, living in the U.S. without papers. She didn't have ID and no one ever knew her full name. Once the airlines started demanding identification to fly, she took to Greyhound. She didn't trust the train. I offered to get her a fake ID so she could fly, but she said that was too complicated. Instead, for the last 20 years, she'd taken the bus on the long trip across the country from Oakland to Grand Rapids and back.

I extracted an annual promise that she would call when she hit Chicago so we knew when she would arrive in GR, but it never happened. Instead, she would call when she arrived at the final stop — a day early, a day late, but rarely on the day expected. If it was in the evening and we had no driver in GR, we would call the hotel nearest the bus station and pay for a room for her to rest and then pick her up in the morning. More than once she called so late no one was around the trailer and she slept outside on top of her traveling gear.

"Lisa, for fuck's sake, I wish you would just call me from Chicago and let me know you're close so we can have someone there when you arrive or arrange a room you can go to!"

We had a relationship with Calder Cab, and they would take her to and from the hotel and allow us to pay the next day, but this meant we had to know. I'm pretty sure she always hoped to fall between the hours of too late for us to come and get her and not so late that she would have to sleep on the sidewalk, a sweet spot that would reap a hot shower and a bed after four days on a bus. But she was as stubborn a dyke as I had ever met, and was prepared to live with the consequences, never complaining.

She worked in the Working Witches' Kitchen back in the day, stirring pots over a campfire with a cigarette hanging out of her mouth and her bare breasts hanging over the pot. Our culinary and sanitary expectations were simple back then — we were grateful for whatever we were fed at the end of a grueling day. If it was accompanied by a bizarre joke and a wink, all the better. She was in her mid- to late-40s then, more than 30 years ago, and was so hard-working. She was the epitome of the Crew of the Willing.

When the Witches Kitchen transformed into Galz Diner and the food morphed into more elaborate vegetarian staples, her personal disinterest in cooking became apparent. She moved over to the Belly Bowl, where her true talents of hobnobbing, flirting, and giving advice to the younger dykes could really shine. The job, which was being the front of house for the Worker's Kitchen, included making hundred-cup urns of coffee, wiping down the tables, keeping the toast table hopping, and cleaning the multitude of silverware that constantly ran out because womyn dragged fork after fork back to their tents or work areas, hundreds arriving back only in the last days on the Land.

As Lisa Lisa aged, she became less able to do the work, less interested in following rules, concocting one workaround after another to never ask for help, even though so many womyn would do anything she asked or allowed. One of her workarounds was to bury silverware in the woods, we assumed so there would be less to wash. When it hit the critical fork emergency moment, someone would slyly tell her that Festival was having to buy more silverware because we were out. She hated causing any undue expense.

She got the double Lisa from an episode one night in the early '90s before the Health Inspection. I walked into the Belly Bowl and flipped a biscuit because it was a shitty mess and the inspection was at 10 a.m. the next day. She, Lisa Mammina, and I shooed everyone out and we cleaned that place until almost dawn. One of us would call out "Lisa" and we would all look at each other — so we went to Mammina, Lisa Lisa, and the single Lisa left to me. As we scrubbed and painted and laid fresh upside-down carpet until dawn, it was clear we were similar and forever bonded in more than having a shared first name.

Lisa was a relentless flirt, not unusual on the Land, but it put a few younger sisters through some changes when she would hit on them with her well-culled phrases.

"Nice legs [pause]. What time do they open?"

I had more than a couple of sex-positive dykes come to me to complain that she was inappropriate.

"Did you tell her you weren't comfortable with her flirting?"

"No."

"You can't have it both ways. You enjoy it when the younger womyn flirt with you, and if you don't, you tell them to back off. She has as much right to flirt as someone in her 30s. If you can't handle someone flirting with you because she's old, I can't help you."

Lisa herself was one the best and most democratic flirts on the Land, always having a little sugar for the sisters as they passed by.

"Hello, Lover," she greeted dozens of womyn each day.

She had pet names for the ones she really liked.

"Cara Mia, can I do anything for you today??"

And her all-encompassing affection bomb: "I love you prodigiously!"

I don't know how many womyn she phoned regularly during the months we weren't on the Land together, but if I had to guess, I would say at least 50. It could be 100. Sisters would send calling cards to her, care of the Oakland office, and we would make sure she got them because this was her conduit to her community throughout the country. Calls where she offered herbal remedies, deep listening, silly jokes, or maybe just to be still on the phone and read a story to one another. She would read to womyn in the hospital and sit next to womyn who had to go to court and had no one. She had a busy schedule of service. She believed in womyn as much as anyone I know and would do everything possible to support a sister.

Language of love

As her physical abilities faded, her mind remained brilliantly weird and her willingness to help around the Land was always alive. She couldn't really fill a crew position by that point, but rotating crews would welcome her to be part of their work, as long as she didn't count as one of their full crew members — and she didn't stay too long. As beloved as she was, she was also a controlling, stubborn pain in the ass, and sisters would get burnt out.

She did dozens of foot rubs on tired, stinky feet every week, snagging workers on their breaks and telling stories as she oiled, massaged, and put love back on those sturdy bases that pounded over unlevel ground. She did Security/Communications shifts where her schedule and position were titled, "The Constant Flower." She folded sheets and towels for the Massage Crew, folded T-shirts at Festiewear, and made teas in Worker Health. She painted backgrounds for the Signz Crew, which she particularly liked because they let her smoke in the tent, and she had her own little corner that she could come and go from whenever she wanted. The signage artists worked with headphones, so they didn't have to engage much, which was a plus all the way around.

One of my most vivid images of the very last Festival was on the last day, when the Carps Crew was taking up the floor from Galz diner, the last wood on the Land. All of us were exhausted — emotionally spent and physically beat — and here was Lisa Lisa, 83 years old, her walker pushed against a tree, scooting along the plywood on her butt, the drill an extension of her hand, screw after screw giving way to her relentless focus as she dismantled the floor.

It had to be a real emergency for her to leave the Land once she was there. I can remember two times when she actually tied a long string around her waist with the other end tethered to the tree near Galz. It didn't matter to her that womon after womon was tripping over her damned string. It was her Land Umbilical Cord, she would say, and she wasn't ready to cut it loose.

Forever an Amazon photo by Katie Yealland

As we were all preparing to leave the Land she would always be on the last shuttle on the last day, hating to leave and asking how early she could come back. Her Worker Storage boxes were identified by the stench of moth balls stuffed into every carton. I would wait to hear from her upon my return to Berkeley, which was always two weeks after that last day on the Land.

She didn't have a phone, so I couldn't call her. She wouldn't accept a phone because she didn't want anyone to find her. She wouldn't accept a burner phone because she didn't want those rays in her head. She didn't want anyone to know where she lived or ever come into her house, but I had to know where she lived because I had falsified income documents for her to be able to keep her housing, and occasionally the people from there called me. Not that I'd ever been inside her apartment. She had me drop her off around the corner and down the block so they didn't see my car. She didn't want anyone to know her business or the business of anyone she knew. So, I would wait for her to call.

In the garden of misfit toys, she was the rainbow unicorn with three horns and two tails. The Festival community, and particularly the working crew, was populated by so many peculiar snowflakes — it was the most stunningly beautiful dimension of the ecosphere of Festival. No matter how maladjusted you were in the patriarchal world, there was room here for you to contribute, to be celebrated, to be cool, to belong. Even those who were so painfully normal and appropriate, who were on the edge of breaking apart, could find their inner freak, and finally let themselves be free.

Lisa Lisa painted so far outside the lines there was no shape. She had no lines. Her liberation on the Land made us all freer. The idea that we had to be a certain way to be loved, respected, and included was buried a little deeper in hell when she walked onto that Land, and it lives on in the hearts of so many dykes all over the world who loved her, for exactly who she was.

When I was making the decision to have the 40th Festival be the last, I was torn up with my own anticipatory grief, but even more so, the extraordinary loss for the sisters who had such difficulty making their way in the outside world, and who thrived so beautifully on the Land. I knew for Lisa it would be a blow, and she dealt with it with a powerful denial. Every time I saw her afterwards, she would ask me when we would be going Home again.

For several years, I arranged for Lisa to clean the office, which really meant she made her way there, found a boom box to play her favorite station, and spit-shined the sink. She wasn't moving well by then, but she had a hard time accepting money without working. So, she cleaned the sink and ate chicken with Terri Lynn one Friday a month, and it gave me a mechanism to get money to her. Once the Festival ended and we were in a constant process of archiving, scanning, and digitizing 40 years of images, papers, and recordings, it was too much to have her there, so Clare would meet her near a bus stop and give her an envelope and tell her we would have work soon. And when the office closed for good, I started meeting her for lunch or at the library to give her the contraband cash envelope and then drop her off at the 99-cent store where she would shop. She never let me help; she said she knew the store like the back of her hand. We had gotten her a walker with a seat, but she only wanted to use that when she got dressed up, and instead preferred a rolling laundry cart with a huge, very used black plastic bag inside, her things buried deep in the folds. Sometimes when I met her, she would have that cart and be wearing a hugely oversized, faded-dark-navy jacket, a stocking cap, sunglasses, and a face mask.

"Wow, Lisa, you're quite a sight in this get-up."

"I go out dressed like this so nobody bothers me. They think I'm homeless or crazy and they don't try and talk to me. Except sometimes people try to give me money. 'Why do I want your money?' I say."

During the last year I saw her, her movement was so compromised that it took her about an hour to cover a city block. She moved painfully, slowly, but with such determination. She still wouldn't let me pick her up at her building or drop her off there. It had to be around the corner and out of sight so no one could see my car. I would watch her inch her way along the street, stopping every 8 to 10 feet to rest.

And then she just stopped showing up. We would make a date to meet at a place of her choosing, and I would wait and worry. No Lisa. When she eventually called, she would say that I had gotten the time wrong, or I had the day wrong. She had been so unusual and so generally cantankerous for so long that it took me awhile to realize that she was slipping away.

When she stopped meeting me, I began going by her building. I would either talk my way in through the office phone to get buzzed in, or I'd wait outside until someone exited to slip through after them, then make my way to her apartment on the second floor and slide an envelope under her door. I could hear her in there rustling around but she would never answer my knock or my voice. Her calls became very sporadic. Various sisters from around the country reached out to ask if I had heard from her, but I stopped being able to say yes. Months started to pass, and this was someone who had left a message on my phone sometimes every day, or five times a day, for years. I had kept my landline, which I called the Lisa Lisa Line, just so we could stay in touch.

It had been 20 months since I had laid eyes on her when I went to her apartment to slip an envelope under her door, my regular tithing. I was always so relieved to see that her Post-It notes were still taped up and keeping everyone in line:

> *Do not knock!*
>
> *Do not put anything under this door!*
>
> *No spraying near this door!*

I could see they were still on the door as I approached, and I relaxed a little. But when I got to the door, I saw the coroner's tape sealing the door, dated that very day.

I had known this time would come, and truly I was only amazed that it had taken so long. But still I was stunned. I took down the case number and phone number from the coroner's tape and called.

"I'm standing outside my friend's door, and I think this only means one thing — what can you tell me?"

The apartment manager had called for a wellness check, and they had found her that morning. She had been there probably two weeks, judging from the signs of her decomposition. The coroner's case manager was so glad to hear from someone because he had found zero in the apartment that would lead to anyone, no trail to follow to find next of kin. No letters, no photos, not a single ID, no prescriptions, no government subsidy paperwork. "Is it possible that someone this age lived with no medical intervention?" he asked. She lived in subsidized housing for the elderly and had been there almost 30 years, but they had no record of other government support. I remembered her telling me how she got that apartment, volunteering next to a womon one day and remarking on how rough it had been sleeping on the bus bench the night before. That womon was on a housing board and hooked her up with that apartment. But there was nothing that could tell him who she was, who her family was, nothing. "She apparently has no one, so I'm relieved that you called."

Oh, she had someone. She had a lot of someones who loved her. She had a whole tribe of people she called out to: "Hello Lover! Have a good day my Cara Mia!"

But she died the way she lived, which was making sure that no one would know anything about her, or about anyone she loved.

I asked what would happen to her now, and they said by law they were required to try for a month to find her legal family. And after that, the county would cremate her and her ashes would go to a place in Napa where unclaimed ashes go.

"What would I need to do in order to claim her? I CLAIM HER."

"After a month of looking, if there is no legal family, a non-family member can claim her if they pay for her cremation, and then they can receive her ashes to spread, but special note, they cannot keep them, they must be spread."

I will do that, and many in her family will contribute to the cost of her cremation; you see, we have a very big family. And we will make sure her ashes get to the Land, where she will join the most awesome group of sisters who have gone on ahead: Deerheart, Paij, Barrie, Ernie, and so many more. I'll spread some ashes behind the Belly Bowl, some at Signz, some more up at DART, and a little out in the Twilight Zone for good measure.

Good night lover — I will always love you prodigiously.

CHAPTER 38

LAST WOC TENT

Karen, who was liaison to the Womyn of Color Tent along with Terri Lynn, came to me early Thursday, the morning after our earth-moving final Opening Celebration, and said that Pat would like me to be there for the Tent Dedication. I was confused, because this was a WOC-only event, one that I understood was sacred. Private.

"Does this have to do with Terri Lynn being off the Land?"

I could only imagine I was being asked to substitute for Terri Lynn at this important moment as she had stood in for me in other ways so many times over the years. By then, Terri Lynn and I had worked together full-time for 12 years. She was central to many areas of Festival production, from crew to campers to artists. The largest of her many responsibilities was knowing the details of more than 400 crew members and juggling crew assignments — some of which changed daily — for all 44 Festival areas. Try and top that, Siri!

Even with all these responsibilities, I often wanted her to be part of the Opening Celebration performance if the opportunity arose and she was willing. An incredible dancer with great performance energy, TL could shoot her love all the way to the back of the listening bowl. When she was in a performance spot in the Opening, it meant she was less available to me in the production of the ceremony, but the trade-off was always worth it.

For this last year, I knew she would want to be in it, and of course I wanted her there present, full, and center.

During the last piece of the Opening Celebration of the last year of the Festival, Terri Lynn danced off the stage and down the ramp like the Amazon that she is, made her way through the crowd, and out of sight, she fell. She snapped her Achilles tendon, was on the ground twisting in pain, and would go to the hospital that night to return two days later in a full medical boot, using a wheelchair, and on some very good drugs. It was an unbelievable heartbreak for her to be injured and sidelined during this last Festival.

Was that why I was being asked to attend the WOC Tent Dedication?

"No," Karen said. "Pat would like you specifically to be at the WOC Tent for the Dedication this year."

My day was well smashed with schedules, and with Terri Lynn out of commission, everyone in Staff Services was closing ranks to pick up her work and assure her parts continued smoothly. She held a lot of things in her hands.

The Tent Dedication was at 11 a.m. The opening of the Day Stage was at noon, and I was always there early, especially on the first day. I had phone calls, a meeting with Kim from the Main Kitchen to assess our changes to the Friday morning Gordon Foods delivery, production schedules to tweak — and personally, I was psychically hung over from the powerful experience that was the final Opening Celebration.

Of course, I would be there at the Tent Dedication. Calls were made, changes were confirmed, approved, or tweaked, and my expected lateness was noted. By 10 a.m., I was fully sorted or close enough. I put on clean and tidy clothes then made my way by bike down the gravel road to the WOC Tent.

A Community Reckoning

As I rode, I was transported in my mind back to the time, years before, when I had biked over to a town meeting on racism that had been called at the Community Center. My bike in those days was a small, pre-loved, no-speed banana bike, not the Trek hybrid now under my feet.

I wheeled up to that long-ago Community Center meeting to find the entire area filled with a growing circle of womyn. I parked myself in the back of it all. There was a mic, and speakers — where did they come from? I stayed in the outer circle, not wanting to pull any attention, and not wanting to spark a dynamic of dialogue between the Festival (represented by me) and the womyn who had called the meeting. I wanted to listen and understand. I wanted to be part of the town.

The conversation had started because white womyn with WOC partners wanted to be included in the womyn of color-only Sanctuary space. This was 1988, and the WOC Tent had been growing and evolving since 1985. By the time this meeting was called, the issues that needed to be addressed had expanded.

Those issues included how to discuss white womyn creating and/or selling things in the Crafts Area that were distinctly drawn from cultures not their own, and how to address artists who made unintentional racist remarks from stage.

I remembered the year when a white artist sang a song about the African American womon who raised her, a song full of love and honor for this womon who had helped her grow up. It did not reflect any understanding of how complicated this story was, that there could be — and were — sisters in the audience whose own mothers were often not with them growing up because they were taking care of white children in order to feed and care for their own. How painful to sit and listen to a song celebrating this reality.

How would we talk about this?

These were complicated and big discussions to grapple with, and a large group of womyn had shown up at the Community Center that day to be in the circle to listen, and to speak to the reality of race and racism in our not-always-idyllic community. From my spot by one of the chokecherry trees toward the back of the group, which had grown to probably 600 womyn, I watched as womyn came to the mic and shared their experiences of being on the Land. The Land that they were personally dedicated to and the community that they had built and committed themselves to for over a decade. The space that was their refuge from the world of patriarchy. This space that was so sacred, but still a place where they faced racism from their sisters, day after day.

Then Papusa Molina, who at that time worked at the Womb, came to the mic and started to speak. Her energy was big, focused, fierce. She called across the field of womyn and pointed to me, her energy a rocket across the field.

"Lisa Vogel — what are you prepared to do to make change on the Land?"

Honestly, it took everything I had to stand there and not evaporate into a puddle of fear or move too fast in deciding how to respond to this sister as she spoke over the mic.

Stand there. Listen.

This was not the first and thankfully it would not be the last time that I was called on to act as the discussion of race and culture evolved on the Land. At that moment, I felt like I was called out. All eyes were on me, and I felt little but fear and self-consciousness. But it was, in fact, a gift. I was called in, and those words came to me in my sleep.

What would I do to make change on the Land?

My way in the world was to learn through empathy, so even if I could not directly relate to a sister's life, I could usually empathize with her, and connect to her experience with my heart, if not my mind. When Papusa asked me this question, I realized that too often I'd felt self-conscious about taking outward steps to be involved personally in anti-racism community work or to speak about racism outside of personal interactions.

I trusted my heart, but not necessarily my actions, my words. I was simply another white womon afraid of doing the wrong thing, and so I did much less than I could, playing it safe, something the color of my skin allowed me to do.

To get in there and be part of change, I had to be willing to look bad, make mistakes, even hurt or anger womyn I loved and respected. I had to own that I was reflexively protecting an image, one that I didn't even believe in myself. I took fewer actions because of my unconscious motivation to not do the wrong thing and be seen doing it. Not only did I have to build my capacity to receive criticism, I had to be truly willing to show my ass.

I was starting to recognize that when I was called to be accountable, it was an extension of trust I could reach for. I discovered that when I showed my ass, I did not fall apart, and it slowly took the value out of hiding behind the privilege of whiteness.

Mid-winter following that Community Center Town Hall, I attended a symposium on racism in San Francisco. I knew Papusa was scheduled to be one of the speakers and workshop leaders. I ducked out to the bathroom at one point, and as I was washing my hands, Papusa came out of one of the stalls. We had never spoken, except that one moment she called to me over the mic at the Community Center. We both were a little surprised to be sharing a sink.

I introduced myself. We said hello. I told her how much I appreciated her work at the conference and asked if she would consider coming to the Land and doing anti-racism work with the Festival crew members. She sized me up, both of us standing by the sinks, and said, "If you are willing, I am willing." Ours would be a long friendship of being allies to one another and confidantes in our complicated lives. We never turned away from one another, no matter how complicated our struggles were over the years.

Papusa came and did workshops with the crew the next summer and other years. It was the start of what would become an ongoing annual all-crew workshop night coordinated by groups of womyn who were on crew, exploring a myriad of issues that had the power to divide us. In that coming together, we grew closer and less fearful of our differences.

The more we talked and realized everyone could survive talking about difficult issues, the more we committed ourselves as a community to do anti-oppression work together in the place it mattered the most, our home. I think for a lot of white womyn the Land was the first place that we were asked to be actively anti-racist and hold our seat if called out for micro-aggressions or acts of ignorance.

It was a place we were not shamed for coming in as who we were, with permission, encouragement, and expectation to grow. For most of us, there was a lot of room to grow. Many womyn of color did a great deal of heavy lifting as teachers, as womyn willing to go through sometimes very painful processes with white sisters, and as sisters willing to take the risk to grow something better in our community.

The overall expectation that race and cultural issues were something we dealt with on the Land steadily grew, and the silences that filled the space of difference grew smaller, less powerful. At the same time, womyn of color's ownership and leadership in the communities on the Land expanded, and with that, the community of womyn of color continued to grow.

The Final Dedication

Now, on that Thursday of the final Festival, as I arrived at the WOC tent — its herstory embedded, its legacy imprinted, at this present moment of its crowning transition — the space was packed. The tent sides were all open, womyn spilling out into the grass and ferns, all the way to the pedestrian path that ran alongside the road.

As the first large gathering at the Tent this year, the energy was joyous as womyn reconnected after their long, dry 51 weeks in Area 51. Sisters I had known through all the years of Festival — either as friends, co-workers, artists, or womyn I had nodded to each year on the woodchip trails — were there alongside womyn I had not seen on the Land in some years. I was so moved to see Lola Wing, who had worked in the WOC Tent in the early years, but to my knowledge had not been back on the Land for well over a decade. This was beautiful.

Fatu was there. I was so happy that she'd made her way to the Land for the last Festival as a camper, after years of having been on the Land as a performer. In those days she was often up before dawn, as I was. More than once I'd sensed someone outside my trailer in the dark. I would glance out the window and there would be Fatu, making her way from Performer Camping down to the fire pit, where she would start the fire for her morning breakfast. She always looked up through my window for a morning hello.

Fatu, 2004 photo by Diane Butler

"I'll have some sausage ready in about an hour, if you're interested."

And she knew I was.

That connection continued even as we no longer saw each other on the Land. In my dining room I have a shell rattle that Fatu gave me one year, a 4-inch turtle shell, painted in yellow, turquoise, and red, a circle of cowry shells and beads along the edge, a spherical design made of waxed string on the belly, and leather closing the shell's opening. She is in my home every day, the beads inside the turtle's belly making the sound that brings Fatu into the room with me.

As I came fully into the center of the Tent, Pat McCombs welcomed me and gave me a warm hug. Pat was the coordinator of the WOC Tent and had been for the past 22 years. Pat balanced the sacred and the sexy, harmonized the political and the party, and generously made room for everyone. She was one of the early womyn who worked with us doing outreach in Chicago, had coordinated Orientation at the Front Gate for a decade, and then moved to the WOC Tent, where she had stayed at the helm all these years. She looked beautiful, as always, her smile so open and warm.

Pat, Amoja, Lola and Lisa, at WOC Tent, 2015 photo by Abena Sharon Bale

I took a seat in the circle. I didn't know if everyone was cool that I was there, but I held my seat on the floor of the tent, making eye contact around the room as sisters settled in. I felt deeply aware of the honor of being invited to join in this gathering, and I let the significance of that invitation sink in.

Over the years, I had observed that in communities of womyn of color there was a smoothness in honoring elders, or founders, that didn't exist easily in white culture. White communities are often much less grounded in or reverent of tradition, to the point of being cut off from it, removed. I felt in my heart as I held my seat that I was being asked to come full circle, for this last honoring of the Tent. I was being asked to witness, to be seen, to be a part.

Amoja Three Rivers, the founder of the Tent over three decades earlier, came over and we embraced, a warm hug that echoed all that we had been through together over the years. We shared a little laugh. She held the center as the elder of the Womon of Color Tent, and I was there holding the center as the elder of the Festival. Amoja would cross over to the other side just four months later, but her spirit that day was flying high, her body whole.

So much of my memory of the hour that followed is a blur of intense emotions, centered on the physical sensation of the energy in the circle and the drumming.

Yaniya Pearson, 2012 photo by J. Bob Alotta

Yaniya, speaking with feather and smudge. Aleah, her eyes always so kind, so steady, holding me in her gaze.

Afia, Ubaka, Fatu — drummers I had booked, worked with, planned Opening Celebrations around — each now drumming 6 feet in front of me. Whatever protective energy I had walked through the Festival with melted. My heart chakra burst open like it flew out of my chest. I was exactly where I needed to be, lifted, and held by the vibration and love in the Tent.

Over the years, I sometimes felt alienated or othered when interacting on the Land with womyn who knew me only as the producer of the Festival. I struggled with this dynamic. I could feel myself some days walking a few feet behind my eyes as I tried to keep my true right size while being personified as the Festival itself.

The amount of projection on me, especially at that last Festival, was exhausting. Through that confusing process, I deflected appreciation awkwardly, which was not the intention of my heart. It was my inept way of trying to bridge the divide I experienced when I was elevated beyond my right size. I felt like I was given too much power in those moments, and in this dynamic, womyn gave me too much of theirs.

Sometimes I felt like I had failed in my most essential task when the credit was all focused on me. I knew how much we had all created this beauty-filled space we loved — it was truly a big US — even as I understood the shorthand of appreciating me for it.

In this circle, I felt witnessed. I felt seen for what I had gone through in recent years, and I could see that so many of these sisters had gone through it with me.

I felt acknowledged for holding it down, and I knew I was not alone in holding it down. There was an exchange of energy and strength. I felt deeply in my body that I could receive and not distance myself from what was happening in any part of my being. Surrounded by sisters, feeling the drum ripple through me, grateful for every struggle, and alive with love.

CHAPTER 39

CREATING THE FUTURE

The day I mailed the letter to the community to say we would hold the 40th and final Festival in August was a jagged exhalation of a long-held breath. I knew that once I communicated this, it was done. And as difficult as the decision was, I knew in every cell of my body that it was right. It was time. The next day, I couldn't get out of bed. There I stayed, laptop on the comforter, nauseous and in shock. My friend, Sara St. Martin Lynne, climbed in with me for part of the day, holding space as I flailed about. I read Facebook posts and looked at emails from friends, kept my phone shut off, and my dog, Billie, close. We got up only to pee.

Sisters were kinder than I expected, and critics were harsher than I feared. It was a whirlwind of emotion and it was excessively real. Everyone was having feelings, big feelings, but the most personal, terrorizing part of my own fear — that the entire community would turn on me with anger fueled by grief — just didn't happen. The community's response was layered with love for our tribe, steeped in the maturity of how we let go with love, voicing deep understanding of the difficult decision that I'd had to make.

Of course, that wasn't everyone. I listened disproportionately to the sisters who were angry about the decision and resentful that it was mine to make. This was a small group, but a group that had to be heard. There were also the quieter womyn, gentle and contemplative about this major shift in our year, in our lives.

While I was propped up in bed that day, I was surfing songs and YouTube videos, praying about what we as a community would need for that summer's Opening Celebration, a moment that could set the intention for our entire last week. I came across Sinead O'Conner's heartbreaking "Thank You for Hearing Me." It broke me open. I played it over and over and then I posted it as the only thing I knew how to say in response to everything sisters were communicating that day to me and to the community. This piece captured what we gave to each other at our best: witnessing, gentleness, respect. I knew this song and this message would be a central part of the Opening, and I knew the Opening, if crafted with this intention, could help us process, grieve, and honor the lifespan of the Festival.

We now had three and a half months to prepare for our final gathering. We wanted to create a celebration of everything we were and make opportunities for the community to mourn and celebrate as one fierce breath. We weren't going to act like nothing was happening, but we also didn't want to act like the ending of the Festival was the only thing happening. We could honor our closure by having the most exquisite Festival of our lives, an entire week an Amazon ritual of remembering and gratitude, and a conscious planting of seeds for what could come next.

After the first flurry of reactions, the announcement that the 40th was the final Festival inspired varying responses. Workers who hadn't worked in many years wanted to come back on crew, and though we needed more crew members for the expected increase in the number of campers, we didn't need EVERYONE who had ever been on crew to be a worker. We fielded many requests from workers and artists and miscellaneous public folks to be given worker/backstage access, always a hot issue for Festival, always one of our most unpopular positions. You really did have to work in order to be in the worker area. That couldn't be bought or bartered, just earned. Within no time we realized that some sisters who hadn't been to the Festival in a long-ass time, decades even, would be returning to the mothership for one final stomp.

It was complicated for the younger sisters in the office to navigate these phone calls with long-ago festies. Terri Lynn and Clare knew the Festival well, understood all the current details, information, and guidelines. They were both so awesome with womyn on the phones; they really cared about everything and everyone, and knew how to take a breath if things got weird. But when the Festival had started, TL was 5 years old and Clare was born the year after we'd moved on to the new Land. It was a real understatement to say that these callers' point of reference from years ago was before their time. They were from completely different Festival generations who had not yet met.

Intergenerational.

One of the most radical veins feeding the heart of our community was the spectrum of age that infused every part of our creation. This truth healed something old, even ancient in us, and replicated a time when elders were not separated from the tribe and when children ran safely among all of us, when young adults witnessed the fierce aging of those who came before them and could see in them the path to becoming an untamed elder. The courage and radical openness of youth gave us the fuel for change — we always remembered, because the explosive fire of youth started our community decades ago. We raised our children in groups and our girls ran in packs, wild and free in the forest.

With the sisters who had not returned to the Festival for 20, 30, or even 35 years, the phone calls at times became a bit thorny. Many things about the Festival had changed over time, but not in their memories.

"What do you mean I can't camp in my RV in downtown DART? That's what I've always done!"

"The last time I came I could get on any shuttle that was at the airport. Are you saying I have to preregister and if a bus time is full and closed, I have to wait?"

*"Wait — If I don't register my granddaughter, she can't go
to Gaia??"*

Things had developed over the years, and in most ways the changes
took better care of the complexity of supporting thousands of womyn and
children. But it was true that our evolved systems came at the expense of
the do-anything-you-want environment of early Festivals. Some of these
"Ladies from the '80s," as I coined them in the office, offered some solid
pushback. Pushback was completely what we were about in the '70s and '80s,
and we needed to work with that if we wanted to welcome these Amazons
back home, even if they had skipped the years when we learned how to talk
kindlier with one another, saving the fiercest pushback for the boys.

We talked a lot in the office about the importance of understanding that
this was a coming home for everyone. It was important for us to understand
the discomfort sisters from long ago felt about the furniture being rearranged
by roommates they hadn't yet met. The announcement of the last Festival
after a 40-year run created a portal into a time and place we were all entering
together, from whenever our Festival experience had been. Our job was to
make that gateway as smooth and loving as possible until we all crossed the
threshold of our shared sanctuary.

Sowing Seeds

As Judith, Tina, and I started to have our meetings about the Opening
celebration, we were in sync about our focus. Gratitude. Amazon Proud.
Celebration. We would have no fear of being in our grief. We would sow
seeds for the future.

On that tumultuous day right after the announcement, a sister had
posted the video of Natalie Merchant's song "Kind and Generous" on my
Facebook page. I must have listened to it 20 times. It captured the essence of
the circle of gratitude that I know all of us felt for our community. It evoked
the strength, love, and self-acceptance we grew together on that Land.

You've been so kind and generous

For your kindness I'm in debt to you

And I never could have come this far without you

So for everything you've done

You know I'm bound ...

I'm bound to thank you for it.

The miracle of this time was that mixed in with the grief I felt at the
ending of the Festival, more profoundly, I felt deep in my bones gratitude for
everything we had created together. At times it was as if I were looking back

from another dimension and could appreciate the complex beauty of what we were, unclouded by the obsessive focus on the endless details that it took to bring the Festival to life.

I started to hear the lyrics of Sly and the Family Stone's song playing in my head, "I want to thank you for letting me be myself, again." This was the miracle of our community: In a world where so many of us did not belong as our true fierce Amazonian selves, it was here that we learned how to find our authenticity. The level of acceptance we gave to one another was something we would never lose.

I ran these song ideas past Judith and Tina and at first, they didn't seem to work together. Then Judith went away and created a masterful mashup of "Kind & Generous" with a full funk refrain of "Thank You For Letting Me Be Myself, Again." Tina choreographed awesome dance sections for each verse of "Kind and Generous," with the inspired idea of having crew members dance down the ramp with signs of gratitude during the funk breaks.

My next call was to Staceyann Chin. She'd first come to the Festival in 2006, after my friend, Karen, had called saying, "Girl! you have to listen to this sister!" Besides what her awesome poetry performances and one-woman theater piece added to our lineups over the years, Staceyann had a brilliant capacity to listen to what I described on the phone about the focus of a given year's Opening Celebration. She would then write a poem that pulled together all the theatrical, lyrical, musical, and movement pieces, encapsulating them into a cogent, fiercely compelling piece of performance art. If you missed what we were getting at in the Opening before Staceyann came out, you couldn't miss it after you heard what she had to say.

Earlier that spring, I'd kept hearing Ferron's song "Shadows on a Dime" in my mind's heart. That line, "But 40 years is 40 years," rang like a lament in my ears. I really wanted it to be part of the Opening. As brilliant as "Shadows" is, I knew that "Testimony" was really the right song for the Opening. I called Ferron from a dog walk and proposed the idea that she do "Testimony" with Marcelle Davies Lashley. We would have Marcelle start, then Ferron would walk out singing the line, "You young ones, you're the next ones, and I hope you chose it well." Though at first, Ferron wasn't quite sure who Marcelle was, when I described her, she said, "Holy shit — I know her. She's beautiful and bald and a badass singer — she should just sing the damn whole song by herself!"

"She is an incredible singer, and the two of you will be amazing together," I said. "I know we'll love hearing Marcelle sing the song — and we need you to take us on the journey into the future."

The music. The dancers. The Opening Celebration was starting to come together, but I knew there were more elements waiting to come into conscious form.

My partner Lia, an amazing triathlete, showed me the powdered Holi colors that were sometimes thrown at racers as they crossed the finish line. "This is right up your alley," she said, and she was right. I looked up the source of this tradition, a cultural festival in India. Holi represents the arrival of spring and the triumph of good over evil, but it also touches on the illusory nature of the material world. The colors used to be made with herbs and flowers, with the beautiful powder meant to go all over everyone, but we knew many of our sisters would not be down with dyes all over their Opening Celebration finery.

I searched and searched, and found bits of color that could be thrown, but nothing that could be seen or felt from a distance. That was the thing about the Opening — everything had to be seen and felt all around the bowl. I would have to let go of this explosion of beauty if we couldn't figure out a way to get the color high into the sky to be seen around the Night Stage bowl. We were already on the Land when I saw a video showing Holi colors packed into fire extinguishers. I found two sources in the U.S. and more in India where I could buy these color-loaded fire extinguishers, but the cost was crazy for the number I wanted. I called the fire-extinguisher company I'd used for 35 years and asked if they could imagine doing this for me.

They had some fire extinguishers that were old and not in use. If I wanted to try one, they were game. I overnighted a bunch of pounds of Holi color to them from Utah and had them load up some extinguishers with different amounts of color for us to test, and we learned the sweet spot was 3 pounds of colored powder to propel thick color 25 feet up into the air, visible from everywhere. Yellow, turquoise, pink, orange, violet, blue, and purple. We could meet the tight turnaround and get 75 pounds of Holi color shipped to our guys in time for them to load 24 extinguishers for us to pick up Tuesday.

At the heart of our vision was the idea of passing seeds to the future, something placed in the hands of every sister at the Opening Celebration as an act of faith toward what would be carried forward. I had originally imagined the seeds would be sea heart beans from the monkey ladder vine that rides ocean currents throughout the world. A beautiful dark mahogany color, and (I thought) heart shaped. How perfect to pass out heart-shaped seeds! Plant a seed of our love and make it grow! In Walhalla, I asked Robin to research where we could get sea heart beans in bulk. The sample packages came and were a beautiful color, but they were quite expensive and not heart-shaped at all.

Then it came to me: We live in an oak forest! The Opening Celebration would unfold in the field surrounding the mighty Mother Oak. The problem was, though, that the acorns left from last year were insect- and squirrel-eaten, moldy brown, and few had their little caps. Not that inspiring. I started to look for acorns online once we got settled on the Land. I asked Erin to see if there were other acorns in the forest on the Land, but at that moment, there were only last year's. Even online in late July, acorns were hard to find. I went ahead and ordered as many as I could from a couple of different sources. As it turned out, only some of the acorns I received were the real deal; others were sweet little wooden creations with acorn-like hats glued on. Elvira made sure my folly was a recurring punchline all Festival!

Then on Festival Tuesday something unexpected happened, as it often does. I was sitting backstage at the Acoustic Stage, on the One World Inspirational Choir risers, when I noticed something amazing on the ground: Acorns, beautiful, fresh green acorns that had just fallen from the trees! Just that much later in the season, only a week or two, and fresh acorns were now on the floor of the forest. We gathered as many as we could for the next night's Opening Celebration.

The Ultimate Celebration

As each wave of workers hit the Land that summer — Put-In, Long Crew, Short Crew, Tech, and Artists — every womon brought a determination to do our very best Festival yet. This was no lame duck Festival! This would be the ultimate celebration of all that we had done. We greeted each other with excitement and sadness, knowing that each moment was precious, and that everything we did had complete meaning for what would fuel the rest of our lives.

Even as we gave our all to being fully present with each other, the coming ending was present too, walking alongside us. Every step of creating the 40th Festival — while simultaneously considering how to approach the ending — was a slow and steady shock to my entire system.

I woke up on the day before Short Crew arrival, still long before dawn with stars in the sky and our city asleep. I knew that if I was ever going to make a plan for what Short Crew had to do with all the things in their inventories, it had to be today. I sat at my tiny computer desk at my end of the Ops Trailer, coffee flowing, and started to type.

We will be setting up depots at the Main Kitchen, DART, and the Womb.

Usable inventory will all be put into storage by like-kind items, not by department. All coolers will be stored together, all pens, all hammers, all tape, all sleeping bags, all tents, all everything — one big inventory. If someone comes forward to produce a different Festival, they will need things, but they would need them in a totally different way than we had them organized, so we will make one large inventory that they can understand.

Reusable items that don't go into the unified inventory will go into a depot, and we will send trucks into town to give these to Goodwill. Feel free to take what you like from the recycle pile but take it off the Land you must. Metal, paper, and glass recyclables will be taken in waves to the recycling center.

Trash — all the things that have no value moving forward, that we have brought to the Land for our most idiosyncratic use or fun but have no recycling or reusable value, or that are fairly trashed, but we continued to love into life — now is when we bite the bullet, they are going into trash.

Worker Storage no longer exists. Your option is to take your things home or put the plywood on the plywood pile and put the foam in the foam pile. We will recycle some locally, save some items for potential future use, and let go of the rest.

Furniture – each area had rough-built furniture, and all of it would be assessed for its potential reuse in a smaller Festival and then stored. Lace Crew would sort and organize all the beautiful furniture built over decades for exactly the right use. We couldn't keep much, and some sisters would want to take some of the smaller pieces, but the rest would go into a bonfire, a fire the Lace Crew would start, feed, and monitor as it burned nonstop for three long days.

Post-Festival, our Inventory Crew became the Badasses of the Universe, organizing the depots, inventorying the combined supplies, boxing and unboxing, taking trips to Goodwill in 24-foot trucks, ordering new roll-offs for the trash. Every trip they took to the barn to unload, they would come back loaded with backstock to funnel into the same process.

We let go of very little over the years, as there would always be another use down the line, and there would always be a down the line.

What Ended the Festival?

Many have said that the trans-inclusion debate is what ended the Festival, and though I understand why that is said, it is only a part of what contributed to the final decision. We had created something truly unique and kept it alive with a full beating heart for 40 years. So much had changed during those years — most importantly, in my mind, the mainstreaming and dilution of the radical feminist movement that was the lifeblood and informing energy of the Festival.

Mainstreaming always serves to capitalize on the energy of a movement, commodifying it and diluting it into meaningless pop culture. At first this often feels like an honoring of the energy of the movement. They really get us! Ellen is on TV! Melissa is at the Grammys! But for radical feminism, it served as a smokescreen to obscure the fundamental issues. It robbed our movement of the passionate rage that fuels revolutionary change, and achieved very little true institutional transformation.

I felt deep in my heart that womyn needed a space like Festival as much in the new millennium as in the '70s, but the mainstreaming of feminism left a vast majority of womyn feeling like the world was now available to them in a new way, even though there had been very few actual systematic changes in patriarchal structure. Fewer of us were aware of the pervasive, rampant violence against womyn than there were in the '70s and '80s, alive with Take Back the Night Marches. We lost our collective awareness of the facts that at least 10 womyn are murdered each day, one-third of those by their intimate partners; that the 600 reported rapes per day are just a fraction of the sexual assaults that womyn experience; and that the tens of thousands of instances of battery are part of our culture.

We stopped talking as much about the huge wage disparity between men and womyn, apparently comforted that they now say womyn make 80% of what men make. The reality is that when averaged over all workers, of all races, and a number of years, that figure is still 49%. In the lesbian feminist community, we settled for a lesbian on TV, a k.d. lang record in the bin, and Amazon.com carrying what was left of independent books, instead of bookstores owned by Amazon womyn in most cities.

And even though almost every major music Festival was still populated by almost all male performers, we stopped enthusiastically supporting womyn's music the way we did in the '70s and '80s. Our overall complacency and hidden desire to assimilate told us we needed each other less. And what Festival gave us was each other. A healthy interdependence on each other.

With so many of us relating more to screens than people and accessing cultural products online, the changes brought by technology no doubt also helped fray our sense of the importance of building in-person community and a participatory culture. And of course, the rise of technology meant misinformation about who we were could spread much farther and faster.

I am NOT saying the trans debate didn't contribute to the cultural shifts and the financial burdens the Festival faced through years of boycott, or that it didn't impact the artists who were targeted. Or that part of our community chose to not attend the Festival in alliance with the trans community or to protest that trans womyn were not specifically invited, although this was often based in the misunderstanding that trans womyn and trans men did not attend.

But I think we lost track of a much bigger picture. In truth, the foundation of Patriarchy was fundamentally threatened by the cultural change that the feminist revolution of the '70s succeeded in creating. They pressed down and pushed back and eventually, the skillfully engineered backlash influenced how womyn who came of age later disowned and dishonored the radical creations of the earlier movement, if not feminism itself.

The Festival was a proud, living enactment of the best of that movement. We never wanted to be mainstreamed, we never took corporate sponsorship, we declined mass media coverage, and accepted all the financial loss and disrespect we accumulated from those choices. Instead, we created a cloistered community of rad womyn in the woods.

Every year we came together, away from the pressure of patriarchy, and rediscovered just how fierce and funky and sexy and smart and strong and beautiful and changeable and playful and vulnerable and loving we are. It doesn't take a Stolichnaya sponsorship to find that out. It takes NOT having a Stoli sponsorship and walking in a world that can't be bought to find in our hearts what is truly important.

Morning was always the witching hour for me on the Land. The week before Festival I always rose by 4 a.m., my eyes popping open and my mind running through the list of things I had been solving in my sleep. The morning came that I had to get the thank you text for our Opening Ceremony gratitude dance over to Mitzi and Leabeth at Signz so they would have time to get them all painted. I sat at my desk and started typing:

THANK YOU HEALERS

THANK YOU BLUEBERRIES

THANK YOU GATEKEEPERS

THANK YOU SWEAT LODGE

THANK YOU KINDNESS

THANK YOU COOKS

The flood of gratitude was a rushing water throughout my whole body.

THANK YOU SHOOTING STARS

THANK YOU LAND WATER

THANK YOU LISTENING

THANK YOU LAUGHTER

THANK YOU COMPASSION

Wise womyn tell us the antidote to fear is gratitude, and I knew this in my bones as I let the typing flow through my fingers.

THANK YOU GODDESS

THANK YOU SAFETY

THANK YOU WISDOM

THANK YOU TENDERNESS

THANK YOU ELDERS

I had to stop at 40 of these refrains because we already had almost 100 crew members participating in other parts of the Opening, and we still had to keep the Festival running through that evening. As tempting as it was to say yes to the areas that asked if they could close for that last ritual, we were still responsible for the town. Sisters would still be arriving, and we had to welcome them home, regardless of when they arrived.

The last gratitude sign I wrote on my list was "THANK YOU AMAZONS."

The concept was that different singers would take a verse of the mashup song Judith had conceived, with Tina and the dance crew dancing on the ramp. As the band broke into the Sly & Family Stone lyrics, crew members would dance, walk, roll, or skip down the ramp with their signs of gratitude for all that we honor, for all that we grew in ourselves when we were together.

The day before the first rehearsal, Judith and Tina came to me and said, "We think you should bring out one of the signs." I couldn't imagine doing something IN the Opening. I was always so deeply involved in the planning, the tech, the building — I was entwined in every part, but to be part of the visual action, that wasn't my role. And then I saw myself with the "THANK YOU AMAZONS" sign, and I knew it felt right.

I want to thank you
For so many gifts
You gave with love and tenderness
I want to thank you

I want to thank you
For your generosity
The love and the honesty
That you gave me

The Opening Ceremony began with Ubaka Hill, who had carried the drum to so many sisters over decades at the Festival. Her drum was answered by drummers coming to her from around the bowl, temple flags on bamboo poles entering from the distance. Pageantry. Power.

Ruth Barrett, the carrier of the Candlelight Concert since Kay Gardner joined the ancestors, called the directions and offered a blessing. Shirley, Aleah, and Yaniyah were with her, holding space, burning herb, setting our intentions. Peace. Focus.

Behind them hung a gorgeous, painted wooden cutout created by Lania, so large she had to transport it from Baltimore in two parts on the roof of her car. It formed two loving hands to hold us. Around us were the phases of the moon on painted discs held high on poles, all rising in the south. There was an altar in each area of the listening bowl, with candles burning. The entrance to the entire Night Stage experience was the most mystical walk-through altar, a space to leave a remembrance, steal a kiss, have a cry.

After the Drum Call and the Blessing, Rhiannon and dancers entered the audience, dressed in red-hooded cloaks. We couldn't see their faces as they processed towards the stage. Rhiannon's plaintive voice was so recognizable, setting every blade of grass vibrating with Sinead O'Connor's song:

Thank you for hearing me

Thank you for seeing me

Thank you for not leaving me

Between the song, the singer, the dance and the dancers, a release of grief and gratitude rolled like thunder over thousands of womyn.

Thank you for staying with me

Thank you for not hurting me

Thank you for holding me

The emotional catharsis shared by thousands of womyn rolled across the bowl, a purifying release of the pent-up energy of anticipatory grief. How will it be at the final and 40th Festival? Now we know. It is real. We are on this ride. Together.

As the procession started to move away, their heads once again covered, they were every womon, any womon, all womyn.

Thank you for breaking my heart

Thank you for tearing me apart

Now I've a strong, strong heart

Thank you for breaking my heart

Then up on the stage, Staceyann burst out.

As the dust settles on our beloved dirt road

indulge your inconsolable ache

lament/weep/wail/cry all need or want

but know too/the seeds of joy we each planted on this Land

will never be dead/instead/the legend of its roots

will grow large inside the heads and hearts

of all of us/who have loved here/and fought here

fucked out loud and without apology here

the memory of it/the spirit of it

will tingle inside the scarred chests

of warriors who survived

BOOM BOOM BOOM. The Taiko drums of the Dance Brigade fell on top of Staceyann's final words, a bone-deep physical cleansing as the waves of rhythm rolled over and over us and opened further our beautiful breaking hearts.

Dance Brigade photo by Desdemona Burgin

We are not afraid of our feelings, our loss, our letting go. This is what the female spirit does — it feels so deeply for the entire world of humankind through every turn of the great wheel of life.

The opening notes of "Testimony" folded in over the Taiko applause. Most of us knew each note so well and sang along and swayed through our tears.

They say slowly

Brings the least shock

But no matter how slow I walk

There are traces

Empty spaces

And doors and doors of locks

But by my life be I spirit

And by my heart be I womon

And by my eyes be I open

And by my hands be I whole

Photo by Desdemona Burgin

As Ferron and Marcelle exited the stage, 146 womyn were on deck, ready for the shared performance of "Kind & Generous," a flat-out fast-paced ceremony of gratitude. Six dancers, nine musicians, 40 crew members to dance down the ramp with Gratitude signs, 26 in the Holi color brigade, 50 sisters ready to move through the audience with acorns of hope, and of course the most incredible sound, lighting, interpreting and stage crews to hold it all in steady hands.

Photo by Desdemona Burgin

Photo by Desdemona Burgin

I want to thank you

Show my gratitude

My love and my respect for you

I want to thank you

I want to ...

Thank you thank you, thank you, thank you, thank you, thank you

I want to thank you.

I was covered in sweat as each piece folded into the next, perhaps our most complicated Opening, so many moving parts, coming off without a hiccup. With each wave of workers who danced down the ramp holding their gratitude signs high, my heart burst open. I could barely remember I was to carry a sign — I was so caught up in the music, the magic, the love.

In the letter I had mailed out in the spring of 2015, I said:

I will meet you there in August — my eyes meeting yours, heart wide open.

And from that day on, I knew I wanted to be prepared to meet the eyes of every single sister I met

Photo by
Desdemona Burgin

on the path, to be present to witness her experience, her joy and her sadness.

As I picked up my sign and started down the runway, my body shook with anticipation

Photo by Desdemona Burgin

and something that could have been fear or could have been manic joy. I held my "THANK YOU AMAZONS" sign high and watched as the ring around the bowl exploded with gorgeous Holi colors as the band rocked so hard and sisters jumped to their feet.

I thought this time with my sign would be a minute, but it kept happening, held by every womon in the bowl on her feet. I grounded myself by looking into the eyes of sisters throughout the field. Thank you. And you. And you.

The dancers came out and danced as the band vamped and the field roared. Thank you. I looked into the eyes of sisters I had known for decades and into eyes I had never seen. Thank you.

I wasn't out of sight at stage right pacing, as I'd been for every Opening Ceremony until that moment. I was right there on the ramp feeling the joy of our community, and the pride we all had in our Amazon tribe.

Thank you for letting me be myself.

Thank you for breaking my heart.

Now I've a strong strong heart.

Thank you, sister Amazons.

Photo by Desdemona Burgin

CHAPTER 40

WHAT YOU TAUGHT ME

We learned as we went and then we passed the learning on to the next woman, who passed it on to the next, because this was the place where we would learn things reserved for men. There are so many pieces of information that make the physical world operate that are intentionally designed to bypass female ears and hands. But we would find that information and make it ours and teach it to the next womyn who came behind us.

Like, it's easier to turn a nut that's stuck on your bolt if you put a pipe on your wrench to make it longer (it's called a breaker bar).

You taught me how to trim a tree in the woods along a footpath. Imagine a sister walking by at night and make sure there are no branches that will poke her in the eye. Trim the branch back almost to where it starts, but not all the way to the branch collar, which could make the tree susceptible to disease.

Having conversations with strong differing opinions is difficult. The most important part is to listen, be eager to understand what the other woman is saying without the inner distraction of trying to plan how you will respond to make your point. Your focus is where your understanding comes from, not changing someone's mind. You taught me to sit in my seat and listen with my heart. We called it radical listening. And we did a lot of listening.

You taught me to put green clay on my bug bites, and never mind the resulting gray-green splotches on my body. Eventually they looked cool, and they drew out the venom and healed my skin so much quicker.

You taught me to wear sunscreen, but I admit, I forgot that a lot.

You taught me how to roll a cable by going with its flow and letting it show me the way it wants to be coiled, nice and soft circles, the way it was coiled the last time, nothing forced and never making a bend in the wire.

You showed me all the wonders of nutritional yeast. On tofu nuggets in the morning. Over my salad at lunch or dinner. In the best damn gravy over biscuits. And, of course, on lesbian popcorn.

Making a mistake isn't the worst thing in the world. Hiding that you made a mistake will eat you up from the inside out. You taught me that making mistakes is an integral part of breathing in and out, and you forgave every one I made.

You taught me not to judge a book by its cover. That it's not possible to assess who would be the right woman for a job by looking at her, especially judging who would be good at a job based on size or gender presentation. I've seen some small femmes kick some serious truck-loading ass, never tiring, never complaining. And I've seen some big, beautiful butches care for the babies with complete tenderness and care. I've seen doctors work hard on the hay wagon and I've seen folks with no medical training run a Womb shift with complete leadership and strength. I've seen babies become coordinators. I've seen elders jump into the mosh pit, canes overhead.

You taught me to tip my chair against the table at night so the morning dew didn't make the seat wet and get another sister's pants damp at the start of her day. I still do that in my yard.

You taught me that even though it looks so cool to release a bunch of balloons into the sky, it endangers birds and animals.

You taught me if I want to be in community with sisters of color, I needed to sit down at the table, get over myself and work through my fears of difference, reach out and form friendships and family, and be a comrade. You taught me that everyone is afraid, and my fear just isn't that special.

Road gravel, 22a to be exact, works a lot better than the bigger rocks I thought should fill the potholes. You taught me that.

Performing artists are workers. We may only see the 45 minutes on stage, but I've witnessed the hours of practice, the humping of equipment, the huddles around the tree, the late nights in the trailer transcribing lyrics, the hours of dancing in the afternoon sun on a red-hot stage, the headphones on in your tent as you learn the new song, the pacing before the show — and I've seen a whole lot of work in a straight-on downpour because that is what you are there to do.

You showed me the ecstasy of dancing naked at midnight.

You taught me to tie my tarp down low in the west, where most of the storms came from.

You taught me self-care is sexy.

You taught me that no matter how little ASL I might know, if I want to communicate with a deaf woman, chances are good we can make it happen if I talk slowly, gesture, and pay attention.

You taught me most cars have 2 gallons of gas left when the low fuel light comes on, but only if the gas gauge still works.

You taught me patience.

You taught me gentleness.

You taught me to be strong.

You taught me to be brave.

You taught me that 40 years is 40 years, and those are 40 years that will last a lifetime.

Photo by Desdemona Burgin